The Business of Digital Television

T0347367

The Business of Digital Television

Chris Forrester

Focal Press

OXFORD AUCKLAND BOSTON JOHANNESBURG MELBOURNE NEW DELHI

Focal Press
An imprint of Butterworth-Heinemann
Linacre House, Jordan Hill, Oxford OX2 8DP
225 Wildwood Avenue, Woburn, MA 01801-2041
A division of Reed Educational and Professional Publishing Ltd

A member of the Reed Elsevier plc group

First published 2000
Transferred to digital printing 2004
© Chris Forrester 2000

All rights reserved. No part of this publication may be reproduced in
any material form (including photocopying or storing in any medium by
electronic means and whether or not transiently or incidentally to some
other use of this publication) without the written permission of the
copyright holder except in accordance with the provisions of the
Copyright, Designs and Patents Act 1988 or under the terms of a
licence issued by the Copyright Licensing Agency Ltd, 90 Tottenham
Court Road, London, England W1P 0LP. Applications for the copyright
holder's written permission to reproduce any part of this publication
should be addressed to the publishers

British Library Cataloguing in Publication Data
Forrester, Chris
  The business of digital television
  1. Digital television   2.   Television broadcasting –
  Technological innovations
  I.   Title
  384.5'5

Library of Congress Cataloguing in Publication Data
A catalogue record for this book is available from the
Library of Congress

ISBN 0 240 51606 0

Typeset by Florence Production Ltd, Stoodleigh, Devon

PLANT A TREE

BTCV
British Trust for
Conservation Volunteers

FOR EVERY TITLE THAT WE PUBLISH, BUTTERWORTH-HEINEMANN
WILL PAY FOR BTCV TO PLANT AND CARE FOR A TREE.

Contents

Acknowledgements

The Internet is a wonderful, if somewhat overwhelming, source of information. A dip one day into my Netscape Navigator™ Newspage_Direct, a 'daily web-paper' for all things televisual (and digital), threw up more than 400 specific stories. These were typically about 600–700 words long, covering subjects such as set top boxes (8), electronic commerce (25), cutting edge multimedia technology (40) as well as the more mundane broadcast satellites (8), network TV business news (6), high definition TV (14) and interactive TV (34). But ask for information on so-called 'superhighway'-related stories and the system goes ballistic, routeing 120 stories into the PC. Ask for anything newsworthy concerning the world wide web and the network responds with 152 stories. It's just another tough day in the digital village.

The position is much the same on news-stands and in the better-stocked book shops. Any month a reader is almost certain to see the face of Bill Gates peering from the front cover of at least one magazine. Business-related weekly and monthly magazines seem now to be wholly dependent on a digital something-or-other on every second page. While books devoted purely to broadcasting are fewer, those with some reference to 'digital' in the title are almost as widespread. It's a nightmare for any journalist hoping to stay a few steps ahead of the pack!

In *The Business of Digital Television* I have attempted to cut through the hype and condense the available information to hard fact and sustainable prediction, free from unsubstantiated assumptions. I want this report to be of value as events unfold, if only as a reference tool or to compare predictions with actual results.

In writing this work I am first and foremost indebted to my fellow journalists in this sector of the business. Their assistance in pointing me in the right direction, as well as their own thoughts and concepts of where the future is taking us, have proved invaluable. First among equals are Barry Fox, Geoff Bains, George Cole, Mimi Turner and my colleagues Stuart Thomson, Julian Clover and Barry Flynn.

I have also been fortunate to talk to a great number of industry leaders who have generously given me their time over the past few years. In particular I'd like to mention Adam Singer, chairman of Flextech, Steve Billinger, then head of BSkyB's interactive division, Graham Mills, director of British Telecom's visual and broadcast services, Dr Abe Peled, CEO of NDS Inc., Jim Beveridge at Microsoft's WebTV, Claire Leproust from Canal+'s interactive division, Steve Oldfield and Phil Braden at Mindport, Barclay Knapp and Jeremy Thorpe at NTL Inc.

Satellite broadcasting has grown to be a crucial player in all aspects of broadcasting and the Internet. I owe a special debt to Giuliano Berretta, director general of EUTELSAT, to Romain Bausch, director general of SES/Astra, and to their respective staff, in particular Vanessa O'Connor and Yves Feltes.

It should be noted that unless stated otherwise, quoted material is taken from extensive interviews I personally conducted throughout the summer of 1999.

Chris Forrester
Richmond, London
August 2000

Introduction

'The Electric Eye'

It is all too easy to presume that it is only in recent times that the world has become obsessed with things electronic, but analogue television broadcasting has been around in an electronic form since 1928. In that action-packed, benchmark year, two separate groups demonstrated wholly electronic television systems. General Electric used a 48-line picture at 16 frames per second (fps), while Westinghouse Electric transmitted a 35 mm film from their KDKA radio station in East Pittsburgh at 60 lines and 16 frames per second.

These were laboratory systems, however, and were unlikely ever to achieve commercial deployment. It would take a few more years of quite frenzied activity to perfect the complex physics and engineering needed to make efficient use of the then rudimentary cathode ray tubes. Dr Vladimir Kosma Zworykin was a Russian engineer who moved to the USA and by 1923 was working for Westinghouse Electric Company. In 1923 he filed a patent on behalf of Westinghouse for a 'camera tube'. In June 1933 Dr Vladimir Zworykin presented his paper 'The iconoscope: a new version of the electric eye'. Later that year he showed his work to two other groups, EMI in Britain and Telefunken in Germany, spurring activity in both countries. The broadcasting world owes Zworykin a great debt.

By January 1934, EMI was showing images on 240 lines/25 fps. That summer Philo T. Farnsworth demonstrated his all-electric system in Philadelphia. The entertainment comprised some vaudeville acts, athletic events and the appearance of various politicians. This was 'modern' television – in that it was electronic, and in its concept of what content would be acceptable, and commercially important.

While John Logie Baird (using a Farnsworth 'electron' camera) and Marconi-EMI (using a 405 line/25 fps interlaced system) battled it out in Britain, Germany actually broadcast a rudimentary television service during the period from March to August 1935. It was not a success. In February 1937 the Marconi-EMI system was selected as the British television standard and some 3000 sets were sold within the first year. When British Prime Minister Neville Chamberlain flew back from Berlin on 30 September 1939, his arrival at Heston Aerodrome was seen live by those lucky few viewers.

A similar standards battle was taking place in the United States, led by David Sarnoff of RCA/NBC. The Federal Communications Commission determined that a commercial television service could start in the USA, once a common standard was established. Although the London Television Service closed down on 1 September 1939 because of the outbreak of war, development work in the USA continued, leading to the adoption of a 525-line system and the first regular broadcasts in July 1941.

The rest, as they say, is history.

The TV pioneers

Alexander Graham Bell In 1876 Bell first demonstrated his telephone.

Henrich Hertz In 1887 Hertz, a German physicist, demonstrated how an electromagnetic wave (itself discovered by Scotsman James Clerk Maxwell) could be made to jump in the form of a spark across an air gap.

Guglielmo Marconi In 1894 Marconi, a young Italian inventor, succeeded in ringing a bell at his parents house in Bologna by sending a radio message across the room. By 1901 his signals were crossing the Atlantic.

Reginald Fessenden In 1906 US physicist Fessenden succeeded in modulating music and speech on to radio waves. The amplitude of the radio wave was altered to carry the sound – hence *amplitude modulation*, or AM.

Lee De Forest In 1907 De Forest, a US inventor, used a triode valve to amplify radio signals.

Armstrong/Levy In 1917, Edwin Armstrong in the USA and Lucien Levy in France independently devised *superheterodyne* circuits that made tuning easier, reduced power consumption and simplified receiver construction.

John Logie Baird   In 1925 Baird, a Scot, transmitted the first recognizable pictures of a human face by means of a mechanical scanning system.

Vladimir Zworykin   In 1931 Zworykin, Russian born, but living in the USA, demonstrated the first practical electronic television camera.

Edwin Armstrong   In 1933, Armstrong devised *frequency modulation*, in which the frequency is modulated by the signal, helping cure the problem of static noise.

1

From dumb box to television that's alive

Digital . . . Convergence . . . Super-highway . . . MPEG . . . The web . . . Pick whichever term you like, it really doesn't matter because our digital future is here now. All we have to do is open our eyes and recognize the signs.

Here are the hard-headed views of some of the industry's leading prophets:

> The notion that TV and/or the Internet will mean anything to somebody in two years is irrelevant. It is my belief that currently the term 'television' doesn't even have the same common meaning that it did even two or three years ago. It is totally changing.
>
> Steve Billinger, then head of BSkyB's interactive division, September 1999

> IP networks are removing distance from the equation. So I can easily see

the Hong Kong community in London having all the Hong Kong channels and services available out there available to them over an IP network of some kind in the London area, or indeed anywhere in the UK. The same would apply to the Japanese or any other ethnic group. The same could apply to Brits who want to hook into the Los Angeles area or elsewhere in the world. It will mean TV is available anywhere, anytime.

Graham Mills, British Telecom's head of Internet and new media, September 1999

At Canal+ we are in a position which is perhaps a little easier than other broadcasters. We can send an e-mail to our subscribers reminding them in their offices that tonight is the night when their favourite show is on. We can also do this on the mobile, saying the soccer match starts in 15 minutes, and even send pictures of the game. Today we are in the middle of the business because we operate the system as a collection point, a clearinghouse, a distribution system. And we have the database, we have the information a commercial broadcaster does not have. We can now e-mail all of our subscribers across the world, and this will become increasingly important as the free-to-air broadcasts become part of the pay-TV offer.

Claire Leproust, head of interactive at Canal+ TV, August 1999

The digital revolution in the broadcasting and telecommunications arena is changing the way we interconnect and working within networks is becoming easier. In the past we had heterogeneous ways of transferring information: there was analogue, there was digital, there were very many proprietary solutions. What is happening now is the emergence of a family of transmission and distribution and contribution systems which are all based on open standards, and on a family of open standards that is relatively small. I refer to the DVB family, the MPEG standard, the IP family of standards and the JAVA family of standards. This is the trend. Whatever is going to happen the infrastructure will be devised within solutions . . . that are public. Any attempt to use proprietary solutions to provide services will be a short-term opportunity.

Antonio Arcidiacono, EUTELSAT's head of multimedia and new products, August 1999

Digital transmission actually means that television no longer is a scarce commodity. The whole of our history is about television being a scarce commodity – one channel, two, three, four . . . Digital transmission means there is no scarce commodity and what that means is that television becomes a variation on the bookstore or news stand theme. So the issue is: when you walk into a bookshop, if you know nothing about a single book, and whether you decide on one or another . . . Given that vast plethora of information you are going to hit certain subjects that have been pre-marketed, or certain brands, and I think we are going to have pretty significant 'info-brands', information in the broadest sense, not just updated train-timetables. And you will have brands that perform their tasks across a number of different ways, each of which access the public.

Adam Singer, chairman of Flextech plc, September 1999

Web-streaming? There is no stopping it. In fact there's something quite nice about it. It reminds me of the evolution of radio and the early days when people had to use a crystal set to start off with, then it got better and better. It's junk today and one would have to be pretty keen to sit and watch or listen at these wonderful 2-inch windows, but in time it is going to be huge . . .

Jim Beveridge, business development manager Europe, Microsoft's WebTV Networks, August 1999

The biggest factor, I call it the sleeper of technology, is the growth in local storage. When the PC first came out, in the early 1980s, it came with 10 Mb of local storage. Today you would be hard pressed to find anything with less than 2 Gb of storage. That's an improvement factor of 200 times. The modem at that time was about 2400 b/s, today the equivalent would be a 28.8 Kb/s, another significant growth factor.

As the prospects for a 10 Gb hard drive become interesting, when it is linked to compression and inserted into a STB. It can expand the content window. In the UK the content window before Channel 5 and Sky was four, a four-channel content window. With cable and Sky analogue, you have a 40-channel content window, more in the USA, perhaps 80 channels. With digital the content window expands to nearer 200. Today's improved compression could give us today 400 channels of content without a problem. But if you add 10 Gb into the STB now, costing around $100 in the year 2000, that would add another 50–80 virtual channels. But go just a little further, and add 100 Gb of hard drive would mean 800 virtual channels. And 100 Gb is suggested for within the next 5 years. So we think the biggest revolution as far as the consumer is concerned will be local storage, which will completely change the paradigm for viewers, which is currently based on time. We ask 'what's on now'. And local storage changes that, and we can start asking 'what would I like to watch'. It is going to be content-driven from your local disk, with maybe 1000 hours of choice, and not necessarily the 200 hours of broadcast channel choice.

Dr Abe Peled, CEO of NDS Inc., August 1999

These quotations are from people whose business interests are very much focused on the new wave of broadcasting. They have, it is fair to say, a vested interest in the prophecies being fulfilled. However, their statements have so much obvious truth about them that they simply cannot be ignored.

As a 'health warning' we might do well to take note of the words of the truly prophetic Ray Hammond in his book *The Online Handbook*:

The linking of computers around the world is going to have far-reaching effects, and the spread of knowledge, the interchange of ideas and the dissemination of information are going to produce a revolution in our society.

Hammond, 1984

Hammond's words, written almost 20 years ago, show how dangerous it is to attempt to be a latter-day Nostradamus. Hammond was completely accurate about the wired future; he was just a few years out in his estimate of how long it would take for us to get hooked. To his credit, in his follow-up volume, *Digital Business* (1996), Hammond admits the network revolution has taken longer to achieve critical mass.

Across the Atlantic there are even more pundits and prophets. Pulitzer Prize-winning writer Joel Brinkley, in *Defining Vision* (1997) states:

> These new machines are wondrous indeed because, unlike the earlier Japanese models, these are digital televisions. A TV that receives its signal digitally is no longer just a dumb box passively displaying pictures and sound. Digital televisions, properly equipped, can be powerful, interactive computers, hardly different from desktop PCs. With those capabilities, suddenly television comes alive.
>
> Brinkley, 1997

In Chapter 3 we look at how the USA has attempted to tie digital television into an introduction of high definition digital television (HDTV), encouraged by two most powerful influences, the US government and the film-making industry. The government viewed the freeing up of most of the analogue TV bandwidth as the answer to its fiscal problems; and Hollywood seemed to want to move its current cumbersome cans-of-celluloid distribution methods into a new paradigm where its latest blockbusters can be delivered direct-to-HDTV set, bypassing the expensive cinema-based middlemen.

However, Dr Abe Peled, a highly-regarded engineer who heads up NDS and is deputy-chairman of Tandberg-NDS (two companies at the cutting edge of televisual technology), described the introduction of HDTV in the USA in 1999 as 'the big yawn'. HDTV is happening in the USA, but at a far slower pace than most experts predicted earlier in 1999.

The USA (at the time of writing) is committed to an analogue switch-off during 2006. In Peled's view:

The original reason for the 2006 date was so that Clinton could settle his budget plans, which he did by auctioning off the spectrum. I think they will postpone it. Already there is an amendment that allows for a delay if 5 per cent of sets have not been converted. Oddly enough, the biggest interest we have seen is for data carriage from broadcasters, of value-added services on top of the HDTV signal for which they can charge. We see some action in this sector, from people seeking income streams from data services.

Peled issues a warning about HDTV:

The other problem of HDTV is only just being realized, and it concerns on-air talent. The *Los Angeles Times* carried a story about a weather-girl who it said needed to shave her armpits a little closer. This is serious for some smaller stations that do not spend lots of cash on make-up or sets. All of a sudden they realize they have to spend more on clothes, on sets, on profes- sional make-up . . . it gets like film. All this costs more money and they are asking 'where does the extra money come from?'

Peled's company developed the multi-camera angle technology used on BSkyB's digital transmissions, permitting viewers to call up their own sub-set of news from its Sky News service.

Look further ahead, look past the current Sky Digital system, which is already the best in the world. Look to even greater fragmentation of the audience. Take the USA, perhaps the most radical example of this, where over the past ten years some fifty per cent of the prime-time audience has disappeared from the major networks. But it's not that they're sitting in front of their PCs, but they are watching one of the dozens of other cable networks. It hasn't changed that much, simply fragmented in sub-sets of an audience. It makes it more difficult for advertisers to reach that mass audience, but in many respects digital allows more targeted advertising, even down to post code advertising. BMW's for Manhattan, and Range Rovers for the country.

Television is already changing as a result of the influence of computing; for example, the tumbling fall in the cost of chipsets, which Peled says already cost 'nothing and next year will be next to nothing'. Storage costs are also in free-fall, and this makes successful digital forecasting possible. 'Cheap chips will make digital set-top boxes even more affordable', says Peled.

However, most developed countries of the world are already migrating to digital transmission. They too want to re-allocate analogue bandwidth for more lucrative uses, and one way or another by around 2008–2010 European broadcasters expect to be fully digital. While viewers may not be enjoying commonplace HDTV transmissions, there seems to be an inexorable slide towards whatever the Hollywood studios want; if Hollywood says HDTV, then it will be HDTV for all.

The cost of entertainment, at least as far as the hardware is concerned, is falling: inexpensive chip-sets, lower-cost flat-screen televisions, free or inexpensive set-top boxes, and not forgetting Dolby multi-channel surround sound (said by more than a few experts to have been responsible for selling more large-screen televisions than any other technological advance since colour). But convergence, from the world wide web and cheap telephony, is also influencing every element of the broadcasting mix.

Take these words from WebTV's Jim Beveridge (in September 1999):

[The industry is] going to be using more fibre, more ADSL, more cable, satellite and wireless. In my view we are going to be using a mixture of broadcast standards and IP-based standards. I see broadcast and IP protocol-based standards coming together. If you are thinking of what the consumer is going to use, then what the consumer is going to have is a number of gateways to getting programming to him. Some will be IP-based and some will be broadcast-based, and I actually think the methods that will work will be when the two base-standards come together which is very much the way [Microsoft] is heading right now.

Beveridge adds:

> Clearly there are bandwidth restrictions on the Internet and I
> see the Internet almost like a sea of technology and services.
> What people will do is take elements of that which is offered
> and build into their own networks what they believe is worth
> including. So you are going to see live streamed media [direct]
> across from Australia to California then it is not going to be a
> great experience. But if you have servers where the material
> has been cached and in addition have access to cellular
> bandwidth then you will be able to receive the video without
> problem at all.

This is the clue: unlimited bandwidth, web-streaming, cellular . . .
Because I am a journalist specializing in broadcasting, I have
tended to skirt around cellular telephone technology, and
even the fast-emerging Palm-type and Windows-CE personal
devices. As 2000 unfolds this is now almost impossible; the creative
people at Nokia, Ericsson and Motorola talk about 'next generation' cellular telephony, with harmonized standards now agreed.
We now have cell-phones that can surf the web, transmit video
and recognize human speech for ease of operation, and far more
is promised.

These are not so-called 'blue-sky' developments. Already on
the market in its second iteration is the famous Nokia
'Communicator': a telephone, keyboard, e-mail and fax machine
all in one. Indeed, the Windows CE-based devices (such as the
Philips 'Velo' and Casio 'Cassiopeia') take this technology and
build in voice-recording functionality on a solid-state circuit. The
Panasonic 'IC' recorder has similar functionality, offering 60
minutes of recording in a tiny machine the same size as a credit
card, while the Philips 'Xenium' is a GSM phone that accepts voice
commands.

All these products exist, and some of them have been about
for a few years. The industry is now gearing up for the next-generation cellular telephones which conform to the WAP (Wireless
Application Protocols) 'media telephone' standard. Nokia released

its first model (7110) in the summer of 1999. It allows users to surf the web and display information in a text format on an expanded LCD screen.

Sweden's Ericsson has similar models (MC218 or R380 dual band), promising simplicity of use and guaranteeing you will be 'surfing' within five minutes of owning the phone. In Japan, NTT DoCoMo, the world's largest mobile phone operator, claimed more than one million subscribers to its new 'i-mode' mobile that uses 'compact HTML' to access the web, e-mail and on-line banking. For 2000, NTT is promising MPEG-4 coding for its next-generation devices based on W-CDMA (Wideband-Code Division Multiple Access) technology. In addition to speech, music and ISDN-type video, NTT believes W-CDMA will allow users to access these 'broadcast' services almost anywhere in the world.

Kyocera's Visual Phone VP-210, suggested as the ultimate in PHS (Personal Handyphone Systems) can receive and transmit live video, send and receive still digital photos and incorporates a visual data bank of 200 numbers and their owners' images.

While all-powerful Microsoft is pushing its Windows-CE technology as the operating system and solution for 'broadcasting' the web to television sets, cellular phones and perhaps even the wristwatch, Europe's cell-phone makers seem to have the edge with their Symbian consortium, using an advanced operating system (Epoc) based on that developed by hand-held computer specialists Psion. One challenge still to be overcome by all these mobile-based technologies, no matter how they operate, is the twin – and usually contradictory – demands of most users. On the one hand, users want small cellular devices; on the other, manufacturers want more functionality; and the moment you build-in a 'TV' screen you have an inherent drift towards bulk and high battery-power consumption.

WebTV's Beveridge thinks most of our new services will be based around web sites.

Look at what the BBC is doing with their 6 p.m. and 9 p.m. news. I see people adding to that sort of concept, so that consumers can pick up their information as and when they want it. In my view the time-shift marketplace is going to be large in that respect, and it might be because they will go direct to the server to pick it up, or the fact that somebody is prepared to stream it to me specifically when I want it.

Steve Billinger, from Sky Interactive, agrees.

First off, all current digital platforms will continue and will have a viable share, and all of their principal roles will be in building the platforms of choice for building compelling media brands, and those brands will be extended to all other digital platforms. Every future platform will be digital and interactive as matter of course. It doesn't matter where or what it is. I am including digital radio, all forms of wireless, all forms of broadband. In my view television will continue to be used to build the primary compelling brand position, and that all of those platforms will deliver slices of the content pie. I use the term 'content continuum'.

Billinger suggests what he calls a perfect example:

Mention family entertainment and you think of – perhaps it's the BBC in the UK but in the USA it's Disney – and when they want to experience family entertainment they need to be able to find a Disney-branded product, and I think they will be able to find that brand and product on every available platform. There'll be times when they are on the radio, and the Theme Park, and on Broadway, and the hockey team in the park on a Saturday night. Each will continue as viable-share businesses, they will be the first choice for building that primary brand value. They will almost certainly be the starting off point. However, all of these platforms must be seamlessly integrated to present a kind of content continuum.

Disney is surely the perfect example of brand extension. Not content with animation, or natural history or even theme parks, their brand can now be found just everywhere. Who would have guessed that a movie (*The Mighty Ducks*) might now be experienced as a Disney-owned sports team?

Content is not King

Disney's attempt shows that the normally accepted truism of broadcasting, that 'content is King' is only partially true. More accurate in a digital, multi-channel, multi-platform age, might be 'The trusted brand is King'. Billinger comments:

> The blur between content and technology, or content and utility, is going to be so fuzzy that it will be difficult to differentiate what is what. For example, in any interactive space what is e-mail? I call it non-category specific content. It isn't news, sports or entertainment, but it's a critical part of the customer offering, and this is the main thing that so-called new media guys don't get. Because increasingly the technology is king, they are both kings.

Some industry experts have suggested that only established brands have any chance of succeeding in this new world. Billinger disagrees:

> Let's go back. Look at the three most recognized brands that have emerged recently, none of which are in the 'content' business that we would normally recognize: Amazon, e-Bay and Yahoo! All three represent utility, and utility has become content in that environment, and that has built their brand value. We all thought that 'content was king' meant CNN and the like. My view is that these are now irrelevant and that customers in an interactive technology-based market, which is what every future platform will be, cannot tell the difference [between CNN and Yahoo!]. One way to do it is to supply better features, better technology, than anyone else or package those utilities, features or technologies better than anyone else, which is what the portal-play is all about, or create platform-specific via the usual types of media structures.

'Portal play' is a neat phrase. The concept that your network TV channel is now also your portal, your doorway to an entertainment-rich nirvana, is a view shared by Claire Leproust, head of interactivity at Canal+. She already sees the Canal+-backed digital bouquet (Canal Satellite Numerique) as being a 'portal' in its own right.

> If you look at a bouquet like ours we already have these channels but also it means that each channel becomes a mini-portal, and if you accept the idea that each channel [focuses] viewers interest and going a step further, each programme can be a sub-portal at that time with each channel playing a role to promote that portal.

Adam Singer is chairman of Flextech plc, the UK's largest digital broadcaster after BSkyB, and the name behind such channels as Living, Bravo, Trouble and Challenge TV. Flextech is also in a huge joint-venture with the BBC (UKTV). Singer comments:

> In my view everything becomes a sub-set of the Internet. The Internet's high-speed capacity is capable of carrying [everything]. If that is a true statement then you just pull down from the pipe the information you want and you utilize it on the device that's most relevant to you. This is already done and exists on the telephone. The telephone line is the pipe, and if it happens to be a fax signal you pull it down to a fax machine, if it's a paging message it goes to a pager or if it's voice to a telephone. It seems to me the same thing happens here. You have your info-brand and you pull down the bit you want onto the appropriate technology. The one thing you don't want to get hung up on is the 'lean-forward', 'lean-back' thing-in-the-corner conversation. Because there will be times when you want to be told a story, and times when you want to interact, and times when you want to know more.

Flextech is already developing this concept; web sites are backing up every one of their channels, but these sites are turning up as channels as part of Flextech's digital TV offering. Singer says:

You will choose the appropriate device for the time and place.
You can already see this on the MP3 player. What is an MP3
unit, but a portable hard-drive? It provides all sorts of
opportunities for mainstream broadcasters. Take *The Archers*
[a popular and long-running radio soap-opera] on the BBC.
Why they have not thought about putting out whole batches of
back-catalogue files of *The Archers* so that people can drop
into the series whenever they want to. . . Or take *Gardener's
Question Time* [another long-running radio show]. Why not
offer listeners the ability to pull down all the answers about
greenfly on roses. You no longer need a radio for this, yet it is
the exact same piece of information. Miss the show on Sunday
at 2 p.m. and you can listen to it on the way to work or the
shops on Monday morning on your MP3 player.

Neither does Singer see there being a 'winner-takes-all' technology
emerging.

It's interesting that there should be any concept of a single
winner. The concept doesn't exist with music, where there are
umpteen ways of receiving music. You don't often hear the
argument that radio was the 'winner' over the concert hall.
They are both forms of distribution and dissemination. So, it
strikes me that it is to do with the right way to receive
information at any given moment. You want to find out where
a local restaurant is, you tune into your Internet-connected,
sat-nav GPS whatsit, pull down the information, push a button
to make a booking and it will give you the 3 star rating, and
that is exactly the right device for that piece of information!
And we could do that perfectly easily right now.

He goes further:

As soon a you start trying to select a winner you are lost. You
can be certain that is not going to be the winner. In 1983 I
decided with my career choice that cable was going to be the
winner! I am not too sure I got it right. If you are in the content
business the job is to get the content out . . . Eric Clapton does

not care how he gets heard, as long as he is on CD, mini-disc, cassette, MP3 and the radio . . . That's the issue. The future is everybody will be a digital home and every home will have the ability to receive significantly more signal than they can receive now and they will all have some ability to interact whether they elect to or not.

That is the basis of this book – during the next ten years every home will be a digital home whether people like it or not. There's one other thought I want to share. A long time ago, when I was still in short trousers, for a bit of extra pocket money I delivered groceries for the corner shop to customers living locally. I had to take special care with the eggs, then sold loose.

Now we have tele-shopping, and I am hooked. I already buy my books from Amazon.com and the big groceries from a home-delivery supermarket and my wine and water from other bulk-suppliers. Currently I do all this via the PC, but I want the convenience of doing it from the television, while e-mailing my family, and ordering a CD. I am not alone, and when every home *is* a digital home and the dumb television, linked to a telephone, has interactive potential, I know consumers will react positively. But I might just also want to do it from my cell-phone, or portable Palm-Pilot when sat on a train or in a traffic jam. It will make my life more convenient, and I am not alone. Whether I'll want them to deliver my eggs only time will tell.

2

The analogue television business today

It is frequently suggested that the 'golden age' of television was during the period 1950–60. It is true that television almost ruined Hollywood's fortunes during this period; but if this was the golden age, then it was one of black and white, somewhat limited creativity, poor reception, lack of competition (except in the USA) and, by and large, public service broadcasting.

In 1950 television was at its most mature in the USA where, during the first six months of that year, some three million sets were sold. Four networks competed for viewer loyalty (NBC, CBS, ABC and DuMont), although NBC and CBS dominated. The DuMont network went out of business in 1956 and ABC struggled through television's first ten years before finding its feet in the 1960s.

In war-ravaged Europe, progress was significantly slower. France established *Radiodiffusion-Télévision Française* (RTF) immediately after the liberation in 1945 but did not initiate full weekday television until 1947. Its millionth television receiver was not sold until 1958, despite the development in 1956 of its *Sequential Coleur à Memoire* (SECAM, Sequential Colour with Memory) colour system.

Germany had managed to maintain a pattern of propaganda television broadcasting to public places until 1944, but it was not until 1949 and the establishment of the Federal Republic that 'modern' television could even begin to blossom. Control of television was ceded to the various regional *Lander*, although the whole system was hamstrung by the notorious *Proporz* method, whereby political parties allocated senior television posts in direct proportion to their parliamentary powers; the programming chief coming from Party A, news chief from Party B, etc. ARD, West Germany's first public network (although supported by advertising), was joined by ZDF in 1962, again with commercial time sold in specific time slots, but not within programmes.

Television broadcasting in the UK recommenced in 1946, under the firm hand of John Reith. With a new Conservative government elected in 1951, approval was given for a second, commercial service to be established with a franchised system of regional operators, licensed by the (then) Independent Television Authority. If sales of television sets are any guide, then the coronation of Queen Elizabeth II in 1953 marked the beginning of the UK's television age.

Japan's television engineers had pioneered many developments pre-war, but television was initiated by public broadcaster NHK on 1 February 1953, and a commercial service (Nippon TV) on 28 August. Services were limited to Tokyo, and not surprisingly receivers were limited – just 866 at year-end. Imported from the USA, a set would typically cost 250 000 yen, equivalent to the annual salary of a middle-class white-collar worker. Another royal event, the wedding of Crown Prince Akihito to Michiko Shoda (10 April 1959), was again the catalyst in selling an estimated two million sets.

Fifty years of progress

If we take 1950 as a generic 'starting point' for modern television broadcasting, then the medium is only now, in the year 2000, celebrating its fiftieth birthday. It has come a long way. While it would be simple to categorize television's development over this fifty-year period, this book has 'digital' in its title, and to get from analogue to digital is not simply a technical quantum leap, it also represents the development and maturity of the analogue system. Without multi-channel analogue television, the mass-market penetration of television sets and general economic prosperity we would not have the necessary base ingredients to make the great leap forward.

A history reminder: In 1957 the Soviet Union launched Sputnik, the world's first artificial satellite.

Analogue television today contains all the necessary components to make a seamless switch to digital – and beyond – fairly easy to achieve. Indeed, for the US people the bulk of their digital signals are simply re-transmissions of their existing analogue TV broadcasts. Wholly new digital services, from satellite operators such as DirecTV and EchoStar, are generally extensions of existing channel offerings, plus a few extra movie services and sports channels (frequently structured into thematic services/events), Pay Per View (PPV) or Near Video-on-Demand (NVOD) movie channels and some extra channels to boost the basic tier.

Virtually all these services exist to a greater or lesser degree on US and Canadian cable systems, in analogue. Besides a clear improvement in transmission quality, digital broadcasting, whether via existing cable or by Direct-To-Home (DTH) satellite transmission, is currently essentially a means of adding channels and viewer choice to the typical 45–60 channel line-up available to US cable viewers.

This situation is changing rapidly. Globally there are exciting changes afoot as cable companies upgrade their analogue networks to cater for digital services (of which more later). Let us refresh our memories as to how the industry arrived at the position today.

'The American way'

Event one: Open house for cable

Until the 1970s, television was a closed business. The established network players, whether in the USA or Europe, had things pretty much their own way. In the USA, however, three quite separate events radically changed the way broadcasting developed.

In 1972 the US television licensing authority, the Federal Communications Commission (FCC), permitted cable operators to enter the top 100 broadcast markets in the USA. At that time, cable companies were specifically limited in the way they could conduct business in cities where the broadcast monopoly was in the hands of expensively licensed over-the-air stations; they thus made their cash by delivering signals to outlying suburbs.

In 1972 just 6.5 million homes subscribed to cable. By 1982 that figure had jumped to 27 million. By 1992 connections were close to 60 million. By May 1999 the number had grown to 67.6 million subscribers out of 95.6 million homes passed (where a cable passes a home, but is not necessarily connected to that home).

Since 1995 the growth of cable has slowed, not surprisingly, considering the high penetration levels; but it is also a result of digital dish sales beginning to eat into this established market. Nevertheless, cable growth, according to Robert Nelson, director of Standard & Poor's Communications and Cable group rate (as at July 1997) shows a buoyant 2–3 per cent annual growth despite competition from digital Direct Broadcasting by Satellite (DBS). Later we will analyse this competition in more detail, but for the sake of comparison, US cable grew by an average 3–4 per cent

Table 2.1   US cable connections 1994–99*

	1994	1995	1996	1997	1998	1999*
US TV households	94.4 m	95.4 m	96.5 m	97.4 m	98.5 m	99.4 m
Cable ho mes passed	91.1 m	92.0 m	93.3 m	94.2 m	95.2 m	95.5 m
Subscribers	58.0 m	59.4 m	62.9 m	64.2 m	65.3 m	67.6 m

*To May 1999

Note: The FCC's declared number of TV households for regulatory calculation is 96.9 million, as at 1998. The television industry estimates a higher number of TV households.

Data: Industry sources; *Cable World,* 1999

Table 2.2   US TV Households – the next thirty years

1999	2000	2005	2010	2015	2020	2025	2030
99.4 m	100.8 m	106.1 m	111.8 m	118 m	124 m	129.6 m	134.7 m

Data: Neilsen Media Research, September 1999. Data on 1 Jan each year

Table 2.3   Twenty-five years of growth: US cable subscriptions

1972	1977	1980	1982	1985	1987	1990	1992
6.5 m	12.6 m	19.2 m	27.5 m	36.7 m	42.6 m	51.7 m	58 m

1995	1998	1999*
59.4 m	65.3 m	67.6 m

*May 1999

Data: Industry sources; *Cable World,* 1999

through the early-to-mid-1990s, and the 2+ per cent figure is better than most analysts were predicting as recently as 1995.

Event two: Channels galore

This second event was a product of the first. With increasing access to major towns and cities via cable, new broadcasters could enter markets previously closed to them. The first to do this was Home Box Office (HBO), a division of Time Inc., which started 'broadcasting' its 'movies-to-exclusive-entertainment service' on 8 November 1972, celebrating its twenty-fifth anniversary in November 1997. Late in 1975 HBO borrowed US$9 million from its parent to secure a long-term transponder lease on what was then a very rare commodity: an orbiting satellite owned by RCA.

> Without HBO there would be no modern cable industry. Through the 70s and early 80s the reasons people subscribed to cable were HBO, CNN and ESPN, but the fundamental driver was HBO. It was something Americans had never been able to get on their TV sets before: 24 hours of uncut, commercial-free movies and R-rated movies to boot.
>
> Larry Gerbrandt: VP, Paul Kagan Associates
> (personal interview, 1994)

HBO intended beaming its programming signal nation-wide, improving its then limited distribution, to cable head-ends (the point from which cable signals are distributed) for redistribution. At the time, according to Scientific Atlanta, there were only two ground-stations capable of picking up the transmissions.

A history reminder: In 1962 the USA launched TELSTAR, the world's first communications satellite used for TV programming.

Within weeks, Ted Turner (who had recently bought the Atlanta Braves baseball team and was keen to 'export' their televised games across the USA) was also after a transponder, a process that took him head-to-head with government. But HBO and Turner's plans galvanized the struggling cable industry. Teleprompter Corporation, then the nation's largest Multiple System Operator (MSO) but reportedly close to bankruptcy, ordered satellite earth stations for each of its systems. Other MSOs quickly followed suit.

Turner received a transmission licence on 27 December 1976. With typical Turner overstatement, he called his modest Atlanta Channel 17 WTCG service: 'The Superstation that Serves the Nation'. The actual 'nation' able to receive Turner's (or HBO's) satellite transmissions numbered no more than 10 000 homes, comprising the few cable operators that had by then installed earth stations. Turner later changed the station's name to TBS, and today the channel is consistently amongst the top three services in cable's basic tier.

Between them, HBO and Turner gave the cable industry a much-needed shot in the arm, providing two channels with counter-scheduling compared with the big three networks NBC, CBS and ABC. Other channels followed, although the next leap forward had to wait until Ted Turner launched his 24-hour Cable News Network (CNN) on 1 June 1980.

Event three: a recording studio in every home

The third development, again hand-in-hand with the growth of cable, was the rapid adoption by viewers (in the USA, Europe and Japan) of video cassette recorders (VCRs). After a slow start, not helped by competing recording standards, VCR sales briskly grew during the early 1980s, from 2.3 m by late 1981, 25 m by 1985 and 65 m by 1990. While viewers were still keen to watch network television, the arrival of a simple method to time-shift cable (or network) programming, gave an added impetus to installing cable.

The American way – today

Analogue broadcasting in the USA is (generally) profitable, diverse and vibrant. At the top of the tree are the 'big three' networks:

Table 2.4   The world's top media companies

		1996	1997	1998	1999
1	Walt Disney	18.7	22.4	22.97	-
2	Time Warner	10.0	13.2	14.5	-
3	Sony	-	10.5	14.4	14.5
4	Time Warner	10.8	11.3	12.2	-
5	Viacom	9.6	10.6	12.0	-
6	News Corp	8.2	9.0	11.9	-
7	Fox Entertainment	-	-	-	8.0
8	TCI	8.0	7.5	7.3	-
9	CBS	4.1	5.3	6.8	-
10	Hughes Electronics	4.0	5.1	5.9	-
11	Polygram	5.4	5.4	5.4	-
12	NBC	5.2	5.1	5.2	-
13	Seagram/Universal	5.1	5.5	5.0	-
14	BBC	-	-	4.4	4.7
15	Nintendo	2.8	3.3	4.3	-
16	CLT-Ufa	-	2.5	3.1	3.4
17	Fuji TV	2.9	3.2	3.3	-
18	Cablevision Systems	1.3	1.9	3.2	-
19	Carlton Communications	2.7	2.9	3.0	-
20	Canal+	1.9	2.3	2.7	-

Notes: (US$billion)

Sony data excludes electronics/insurance businesses.

1999 data shows results where announced prior to press time.

All local currencies shown in US dollars at constant 1998 rates.

Data shows companies by latest annual turnover, consequently does not show those companies (Viacom/CBS, NBC/Paxman) involved in late 1999 merger activity.

Source: Screen Digest, July 1999

The so-called 'Peacock Web' of NBC (owned by General Electric), the 'Eye Network' of CBS (since September 1999 owned by Viacom) and the 'Alphabet Web' of ABC (owned by Disney).

From a viewer's perspective, the three networks are much the same. Each network owns and operates (the 'O&Os') a limited number of stations. The formula for permitted station ownership is complex: networks can themselves own either twelve stations or reach a maximum of 35 per cent of the US population; but high-dial positioned UHF stations are considered only 50 per cent of the 'value' of low-dial VHF stations, helping distort the actual penetration figures. Suffice to say the major players are operating in the most lucrative 'big city' markets.

However, extended might and power comes from 'affiliate' stations, who carry network-provided programming to a near 100 per cent national penetration in return for a portion of the advertising revenue gained. The income structure for an affiliate station is also highly complex, but the end result sees the 'winning' network reward its affiliates with more favourable advertising rates.

All three networks have spent ample time in the financial doldrums. As at mid-summer 1997, ABC, as a core network, was only just profitable and struggling in the ratings. ABC is now part of the much larger Disney empire, a move that may simply be calculated to make the network a shop-window for Disney output and merchandise. But Disney provides a perfect example of the risks facing any of these new network owners. In the four years following Disney's acquisition of ABC (for US$19 billion, in 1995), ABC has seen profits plummet from around US$400 m a year to a loss of $100 m.

In September 1999 Viacom 'merged' with CBS in a deal valued at US$36 billion, creating another USA-based broadcasting powerhouse with annual revenues of more than US$20 billion. For its last complete year (1998) NBC saw profits evaporate by one third, while CBS barely broke even. It will be interesting to see how CBS, under Viacom's control, fares over the next year or so.

Since 1995 the prime-time ratings winner has tended to be NBC, thanks to seven out of the top ten shows (including *Seinfeld*, *Friends*, *Frasier*). In 1997 its profits were around US$500 million.

However success is conventionally measured, these three networks must be considered as dinosaurs. It matters little who is the current 'top dog', only that they are collectively losing audience share at a frightening rate. The facts are that in 1977, the three networks dominated prime-time television capturing 93 per cent of viewing. This figure was down to 89 per cent by 1980, to 74 per cent by 1985, 71 per cent in 1987 and 65 per cent in 1990. During the winter 1996–97 season, their share had dropped to 49 per cent of prime-time viewing according to Nielson Media Research, the first time their collective share dropped below the 50 per cent mark.

Even worse, any network might have an individual high-spot but it comes at the expense of the other two, tending not to eat into basic cable's audience share at all. In other words the 'big three' networks are eating each other alive.

> Part of [the problem] is that there are more entertainment options out there, and not just on the television dial.
>
> Giles Lundberg, Fox TV's head of research and marketing.
> *Variety* magazine, May 1997

Network television's decline

The reasons for this decline are two-fold. First, as its penetration increased, cable viewing eroded the network share of viewing. While some cable channels slightly increased their own viewing share, it was the growing number of channels available through the late 1980s and 1990s, plus the 65+ per cent penetration of cable, that has worn down the network's domination.

In mid-1999 there were more than 200 analogue niche channels already transmitting to US viewers, many of them achieving less than 0.1 per cent audience share, and with dozens waiting for extra capacity to be created. Fewer than 50 of those broadcasting found nation-wide carriage owing to the previously mentioned capacity limitations, suffered by virtually all cable operators. An increasing number of channels are finding carriage on new digital networks, and on digital satellite, of which more later.

Secondly, the three networks were challenged by new entrants to non-cable network television, that is, conventional over-the-air broadcasting. In 1970 there were only 65 independent (non-affiliated) television stations; by 1980 the number had grown to 115. Lower cost transmission equipment and the attractive advertising market made owning a television station desirable, particularly to publishing groups. In the 1990 television census, there were 339 independent stations. We will look at the prospects for emerging 'micro-TV' stations in a later chapter.

Rupert Murdoch started building his Fox Network in 1986, buying the Metromedia group of stations and then, through further purchases and affiliate relationships, launching Fox as a rated network in time for the winter season 1990–91. Initially Fox was very much a part-time network, ignoring some weeknights completely, and leaving breakfast and day-time alone. In mid-1997 Fox started to offer a near-complete schedule. Their winter season (1996–97) achieved a 13 per cent share of prime-time across all viewing.

A typical week on Fox TV (late August, 1999) saw *The Simpsons* gather a 13 per cent share of all viewing, helping to drive the network to an average 12–14 per cent (dependent on which week one examines). This is behind the 'big three' of ABC, CBS and NBC, but Fox is less interested in 'all viewing', preferring to target the more lucrative 'teens and twenties' age group. It has largely succeeded in its goals.

Fox TV consistently wins the weekend morning slots, with a typical 20 per cent share, with only the Disney-backed ABC Network's 10 per cent share coming close to Fox. Fox owns 23 stations, reaching 34.8 per cent of FCC-calculated television households. At mid-August 1999 Fox was the biggest American television group, bigger than CBS, NBC or ABC when measured by audience reach.

In addition to Fox, the 'big three' have had to cope with challenges from two other mini-networks (usually referred to as 'baby-nets'). United Paramount (UPN) broadcasts on five evenings a week (Monday to Friday) gaining a typical 4–5 per cent audience share, while the Warner Brothers Network (WB) transmits programming on Sunday to Thursday achieving around 4 per cent share.

Table 2.5   The top 20 USA TV groups*

Rank	Group	No. of stations	FCC audience coverage (%)
1	Fox TV Stations Inc.	23	34.8
2	CBS Stations Inc.	14	30.9
3	Paxson Communications Group	44	26.8
4	Tribune Broadcasting	17	25.9
5	NBC Inc.	11	24.6
6	Walt Disney/ABC Inc.	10	24.0
7	Gannett Broadcasting	18	18.0
8	Chris Craft/BHC/Utd	8	17.6
9	HSN Inc/Silver King	17	16.4
10	Telemundo	8	10.7
11	A H Belo	16	10.5
12	Paramount Stations	13	9.1
13	Univision TV Group	12	9.9
14	Cox Broadcasting	12	9.5
15	Hearst-Argyle TV	16	9.2
16	Young Broadcasting	15	9.0
17	E W Scripps Co.	10	8.7
18	Sinclair Broadcasting	28	8.2
19	Post-Newsweek Stations	6	7.1
20	Meredith Corporation	11	6.2

*Data: *Broadcasting & Cable,* 1999

Table 2.6   USA network rankings*

1	NBC
2	CBS
3	ABC
4	Fox
5	UPN
6	WB

*All-adults, prime-time average 1997–8 winter season
Data: Industry sources

In addition to these newcomers, analogue over-the-air transmissions have other challenges, again eroding network share for the majors. Two Spanish-language broadcasters are achieving notable success in highly-regional markets: Univision (carried to 92 per cent of Spanish-speaking households) and Telemundo (carried to 80 per cent of Spanish-speaking households). In 1998 Univision regularly attracted 80 per cent of Spanish speakers, putting the broadcaster ahead of all the major networks in Hispanic neighbourhoods. With a diet of *telenovellas* and game shows Univision's network even outperformed UPN and WB nationally. About half its programming is original, mostly produced in Miami, the rest bought in from Venezuela, Argentina and other Latin American markets. Telemundo, the second largest Hispanic network has production facilities in Hialeah near Miami, Los Angeles and Puerto Rico, although its daily output is less than Univision.

There are other network groupings, of which the most significant is Barry Diller's Home Shopping Network/Universal. Other groups predominantly transmit religious programming.

It has frequently been said that Fox, UPN and WB are just cable channels that have a mainstream distribution chain. Certainly the programming on offer, themed and stripped across schedules, has far more in common with cable than with the 'conventional' networks, who attempt to satisfy the interests and tastes of a much wider audience.

The growth of cable

Cable distribution in the United States was recently described as the '57 Million Club', whereby the top 25 multiple system operators (MSOs) controlled some 88 per cent or 57 million of the USA's 67 million cabled homes. Any examination of US cable can only ever be a snapshot in time, as the industry is highly volatile with frequent buying, selling, swapping and merging of systems.

Cable companies offer a mix of local programming; the FCC 'must carry' regulations obliging them to supply all local network channels. As described earlier, specific channels like HBO, CNN and ESPN were designed exclusively for carriage by cable (and

Table 2.7   The top 25 US cable companies

Rank	Company	Subscriptions (m)	Penetration (%)	Pay/Basic* (%)
1	Tele-Communications Inc	14.3	60	108
2	Time Warner Cable	12.3	68	65
3	US West Media Group	5.2	63	83
4	Comcast	4.3	62	92
5	Cox Communications	3.2	65	61
6	Cablevision Systems	2.8	65	150
7	Adelphia Cable Communications	1.8	71	50
8	Jones Intercable	1.4	62	80
9	Century Communications	1.2	59	n/a
10	Marcus Cable	1.19	64	56
11	Suburban Cable	1.15	76	65
12	Charter Communications	1.07	56	54
13	Falcon Cable	1.05	80	29
14	Prime Cable	0.85	53	87
15	InterMedia Partners	0.82	63	66
16	TCA Cable Television	0.7	76	65
17	Cable ONE	0.63	74	64
18	Fanch Communications	0.50	69	38
19	Multimedia Cablevision	0.47	61	69
20	Triax Communications	0.45	69	63
21	C-TEC Cable Systems	0.37	65	n/a
22	Rifkin & Associates	0.31	71	54
23	Service Electric Cable	0.29	72	37
24	Tele-Media Corp	0.28	77	31
25	SBC Media Ventures	0.27	66	100

*Pay/Basic, the number of customers who take a premium channel

Source: *Broadcasting & Cable*, June 1997

Author's note: This 1997 listing remains interesting, if only to show the wide disparity between different companies on both the all-important cable penetration rates and pay-basic ratios.

more recently the growing number of digital Direct Broadcasting Satellites, DBS). Cable operators throughout the world use the US model, in which MSOs split channels into two quite distinct types: a basic tier usually priced to include anything between 20 and 40 channels, and premium services charged on an individual or à la carte basis.

Table 2.8 The top US cable operators*

1	TCI/AT&T	$5.0 bn
2	Time Warner	$3.7 bn
3	Cablevision	$2.4 bn
4	Cox Communications	$2.0 bn
5	Comcast	$1.25 bn

*By turnover (US$)
Data: Screen Digest, July 1999

Squeezed out

Far from the much talked-about '500 channel universe', even the USA, the most mature television market in the world, cannot find adequate space for more than a third of the channels currently available.

> We've got four not-fully-distributed networks out there in Cartoon Network, Turner Classic Movies, CNN/Sports Illustrated and CNNfn, so I don't know at this point that it makes any sense to try and put any more out there.
>
> Brad Seigel, president TNT/TCM,
> personal interview March 1997

In 1995 there were four proposed networks wishing to cover the 'family/parenting' sector. Only one remains. Speaking in March 1997, James Zeilinger, president of Parent Television, said that more Americans subscribe to parenting magazines than food or health titles, but his network still couldn't find carriage space. 'We came close many times to signing a deal,' he said. '[but] it's a chicken and egg situation . . . we can't afford to bleed that much [cash] until there are more than a few million [digital boxes].'

The US cable market is beginning to address this capacity shortage by overlaying and converting its current analogue copper co-axial systems to glass fibre and hybrid-fibre/co-axial ready for digital. (Chapter 3 describes how cable companies are converting to digital.)

In North America there is other broadcast activity besides cable. We need to mention the direct-to-home satellite market that grew up in the whole of North America. During the 1960s and 1970s, the radiated power from an orbiting satellite was weak, needing very large receiving dishes on the ground. Nevertheless, some enthusiasts started eavesdropping on this signal in much the same way radio amateurs have always sought out weak and distant signals.

By the early 1980s satellite power outputs were increasing, and dishes commensurately reduced in size, enabling a wider audience to invest in what were then called TVRO systems (Television Receive Only Earth Stations). Now we would simply call them dishes. HBO, for example, were forbidden to distribute their signals via cable in Canada, and many Canadians bought two and three-metre dishes to receive signals, even though viewing such signals was technically illegal in Canada.

For many years reception of such signals (in the USA as well as Canada) was ignored by the broadcaster. The market was small in comparison to that of cable, but by the early 1990s this had grown to some 4 million 'backyard' dish systems. Scrambling, already common to cable viewers, was becoming increasingly normal on all satellite transmissions thus forcing viewers to subscribe, usually to a programme packager.

By mid-1999 this analogue market was in steep decline in the USA and Canada, as digital broadcasting became more commonplace, and viewers saw the benefits of digital transmission over analogue. During the first half of 1999 this market declined, losing another 94 000 subscribers to a new low of 2.18 million 'backyard' dish homes. It is expected to fall back to a level where viewing with large, steerable dishes is again limited to enthusiasts. This is already happening and by mid-2000 numbers had dropped below 2 million.

The European way – today

Describing analogue television in Europe represents something of a challenge when compared with the US model. Besides the obvious linguistic and cultural differences, there are significant contrasts among the European countries in how broadcasting has evolved since the Second World War.

A history reminder: News International buys struggling Satellite TV, and renames it Sky TV, 1983. In 1988 News Corp launched a four-channel Sky service.

According to the advertising industry, in television terms Europe comprises 33 countries and 35 sales markets (the difference being the linguistic splits in Belgium and Switzerland). Some pan-European satellite channels have attempted to break through these national and linguistic barriers (notably the original Sky channel in 1982, 'SuperChannel' which launched in February 1987 and MTV which launched in August 1987). However, Europe remains a fragmented television market.

Even though the official line from the European Community is to support and encourage the concept of 'television without frontiers', the reality is that European harmonization of television services simply has not happened. There is some limited cross-border traffic in complete channels (French channels in Wallonia, Dutch channels in Flanders, BBC services in Ireland and The Netherlands), but these are the exception and generally restricted to linguistic groupings.

Europe shares at least one common trait with the USA, however: an ability to create super-large TV groups, frequently headed by a so-called media mogul. While the US giants (Time Warner, Viacom) are significantly larger than their European counterparts, in many respects the European 'mogul' has a high visibility outside the media sector, notably Leo Kirch, Silvio Berlusconi and of course, Rupert Murdoch (an 'honorary' European in this case because of his significant European media interests). Though the USA has important names like Ted Turner and Bill Gates, one suspects that few ordinary members of the viewing public could name the various conglomerate chief executives now running NBC or ABC, or even important media figures like Gerald Levin (Time Warner) or Sumner Redstone (Viacom). Most people in the USA would almost certainly recognize Rupert Murdoch, however.

It is also worth bearing in mind that, as already mentioned, television in Europe is a relatively modern phenomenon. Whereas the USA had an estimated 36m television households by February 1955, the whole of Europe possessed only some 4.8 m television sets (Smith, 1995).

There is one other important similarity with viewers in North America. Europeans are turning away from the established public 'free-to-air' networks (both publicly supported and commercial). In the 'big five' European markets, for example, only France held on to market share in the period 1990–1995.

Table 2.9   Public broadcasters' viewing shares

	1990 (%)	1995 (%)
UK	57	54
Germany	58	35
France	33	42
Spain	74	37
Italy	50	49

Source: Zenith Media, Feb 1997

Since 1995, the decline of public broadcast viewing has been more rapid, as multi-channel television gained wider acceptance in virtually all key markets and in the UK especially.

Analogue cable

An analysis of European cable (and satellite) connections shows how far more widespread multi-channel viewing has become since 1990. Indeed, prior to 1990 cable distribution was far from widespread. Only in Belgium was cable available nation-wide (1988, passing some 97 per cent of homes with 87 per cent connections), followed by The Netherlands (1988, 76 per cent of homes passed, 72 per cent connections). By comparison, in West Germany in 1988, while cable passed well over three-quarters of homes, actual subscribers measured less than 19 million television households.

> **A history reminder:** The first Astra (1A) satellite was launched aboard an Arianespace rocket from Kourou in French Guiana in December 1988.

Just as HBO, Turner and the other broadcasters in the USA had sought to reach their viewers exclusively by cable, so various broadcasting groups attempted a similar approach in Europe. The early operators tried to imitate the US broadcasting model; intending their signals to reach cable distributors and deliberately making their channels near-copies of commercial television services, although heavily (indeed, almost exclusively) dependent on inexpensive, imported programming.

Along with Sky Channel, TEN (The Entertainment Network) was launched in March 1984. It failed a year later, to be re-launched as Mirrorvision, owned by Robert Maxwell. Mirrorvision merged with UK-based Premiere in April 1986. Premiere closed in 1989 and Sky Channel, despite News Corporation's involvement, struggled, as did SuperChannel.

These pan-European services, lured by the concept of broadcasting a common entertainment channel to a growing number of well-heeled viewers, found some enthusiastic support from younger viewers but the numbers were never enough to attract adequate advertising support. The early satellite broadcasts were made from low-power orbiting, effectively ruling out their reception 'direct to home'.

The universe of homes is not big enough to support thematic channels.

R. Hooper, managing director, SuperChannel
Cable & Satellite Europe, September 1987

Table 2.10 European cable penetration

	1988	1989	1990	1991	1992	1993	1994	1995	1996	1997
TVHH	118 m	120 m	122 m	132 m	133 m	134 m	135 m	136 m	138 m	141m
Passed HH	–	32.4 m	37.5 m	36 m	40.4 m	44.7 m	48.3 m	52.3 m	55 m	66.9 m
Connected	15.4 m	18 m	21.7 m	25.1 m	28.1 m	32.8 m	35.7 m	38 m	39.8 m	41 m
Connected%	–	55.7	57.9	69.7	73.4	73.8	72.7	73.8	72.4	72.6

Notes: Percentage connection is of homes passed.

In 1991 the former East Germany was included in data.

Source: European Audiovisual Observatory/European Cable Communications Association, 1998.

Table 2.11 European cable/satellite: 1999*

Country	Popu-lation (m)	TV households (m)	Homes passed (m)	Cable Subscriptions (m)	Satellite Subscriptions (m)
Austria	8.1	3.15	1.7	1.1	1.04
Belgium	10.2	4.17	4.0	3.86	0.1
Denmark	5.3	2.44	1.66	1.35	0.88
Estonia	1.47	0.54	0.22	0.12	-
Finland	5.15	2.47	1.3	0.90	0.9
France	60.0	24.0	7.72	2.66	1.75
Germany	82.0	33	26.0	18.7	13.6
Ireland	3.7	1.2	0.97	0.96	0.09
Israel	6.1	1.7	1.6	1.1	-
Italy	58.0	21.5	0.9	0.07	2.0
Netherlands	15.6	6.69	6.3	6.0	0.32
Norway	4.45	1.8	0.9	0.77	0.3
Portugal	9.8	4.18	1.8	0.56	0.02
Romania	22.5	8.1	5.6	3.0	0.2
Slovenia	2.0	0.6	-	0.24	-
Sweden	8.85	4.09	2.6	2.0	0.4
Switzerland	7.1	3.1	2.6	2.6	2.8
UK	58.8	23.8	11.9	3.9	3.5

*Data: European Cable Communications Association, 1999

Sky Channel was Europe's first satellite television channel, launched in April 1982. In 1983 News International bought 65 per cent of its shares, and by 1988 it owned 82 per cent. In 1987 Sky increased its capitalization by raising £22.63 million, but its losses up till then (and subsequently) were substantial, amounting by the end of its 1987–88 financial year to almost £39 million.

Table 2.12 Sky Channel losses

15 months to June 1984	−£5.7 m*
12 months to June 1985	−£8.6 m
12 months to June 1986	−£5.6 m
12 months to June 1987	−£10.2 m
12 months to June 1988	−£8.4 m

*All pre-tax.
Source: Company Reports

Even early launches of popular thematic channels like MTV had tough times, and many forget that Viacom's first partner in Europe for MTV was Robert Maxwell (who owned a 51 per cent share of MTV Europe, with another 24 per cent owned by British Telecom). Cabled homes (less than fifteen million over the whole of Europe in 1988) were still insufficient to provide a viable market for international services.

Analogue satellite

Analogue satellite broadcasting in Europe had developed in a very haphazard way prior to 1988. During the 1980s there were eight active satellites over Europe, ranging from some with a single channel up to EUTELSAT's busy EUTELSAT 1-F4 with fifteen channels by early 1989.

In 1988 Sky Channel estimated its maximum potential audience as some twelve million households.

The market needed something else to spur it to action, and that happened on 11 December 1988 when Astra 1A blasted off from Kourou in French Guiana. Astra was owned and financed privately by a Luxembourg consortium, Societé Europeenne des Satellites (SES), incorporated in the Grand Duchy of Luxembourg in 1985.

Luxembourg holds a special place in the hearts of most Europeans of a certain age, as the home of Europe's first free-enterprise broadcasting, namely Radio Luxembourg, which established itself during the 1930s on an output of popular programmes supported by advertising and sponsorship. The original company (Compagnie Luxembourgeoise de Radiodiffusion) went on to become CLT, of which more later.

In 1983 a percipient Luxembourg government took the decision to enter the so-called satellite age, a decision that was considered brave by many commentators at the time. SES/Astra's early publicity proclaimed the Brussels-backed message of 'Television Without Frontiers – Entertainment from the Stars'. Its first satellite (Astra 1A) was launched successfully on 11 December 1988, from which broadcasters supplied a mix of English and German

Table 2.13   Some of the early analogue channels

Name	Original ownership/notes	Launched
Sky Channel	Brian Haynes (backed by Guinness Mahon, etc.)	Apr 1982
Screensport	W.H. Smith, ABC (ESPN)	1983
Children's Channel	BT, Thames Television, D.C. Thompson, Central Television, EMI	1984
Teleclub	Rediffusion AG 60%, Beta Taurus (Kirch) 40%	1984
TV5	A 'best of French broadcasting' channel	1984
Premiere	EMI, Goldcrest, Fox, Columbia, HBO	Sept 1984
Sat Eins	PKS 40%, Axel Springer 15%, APF 15%	1985
CNN	Turner Broadcasting	Sept 1985
Lifestyle	W.H. Smith, TVS and Yorkshire Television	Oct 1985
SuperChannel*	Granada, Virgin, Yorkshire Television	Feb 1987
Satellite Info. Serv (SIS)	Ladbroke, Mecca, Coral, Grand Met, Wm Hill	May 1987
MTV	51% Maxwell, 25% Viacom, 24% BT	Aug 1987
TV3 ScanSat	Kinnevik 96%, Nora (Norway) 4%	Dec 1987
The Movie Channel	British Satellite Broadcasting (BSB)	Mar 1990
NOW	BSB	Mar 1990
Galaxy	BSB	Mar 1990
Power Station	BSB/Virgin	Mar 1990

*SuperChannel had started out life as Music Box.

analogue programming designed for reception on small (typically 60 cm) roof-mounted dish antennas.

The potential market for direct-to-home satellite reception was minuscule, with no more than 113 880 installations across Europe, according to *Cable & Satellite Europe* magazine (see Table 2.13). The market was ready to expand, however, a fact noted by many potential broadcasters across Europe.

The emergence of BSkyB

The UK had been allocated five direct broadcasting by satellite frequencies as early as 1977, but it took until December 1986 for

Table 2.14   European satellite dish installations – 1988

Austria	6000
Denmark	8000
Finland	3600
France	10 000
Greece	1500
Ireland	2000
Italy	2000
Luxembourg	80
Netherlands	2000
Norway	3700
Portugal	2000
Spain	19 000
Sweden	17 500
Switzerland	1000
W. Germany	19 500
UK	18 000
Total	113 880

Source: *Cable & Satellite Europe*, October 1988

the then Independent Broadcasting Authority to select British Satellite Broadcasting as the operator. BSB, which achieved fame and then notoriety with its 'squarial' dishes, had a troubled time of it. Promised starting dates were broken; technical problems beset the project; and financing cash was spent at a spectacular rate, with accusations of profligacy at board level. BSB eventually commenced transmissions in April 1990, more than a year after Rupert Murdoch had launched his Sky service.

On 8 June 1988, what has been described as the 'rumpled' figure of Rupert Murdoch announced to a press gathering that News International would launch four 'Sky' channels broadcasting from an Astra craft by February the following year, less than 9 months away. 'We are seeing the dawn of a new age of freedom for the viewer,' said Murdoch.

What followed was probably the bloodiest period in British broadcasting, or perhaps broadcasting anywhere. Two companies, Sky, backed by News International, and British Satellite

Broadcasting, backed by more than £1 billion of private finance, were locked in a battle for the eyes, subscription cash and loyalty of British viewers. BSB used a new broadcasting standard, the D-MAC system; this needed specially-developed receiver/decoder boxes, although, using fairly high-power satellites, the receiving dishes could be small, no more than about 40 cm across.

Astra 1A went 'live' on 5 February 1989. Although designed as a telecommunications craft, rather than a broadcasting satellite, it was the vehicle that enabled many more viewers to access satellite television with low-cost, rudimentary receiver boxes and small satellite dishes. Up to this point viewers had needed dishes of at least 90 cm diameter (and ideally 1.2 m) to obtain a decent screen image.

Murdoch was first to market, with a low-cost receiver box developed by Alan Sugar's Amstrad company. His launch in February 1989 was itself not without problems, with a promised Disney channel just one of the stumbling blocks; but well within a year of launch Sky was reporting operating losses of £95 million on top of start-up costs of £121 million (News International Annual Report and Accounts, June 1990). These were bad, but BSB's losses were worse. By October 1990 the two companies had started merger talks, which were completed in November. According to published estimates, by the time BSB and Sky had merged (to become British Sky Broadcasting) they had spent a total of £1.25 billion creating a direct-to-home market in the UK.

Murdoch and his low-cost service, transmitting its channels on the Astra telecommunications satellite, had won the day, even though losses would continue. Indeed, two reports circulated in 1988 were not that encouraging of satellite's prospects as a broadcasting medium. Logica estimated a UK dish population by 1994 of 600 000. Even more depressing was a CIT document predicting Europe-wide dish ownership of just 1 million by 1996 (see Collins, 1992). There were many similar doom-sayers.

Table 2.15 The Astra constellation – 2001

Name	Manufacturer	Launch date	No. of transponders/ channels	Expected life (years)
At 19.2 degrees East				
Astra 1A	GE Astro Space	Dec 1988	16	12
Astra 1B	GE Astro Space	Mar 1991	16	12+
Astra 1C	Hughes HS601	May 1993	18	15
Astra 1D	Hughes HS601	Nov 1994	18	13+
Astra 1E*	Hughes HS601	Oct 1995	18	14
Astra 1F*	Hughes HS601	Apr 1996	22	15
Astra 1G*	Hughes HS601	Oct 1997	28	15+
Astra 1H*	Hughes HS601	Jun 1999	28	15
Astra 1K*	Aerospatiale 3000B3S	Q3**/2000	52	16+
At 28.2 degrees East				
Astra 2A*	Hughes HS601	Dec 1997	28	15+
Astra 2B*	Matra Marconi	May 2000	28	15+
Astra 2C*	Hughes HS601	1H***/2001	28	15+
Astra 2D*	Hughes HS376	late 2000	16	12+

Notes: *These craft are intended for digital broadcasting.

Some craft (notably Astra 1G/1H/2A/2B) have extra transponders, generally 4 per craft, providing on-board redundancy and thereby guaranteeing the satellite ends its working life with at least the designated number of transponders.

Astra also have an option to purchase an additional Matra-Marconi craft.

**Q3 = quarter 3 of the business year.

***1H = first half year of the business year.

Table 2.16   Astra's growth and penetration of TV homes*

	1991	1992	1993	1994	1995	1996	1997	1998	1999*
DTH/SMATV**	7.36	11.22	15.43	19.99	21.73	22.97	24.78	26.51	33.2
Cable		24.60	29.50	33.75	36.59	39.60	44.0	45.74	48.03	50.5
TOTAL		31.96	40.72	49.17	56.58	61.33	66.97	70.52	74.54	83.7

*TV households in millions, at year end except 1999 (half year).
**SMATV: Satellite Master Antenna TV distribution system.
Source: SES/Astra

Analogue satellite television – a European success story

If the 1988 predictions of barely one million dish installations across Europe by 1996 were compared to today's real position, then by any measure the enthusiastic adoption of satellite broadcasting has been a huge success.

Astra's own 1987 predictions of its 1996 position have also been exceeded, as revealed recently by Marcus Bicknell, Astra's first marketing manager. He admitted that some people thought his forecasts optimistic, but they were based on the ownership of VCRs in any given market. On that basis, Astra predicted that in 1996 there would be 20.2 m DTH and SMATV viewers across Europe (some 17 per cent of European TV homes, claimed Astra). The actual 1996 figure was 22.97 m, as Bicknell stated, not only ahead of Astra's own estimate but reasonably accurate as to the actual market position at the time. At mid-1999 the figure stood at more than 33 m homes.

However, Bicknell's forecast of European cable connections has proved to be significantly underestimated. In 1987 Astra suggested total cable viewing of 23 m homes in 1996. The reality was near double, at 44 m homes in 1996 and 50.5 m at mid-year 1999. Astra's predicted combined total (DTH and Cable) for 1996 was 43.2 m homes, but the actual numbers were 66.97 m and mid-year 1999 stood at 83.7 m homes. Bicknell recently suggested that

Table 2.17 The EUTELSAT constellation 1999–2001

Name	Manufacturer*	Launch date	Position	No. of Transponders	Expected Life (years)
EUTELSAT II-F1	Aerospatiale	Aug 1990	48° East	16	9
EUTELSAT II-F2	Aerospatiale	Jan 1991	12.5° West	16	9
EUTELSAT II-F3	Aerospatiale	Dec 1991	36° East	16	9
EUTELSAT II-F4*	Aerospatiale	July 1992	10° East	16	9
EUTELSAT II-F5	Aerospatiale	Mar 1995	Launch Failure		
DFS-Kopernikus	MBB	July 1990	28.2° East	11	10
Telecom 2A	Matra Marconi	Dec 1991	8° West	11	10
EUTELSAT HB1	Aerospatiale	Mar 1995	13° East	16	11
EUTELSAT HB2	Matra Marconi	Nov 1996	13° East	20	14+
EUTELSAT HB3	Matra Marconi	1997	13° East	20	14+
EUTELSAT HB4	Matra Marconi	1998	13° East	20	14+
EUTELSAT HB5*	Matra Marconi	Oct 1998	13° East	22	14+
EUTELSAT HB6	Alcatel	Q4**/ 2001	13° East	28	12+
EUTELSAT W1-R*	Aerospatiale	2000E	28.5° East	24	14
EUTELSAT W2	Aerospatiale	Oct 1998	16° East	24	14
EUTELSAT W3	Aerospatiale	Apr 1999	7° East	24	14
EUTELSAT W4	Aerospatiale	Spring 2000	36° East	41	14
EUTELSAT AB-1*	Aliena Aerospazio	Q1***/2001	12.5° West	20	14–15
SESAT*	NPO-PM/Alcatel	Apr 2000	36° East	18	10
RESSAT	Matra Marconi	Q4**/2000E	10° East	28	12+

Notes:

* HB = the EUTELSAT Hot Bird series.

HB6 will replace HB5 which has technical problems. HB5 will be moved to a new location.

ESAT = Siberia Europe Satellite.

W1 was lost as a result of water damage while under manufacture. W1-R is its replacement and will probably replace DFS-Kopernikus at 28.2 degrees East, probably being called 'Eurobird'.

AB-1 is 'Atlantic Bird 1', designed to boost transponders at 12.5 degrees West.

Three EUTELSAT I series (British Aerospace craft with 7-years design life), launched in 1983, 1987 and 1988, are in inclined orbital operation at 12.5 degrees West, 36 degrees East, 25.5 degrees East and 21.5 degrees East.

RESSAT was originally ordered as a flexible replacement for the 'W' series.

Aerospatiale is now part of the Alcatel conglomerate.

**Q4 = quarter 4 of the business year.

***Q1 = quarter 1 of the business year.

Table 2.18   EUTELSAT's household coverage: end 1998

	1994	1995	1996	1997	1998
DTH/SMATV*	8.2	10.1	12.3	-	-
Cable	40.9	45.3	47.8	-	-
TOTAL	49.1	55.4	60.1	64.1	70.6

Notes: In millions of TV households

From 'Hot Bird' 13 degrees East position

*SMATV = Satellite Master Antenna TV distribution system

Source: Eutelsat Analysis, 1999

instead of basing his forecast calculations on VCR ownership, a better guide might have been total television ownership.

EUTELSAT claim much higher penetration rates, largely as a result of their wider coverage and relative strengths in Eastern Europe. They claim an enlarged Europe has some 269 m TV homes, of which 80.7 m receive satellite signals by means of satellite, cable delivery or SMATV distribution.

Table 2.19   Europe's highest penetration cable channels*

CNNI	44.421 m
Eurosport	40.599 m
NBC Europe	36.83 m
MTV	35.73 m
TV5	34.552 m
Arte	29.634 m
Viva	22.72 m
TNT/Cartoon	21.945 m
RTL TV	21.263 m
EuroNews	20.997 m
ARD	20.917 m
VH-1	20.07 m
Sat 1	19.40 m

Data: *Q1 = January–March 1997

Source: *Cable & Satellite Europe*, June 1997, from data supplied by channels

UK analogue cable and satellite viewing in mid-2000 consistently takes a 40 per cent share (in multi-channel homes), with terrestrial viewing (originally of four networks, BBC1 and BBC2, ITV, Channel 4, and since March 1997, Channel 5) down from 70+ per cent, to 41 per cent in June 1997. When taken as a percentage of viewing in all TV households (not just multi-channel homes) satellite and cable is taking an 11.7 per cent share of all viewing (April–June 1997, Broadcasters' Audience Research Board (BARB) data). The trends are clear, and the UK's terrestrial broadcasters (including the BBC and all of the ITV regional companies) have launched niche channels to secure some degree of presence in the sector.

The UK's Broadcasters' Audience Research Board (BARB) data shows that within this 11.7 per cent share of all viewing, the UK's analogue niche channels are very popular amongst the young and better-off, and less welcome in homes of the elderly (55+) and in socio-economic groups C2DE.

The importance of the period April–May–June 1997 in the UK for cable and satellite channels cannot be understated. At the end of March, Channel 5 launched, to around 80 per cent of the UK audience, and BARB data shows that C5 gained a typical 3 per cent of all viewing. The BARB data shows this 3 per cent was won at the expense of the other four 'network' channels, and not at the expense of cable and satellite broadcasters, whose audience share remains steady – and gently increasing.

Elsewhere in Europe, multi-channel viewing of the non-publicly* supported channels is considered more commonplace. In Germany the audience for cable and satellite-supplied private channels is typically 60 per cent of all viewing. Comprehensive audience measurement from Eurodata confirms, in their words, 'cable and satellite cover has been increasing in every country.' If satellite and cable distribution is flourishing, together with a concurrent growth in viewer choice, it follows that viewing of the once dominant national (public) networks must be shrinking.

*Note: 'Public' here means free-to-air network channels, including licence fee-supported national channels as well as nationally-available private channels.

Table 2.20   UK niche channels, percentage share by demographic (All individuals, 13 weeks ending 29 June 1997)

	24 hours	Peak time
All individuals	11.7	9.3
All adults	10.5	8.5
16–34	15.9	13.0
35–54	13.1	10.6
55+	5.2	4.4
ABC1	9.3	7.6
C2DE	11.3	9.2
16–34 ABC1	14.5	12.0
35–54 ABC1	11.0	8.8
55+ ABC1	4.2	3.3
16–34 C2DE	17.0	13.8
35–54 C2DE	14.9	12.2
55+ C2DE	5.8	5.0
Children	21.1	16.9

Data: BARB/Incorporated Practitioners in Advertising (IPA) July 1997

Asia-Pacific analogue trends

The American and European viewing patterns are echoed in the Asia-Pacific region, with some notable local differences. Daily viewing of television in Japan (205 minutes) is higher than in many European countries (UK 215 minutes, Germany 183 minutes, The Netherlands 157 minutes), although still lower than the USA (239 minutes).

Many Asian homes have multiple television sets. For instance in Taiwan, two out of three households own two or more sets, but this does not lead to high television viewing. However, in Thailand there are still broadcasters who do not air a complete 24-hour schedule. Politically-controlled and state-run channels existed until very recently in some countries (for example, Malaysia). There are other viewing oddities, quite alien to 'western' viewers. In Taiwan the television weather report runs more than ten minutes (and frequently gets into the 'Top 10' programmes) and the main evening news is a one-hour show.

Table 2.21 1996 Daily viewing time per individual*

Poland	242
United States	239
Turkey	216
Italy	216
United Kingdom	215
Spain	214
Hungary	213
Japan	205
Greece	202
Canada	192
Argentina	191
Belgium, South	191
Australia, Sydney	189
Ireland	189
Germany	183
France	179
Portugal	169
Finland	161
Denmark	159
Netherlands	157
Belgium, North	153
Norway	150
Brazil, Rio de Janeiro	146
Sweden	140

*Note: All times in minutes.

Source: Eurodata TV, 1996

Table 2.22 1996 Asian viewing*

Japan	4.0
India	4.0
Indonesia	3.7
Philippines	3.5
Singapore	2.4
Malaysia	2.2
South Korea	2.2
Taiwan	2.0

*Note: All times in hours per household.

Source: Survey Research Group, Singapore, 1997

Despite these regional differences, the trends are quite clear. Cable and satellite viewing is fast-developing, rapidly changing the way television is watched in most countries. In Taiwan, cable and satellite reach three TV homes out of four (and some four million subscribe to STAR TV, a DTH multi-channel bouquet). While subscriptions to new satellite channels are increasing in some key markets, it may be that the notoriously hard-working Asian communities have yet to adopt western 'couch-potato' habits.

Table 2.23   1996 Asian multi-channel penetration

China	49.0 m
Hong Kong	0.4 m
India	22.0 m
Japan	10.8 m
Philippines	0.6 m
Singapore	0.07 m
Taiwan	3.5 m
Malaysia	0.2 m

Data: *Cable World*, 1997; Industry sources

Japan's analogue national networks have been protected and cosseted from external competition. Despite the growing number of analogue satellite channels, penetration from the new breed of multi-channels amounted to only 1.1 per cent viewing share in 1996 (Eurodata) and to no more than 3 per cent by the end of 1997, predicted to rise to 11 per cent by 2010. Satellite/cable television achieved penetration of 32.2 per cent at December 1996 and digital satellite/cable is expected to reach 85 per cent penetration by 2010.

Five network channels (all Tokyo-based) take 89 per cent share of Japan's television advertising revenue, leading to high profitability for the NHK, NTV and Fuji TV systems. However, Japan's Ministry of Posts and Telecommunications (which is also Japan's TV licensing authority) predicts that by 2010 the established networks will see their viewing share decline to 67 per cent. Even more damaging, the ministry predicts that terrestrial network's share of a more than doubled advertising cake will only grow 1.6 times in the period to 2010. In contrast, the ministry believes digital cable television revenues could expand more than six-fold, and satellite more than seven-fold, by 2010.

The adoption of digital

Over the last 75 years, analogue television has been developed to its technological and spectrum limits. There is not a developed nation that could find unallocated spectrum to create another national television channel. The UK's Channel 5, barely reaching much over 70 per cent of the terrestrial audience in analogue, is a case in point, showing what can be achieved by mopping up the last remaining unallocated slices of spectrum. Channel 5 gets 100 per cent coverage from satellite and will get improved distribution from its digital terrestrial distribution.

The UK is typical of the rest of Europe – and most developed countries – in fully utilizing its analogue broadcast spectrum. In the UK, this equates to potential 44 channels, each 8 MHz in size. Some European countries use a 7 MHz bandwidth and North America uses a 6 MHz system. Most countries use a five- or six-channel network system, broadcasting from a central antenna transmitting for up to 70–90 km radius depending on local terrain and radiated power. Lower power transmitters are used to fill in local gaps and black spots.

Each of these broadcast regions would be surrounded by other broadcast regions using a different set of channels, with the original set now lying dormant or fallow to avoid cross-channel interference. The 'cordon sanitaire' system normally works perfectly except at times of the year when atmospheric propagation takes place (usually during summer-time high pressure); at this time cross programme interference from 300 or 1000 km or more distant is not uncommon. It is worth remembering that some broadcast antennae (for example, Crystal Palace near London) operate at 1 m W (one million watts) and interference of only 1 per cent of that is enough to visually corrupt an analogue signal.

While the current analogue broadcast system works perfectly well, it is easy to see that at any single location some five or six channels are in use, leaving 38 analogue channels that are not being used.

Today, a 625-line Phase Alternating Line (PAL) or French-developed Sequential Colour with Memory (SECAM) image has already been improved significantly, as viewers will instantly recognize. The US NTSC signal (National Television Standards Committee, or colloquially 'Never Twice the Same Color') is a less robust signal, with fewer scanned lines (525) and some notorious broadcast deficiencies. The European PAL system actually evolved from NTSC and might be considered as NTSC Mk 2.

While broadcast engineers have developed technical fixes which enable wide-screen (PALplus) and even higher-definition broadcasts using analogue (MAC) technology, analogue has increasingly been seen as having reached its technological limits.

The status quo might have remained ever thus were it not for the problems in PAL/SECAM and NTSC within the broadcast centres. There can be a measurable loss in quality at editing and duplication stages with taped material. This can easily be seen at home if a viewer makes a copy of another VHS recording. Each subsequent copy causes further degradation in quality.

To overcome these problems at the professional end of the transmission system, many broadcasters have long adopted digital editing facilities. Using digital technologies within the studio eliminates this degradation. Until recently, however, the digital image was converted back to analogue for transmission after any post-production stages. Again, it will be instantly recognized by viewers that 'live' studio broadcasts in PAL/SECAM and NTSC still represent the best images possible in the analogue environment.

There is another problem for analogue, which affects the text messages used in most countries. Despite the exploitation in some countries of some of the analogue transmission lines (the vertical blanking interval or VBI) for Teletext-type use, the resulting text and graphic images are rudimentary, and again have been developed to the limits of its technology.

These technological limitations are but one side of the coin. The other side represents the tangible benefits that digital can offer, some of which are already with us. In Europe, for example, some broadcasters transmit the audio element of the television picture in a format known as NICAM. A NICAM signal is digital, and represented a significant audio breakthrough in television broadcasting.

However, the most dramatic benefit that digital offers over analogue is a more efficient use of the broadcast spectrum. The broadcasting spectrum is finite and there are huge pressures from a vast range of new non-broadcast technologies for an increased portion of the spectrum, not least the cellular telephony market. Analogue signals cannot be themselves compressed or reduced in size or made more spectrum-efficient.

Neither can analogue signals be themselves genuinely interactive, or provide any sort of sophisticated integrated 'return path'. Canadian cable company Videotron, among others, developed intriguing systems which used the set-top box as a device to give viewers an element of pseudo-choice. It would be fair to call this 'interactive' insofar as the viewer does interact with the television set, but this cannot be compared to what is now understood by the term interactivity. It is possible to use the telephone as a 'return path' to the studio or head-end, but analogue transmission itself has no inherent facility for interactivity.

While analogue signals can be tweaked to provide marginally improved images (and sound), the bandwidth occupied is still the same. The adoption of digital technology for television and radio broadcasting will, over time, free up the existing analogue spectrum for new, more lucrative uses. A digital 'multiplex '(mixture) of channels occupying the same bandwidth as analogue (6–8 MHz depending on the country) can certainly contain four and, more typically, six channels. There is even the strong possibility that more channels could be accommodated within a 6–8 MHz bandwidth, but that would be dependent on higher levels of compression.

However, the prospects that in time (in European terms) some 36–8 analogue channels might be returned presents government and business with some appealing options, which are replicated world-wide and are immense. Even if half the frequencies were turned over to cellular telephony (the likely target for most governments) the other half could be allocated to digital television, creating immediate space for around 100–150 extra digital channels to be broadcast terrestrially. It could even be many more.

Digital broadcasting currently uses significantly lower power transmissions, of the order of 10 kW (10 000 watts) compared with the 1 million watt output of a transmitter like Crystal Palace.

Digital has two other key characteristics which we examine in detail later, but essentially they are as follows.

■ More channels and services become possible from the same bandwidth.
■ Interactive services can be included.

We can summarize the points so far as:

■ analogue transmission is inherently inefficient
■ image can suffer dramatically from degradation in the production stage

- images are broadcast-neutral, that is they use the same bandwidth whether it is a schools programme or high-quality drama production
- analogue is limited in the amount of extra data it can carry, e.g. Teletext
- analogue cannot be interactive.

Digital compression and multiplexing

A standard uncompressed digital signal would use some 133 Mbps (megabits per second) and would not be economic to broadcast, taking as it would almost as much bandwidth as an analogue signal. Digital television overcomes analogue's limitations and permits more efficient use of the available bandwidth, because of the compression of the broadcast signal. This process is far from straightforward but image digitization technology follows the sampling theorems that are now the basis for all-digital photography and image capture. However, television is not a 'still' image (although in essence made up of many still 'snapshots' of an event) and is constantly seen as 'moving'.

The main digital video standard is that adopted by the Motion Picture Experts Group (MPEG). Their second-generation standard (MPEG-2) has been endorsed and adopted throughout Europe and many other parts of the world but at the time of writing not for North America or Japan.

What is MPEG?

The Motion Picture Experts Group (MPEG) working under the umbrella of the International Organization for Standardization (ISO), develops video compression standards. MPEG-1, MPEG-2 and other versions are adopted as global transmission standards. MPEG1, developed in the 1980s, specifies a data rate of 1.3 Mbps. However, MPEG-1 video on personal computers did not meet the quality standard set by broadcast television.

MP3, or to give it its correct title MPEG-1 layer 3, is the standard for compressed audio to which metadata, such as basic information recording status, artist name and details etc., are added. The most common application today is for the distribution of music on the Internet. However, it might be that radio broadcasters could start transmitting their own archived material in MP3 form quite separately from the conventional broadcast.

MPEG-2, in comparison, has much better image quality and is suitable for delivering entertainment-quality video, including films and television programming. MPEG-2 was approved and 'fixed' as a standard in 1995 and is widely supported by the broadcast, cable, computer and satellite television industries.

MPEG-4 has been established as a compression standard suitable for low-bandwidth applications such as video phones, mobile video and hand-held games. It is designed to support full multimedia conferencing, integration of natural and synthetic audio/video, and simultaneous handling of audiovisual material to multiple destinations from multiple sources. Some insiders also suggest MPEG-4 might be the follow-on compression standard to MPEG-2 for full-motion video. However, there is now an enormous acceptance within the industry that MPEG-2 is quite sufficient; equipment has been bought and studios and post-production facilities have been equipped to handle MPEG-2. Any new compression standard would have to overcome this huge installed base.

MPEG-4 already has a sibling, though in the form of MLVC, or multi-layered video compression. Its developers (Matsushita, the Japanese electronics company perhaps better known as Panasonic) say it will produce higher quality and smoother motion video. In MLVC, a video sequence is treated as a multi-layered task, with each layer tackled separately. An example would be an image of someone passing in front of a wall. In this case the wall forms one layer, while the person is another. MLVC allocates a different number of bits according to the various tasks in hand. The fixed wall will be less demanding than the person, who will be moving. The human eye is much more demanding of the moving image than the still, as we tend to follow the action, and in MLVC a greater bit-rate will be allocated to the human.

Various bodies worked on the original concepts of compressing still images, following the work done by the ISO and what the industry calls Discrete Cosine Transform Coding (DCT) technology. Associated standards are generally dubbed JPEG, with the results of these developments seen in audio CDs, CD-ROM, picture CDs (from Kodak) and more recently the digital still cameras now increasingly commonplace, as well as mini-disc developments. All depend on the elimination of redundant information, and the ability to rebuild correctly an image (or audio element) faithfully for viewing or listening.

There are five commonly accepted levels, or subsystems within MPEG-2, as specified by the European Broadcasting Union and the Digital Video Broadcasting group, which have resulted in the MPEG-2 DVB variants.

1   The base source for signals, either a broadcasting studio or data-broadcasting centre.
2   A source coding and compression system. There are now many proprietary systems on the market; each processes the studio signal to achieve a bit-rate reduction. This provides a signal at a data rate low enough to be carried along the transmission path. Europe has adopted a series of MPEG-2 standards complying with ISO/IEC IS 13818.
3   A data multiplexing and transport system. This takes the individual streams of compressed data and assembles them in well-defined packets which can then be multiplexed (or mixed) into a single data-stream. This data-stream, for each channel, will contain in addition to the video and audio-bit-stream, extra information for some basic engineering controls commonly known as Service Information, Forward Error Correction and the like.
4   A channel coding, modulation and radio frequency transmission section. The channel coder processes the digital-bit-stream into a form suitable for it to be transmitted over the appropriate frequency.

5 A receiving, decoding and display system. This includes a radio frequency demodulator, a channel decoder and a source decoder which converts the bit-stream back into image, audio and data/text for display on a television set.

In addition to the above the signal may be scrambled and consequently have to carry a Conditional Access Interface.

The Service Information Data-stream (sometimes called Service Description Tables) covers a huge list of technical requirements that the system must recognize within the specification. The more common, within the DVB specification, are:

■ bouquet* name descriptor
■ conditional access descriptor
■ country availability descriptor
■ data broadcast descriptor
■ digital stream indicator descriptor
■ ISO 639 language descriptor
■ linkage descriptor
■ mosaic descriptor
■ multilingual service name descriptor
■ parental rating descriptor
■ private data specifier descriptor
■ stuffing descriptor
■ telephone descriptor.

In addition, the Network Information Table needs other data, for example;

■ copyright descriptor
■ frequency list descriptor
■ satellite delivery descriptor
■ cable delivery system descriptor
■ terrestrial delivery system descriptor

*A bouquet is a group of channels, usually under one broadcaster's control.

Digital video broadcasting*

The Digital Video Group explains the concept neatly:

> The basic building blocks which are the currency of the DVB System are the MPEG-2 data packets. The DVB Multiplex may be seen as a kind of bridge:

> In this metaphor, the traffic across the bridge carries Data Containers, holding MPEG-2 packets. The contents of each container are indicated by Service Information, much like writing on the side of a truck.

> MPEG packets are fixed-length containers with 188 bytes of data. MPEG includes Program Specific Information (PSI) so that the MPEG-2 decoder can capture and decode this packet structure. This data, transmitted with the pictures and sound, automatically configures the decoder and provides the synchronisation information necessary for the decoder to produce a complete video signal at its output.
>
> *Courtesy: The DVB Group, 1995 data

While this talk of packets and bit-streams can be fascinating, it may not be sufficient to convey fully to the non-expert how the data is compressed. An easier way to comprehend it may be to imagine a news broadcast. The camera will scan the image of the newsreader many times a second. Each image will be compared in 'real time', with every frame compared with successive frames, analysing each pixel of information for colour and shade.

If our newscaster is broadcasting against a blue background, it is likely that much of the image will remain constant from one split second to another. If this is the case then the instruction will be, effectively, to 'hold blue pixel 123 in position x'. That instruction will hold true for all the pixels where the blue colour remains constant. In other words, instead of sending a complete image many times a second, the redundant information is discarded until the pixel changes.

This highly simplified explanation excludes motion, a vital component of the specification. This can be accommodated by imagining a basketball player moving swiftly from left to right and throwing his ball towards a net on the right. The MPEG encoder has the ability to identify this motion within each pixel or macroblock of data, and to a certain extent estimate the position within the next frame.

The challenges

The most challenging images to compress are those broadcasts that contain lots of fast-moving information. Sport is top of the list, with indoor basketball and swimming said to be the most difficult to compress: swimming, because of the complexity of the water itself, with tiny waves, reflections, and splashes of water droplets; and basketball, because of the floor area, usually with painted zones, fast-moving court action and the relative nearness of the crowd.

In comparison, movies represent one of the easiest of compression tasks. Movies are shot at just 24 frames a second (much slower than television's 50 or 60 frames per second) needing less real-time compression work. One California-based company (Imedia Corporation) has managed to compress movies at a ratio of up to 24 to one, that is 24 movies or channels occupying a single 8 MHz bandwidth. This technology is not MPEG-2 DVB compatible but it shows what might be achievable in the near future.

Imedia's patented technology, which is highly applicable to movies, uses what they call a StatMux, a statistical multiplexing operation, which recognizes that, even in fast-moving Hollywood action films, much of the time requires only modest compression activity. The few moments of explosive action, when the screen is filled with rapid movement, can be compensated for by 'stealing' spare bit-rate from another channel with less demanding on-screen action.

This permits ultra-high compression and low transmission rates of around 1 Mbps.

Data rates employed

The generally accepted data rates currently employed in digital transmission vary according to source material and the quality level acceptable to the viewer. For example, a corporation might happily accept a sub-VHS quality for its own internal video-conference needs, but would not wish to 'transmit' a corporate video – even to its own employees – at anything other than broadcast quality. The same company, for a public or trade exhibition, might want its corporate video presentation to be made and shown in high-definition.

There are many concerns over the employment of various bit-rates by broadcasters, especially since movies are the least demanding and fast-moving sports the most demanding (excluding true high-definition). At the very least sport will be around three times as greedy as movies in terms of bit-rate.

Various equipment manufacturers and broadcasters, in the period up to the start of widespread digital transmission, have calculated the likely data-rates for compressed material. In 1997 these were given as follows, with the originator's terms also provided for guidance.

Table 3.1

Quality	Data rate	Source reference
Video-conferencing	1–2 Mbps	Compression Labs Inc
'Micro Television'	1–2 Mbps	EUTELSAT
Films	3.5 Mbps*	TV/COM
Live sport	4.6 Mbps	TV/COM
16:9 wide aspect	5.76 Mbps	TV/COM
'Broadcasting'	4.8 Mbps	EUTELSAT
High definition	≥14 Mbps	TV/COM
	25 Mbps	Compression Labs
	21 Mbps	Scientific Atlanta
Broadcast HDTV	20–40 Mbps	EUTELSAT
Studio HDTV	40–70 Mbps	EUTELSAT

*Films can be shown at bit-rates from about 2 Mbps, with a trade-off in broadcast quality.
Data: Orion Satellite, 1995

In the period to 1999 encoding improvements have come thick and fast. Better noise-reduction units, now increasingly built-in to the codec (coder-decoders) sets used by compression engineers, are helping overall to improve compression ratios. 'Good signal in means a good signal out' might seem an obvious statement, but never has it been truer than in digital television. A good, clean image at the start of the compression sequence means an easier task for the equipment, and less corrupting on-screen artefacts at the end of the sequence. It also potentially means less bandwidth consumed.

The European Digital Video Broadcasting group, within their DVB standard for MPEG-2 compression, has set standards for various image qualities, which they range from low to high under five 'profiles' or levels. However, even their 'low' category will deliver an image (depending on source material) that is at least equivalent to images currently broadcast in analogue.

The five profiles in the MPEG-2 system are:

- Simple Profile
- Main Profile
- Scaleable Profile
- Spatially Scaleable Profile
- High Profile.

DVB states that for a conventional 4:3 image (the shape of normal television sets), which would contain (in Europe) 352 x 288 samples refreshed (101 376 samples/sec) or scanned at 25 frames per second, a bit rate of 4 Mbps would be the maximum needed.

As one moves progressively higher through the resolution chain, DVB specifies around 24 'conformance points'. The top of the value chain, and the most expensive in terms of bit-rate and therefore bandwidth occupied, is high-definition television at a scan rate of 1920 samples per line, or scanning 1920 x 1152 lines (2.2 million samples) scanned 25 times per second. This would translate into at least 80 Mbps.

It is perfectly possible to achieve wide screen (although not the highest-quality HDTV) at a lower bit rate. Indeed, the DVB group themselves suggest a sample rate for 720 x 576 (414 720 samples, 25 times a second) would occupy a 15 Mbps bit-rate.

Transmission

Transmission is carried out by various means: satellite, cable and terrestrial. Depending on the country, some broadcasters own their own transmission systems, others use a public or privately owned transmission system. Two broadcasting methods have been adopted. In Europe (and also in Australia) the chosen method is Coded Othogonal Frequency Division Multiplex (COFDM) and backed by the DVB standards. In the USA the Federal Communications Commission (FCC) has adopted Vestigial Sideband Broadcasting system (VSB).

OFDM uses a data-stream, which is divided into several bit-streams running parallel to one another. These parallel data-streams are modulated into individual carriers, each of which occupies a small slice of the total 8 MHz bandwidth. Frequency separation is easier to achieve and the resulting transmissions are said to be more robust and less susceptible to interference.

The USA has chosen a different system, 8-VSB, which uses their entire 6 MHz bandwidth as a single frequency, with all the component parts multiplexed together. Its claimed benefits include lower broadcast power and the possibilities of extended station coverage. However, (as at April 2000) there are problems. It is strongly argued by some transmission and studio experts that the USA has chosen the wrong system. In numerous tests 8-VSB seems not to be as robust or practical. In February 2000 the Brazilian broadcast authorities decided against the US system, selecting Europe's DVB system. Meanwhile the US broadcaster CBS, in private tests during the winter of 1999–2000, determined that the 8-VSB system showed 'dramatically disappointing results'.

The reported differences between COFDM and 8-VSB are that in practical terms COFDM has less multipath interference (for COFDM), a more robust signal, greater distance coverage and better indoor reception on portable sets.

Carriage

In the UK there are now two terrestrial transmission operators: Castle Transmission, which in early 1997 acquired the network transmission assets of the BBC; and NTL, the privatized arm of the independent (commercial) television sector. Castle has the contract to transmit the BBC digital (and analogue) channels and also the British Digital Broadcasting group's three multiplexes. NTL are contracted to transmit ITV, Channel 4, Channel 5 and S4C's digital services.

Terrestrial transmission of digital services in the UK started in November 1998. Six multiplexes, each capable of transmitting 18 Mbps, were licensed by the UK's Independent Television Commission:

Multiplex A Occupied by the BBC
Multiplex B Occupied by ITV (Channel 3), Ch 4 and Teletext Ltd
Multiplex 1 Channel 5, S4C, ITN
Multiplex 2 British Digital Broadcasting (ONdigital)
Multiplex 3 British Digital Broadcasting (ONdigital)
Multiplex 4 British Digital Broadcasting (ONdigital)

Cable operators are responsible for their own transmission systems, while satellite broadcasters depend on the satellite platform owners (for example, Astra, EUTELSAT and Telenor) to provide transmission facilities.

In Europe, France (under the direction of the Conseil Superieur de l'Audiovisuel – CSA) is examining proposals which, in addition to national terrestrial digital services, would also see a Multichannel Multipoint Distribution System (MMDS) adopted. MMDS is a wireless system, offering up to about 60 digital channels over a tightly defined area, for example, a single town. France is unlikely to see such transmissions start before 2002–3.

Germany has a well-developed cable system (especially in the former West Germany) so the pressure on establishing a digital terrestrial network is considerably less. There is the added complication that Germany's federal government system gives the responsibility for initiating and controlling such developments to the individual Lander states, although telecommunications falls within the competence of the national media authority.

Italy, as yet, has no detailed proposals underway to initiate digital terrestrial broadcasting and while both public and private broadcasters have embraced digital transmission enthusiastically, they have concentrated on cable, telephony (Stream) and satellite as the delivery mechanism.

Spain was expected to be the next major market to implement digital terrestrial nation-wide during late 1999.

The Nordic countries, especially Finland and Sweden are also introducing digital terrestrial television services during 1999–2000. The Scandinavian region has two MPEG-2 DVB digital satellite platforms and cable services are also beginning the changeover to digital.

Australia is also pushing very hard to see its analogue networks convert to digital, and while a provisional date of 2002 has been put on the introduction of digital terrestrial services, that date could be brought forward. Australia has also adopted the European system of MPEG-2 DVB digital satellite broadcasting.

The Federal Communications Commission in the USA has pursued an aggressive switch-over to digital terrestrial. The 'big three' networks of NBC, CBS and ABC all made noises about starting digital broadcasts before the end of 1998 and this deadline was met. National deployment was generally reached during 1999. Both the USA's satellite broadcasting platforms are transmitting in MPEG-2 DVB (DirecTV and EchoStar's DiSH system).

Mexico's second largest television network TV Azteca entered the world of high-definition digital television in late-December 1997 with an initial investment of $1.5 million that has started up the corresponding high definition transmission signal. Another $15 million will be spent on the acquisition of equipment and cameras to handle high definition transmission. The new signal, together with high-definition television sets from Sony, Mitsubishi and

Panasonic, will enter the Mexican market towards the end of 1998. The new sets are expected to carry a price tag of around $5000.

Conditional Access

Many digital broadcasts are already taking place, especially from satellite over Europe, and these are covered in later chapters. However, some of these broadcasts are 'in-the-clear', that is, they are digitally encrypted but not scrambled. In other words, anyone with a digital set-top box will be able to view the broadcast without having to subscribe. Most digital broadcasts, however, will be scrambled, especially those supplied by the various pay-television platforms of Canal+, BSkyB and others.

In addition to coping with variable bit-rates, the encoding–decoding system has to cope with whatever Conditional Access (CA) and scrambling method the broadcaster may overlay upon the signal. The scrambling will also require that data unique to the broadcaster are incorporated, which will include Subscriber Management data. Each digital receiver box thus comprises two parts: the decryption system as well as the unscrambling element.

Europe has adopted an open architecture Conditional Access system, based on recommendations of the DVB group. Seven points of common agreement have emerged:

- Set-top boxes can be fitted with either a single CA system (Simulcrypt) or a common interface suitable for the reception of more than one CA system (Multicrypt).
- A common scrambling algorithm has been defined
- A code of conduct for access to decoders has been established
- The DVB group has developed a common interface standard
- Anti-piracy recommendations are drafted
- CA licensing should be on 'fair and reasonable terms'
- CA systems used in Europe should allow for simple Transcontrol, for example, cable operators can replace CA data with their own CA data.

The DVB standards are deliberately open and have been ratified by various European standards bodies. The DVB project has also been adopted outside Europe, generally by means of satellite broadcasters operating over North America, Central and South America, Africa, the Middle East, India, Asia and Australasia.

Many Conditional Access and scrambling systems are currently in use by the various broadcasting groups. Some examples are shown in Table 3.2.

Table 3.2   Conditional Access and scrambling systems

Broadcast Platform	Conditional Access	Operating System
AB Sat (France)	ViaAccess	ViaAccess
BSkyB/Open. . . (UK)	News Digital Systems	Open TV*
Canal Digital (Scandinavia)	Conax	Mediahighway
Canal Satellite Digital (Spain)	Mediaguard	Mediahighway
Canal Satellite Numerique (Fr)	Mediaguard	Mediahighway
DF-1/Premiere	Irdeto/Mindport	d-box
Tele+/Telepiu (Italy)	Irdeto/Mediaguard	d-box/ Mediahighway
TPS (Fr)	Viaccess	Open TV
Via Digital (Spain)	Nagravision Digital	-

*Open TV Inc. is owned by a consortium led by Mindport Holdings and Sun Microsystems.
Source: *Screen Digest*, 1997

The following manufacturers are some of those active in the market, supplying or licensing their technology to the broadcasters listed:

Beta Research (owned by Kirch, Deutsche Telekom and
 CLT/UFA): DF-1/Premiere
News Digital Systems (News Corp): BSkyB/Open. . ., DirecTV
Irdeto (Mindport, MIH Holdings): Tele+/Telipiu, 1st Net, Gulf
 DTH, M-Net
Viaccess (France Telecom): AB Sat, Television Par Satellite
 (TPS),
Nagravision (Nagra Kudelski, Canal+): Via Digital

Mediaguard/Mediahighway: (Canal+, Bertelsmann) Canal
Satellite Digital/Numerique
Next Level (General Instrument): TCI, ComCast, Cox
Communications in the USA, plus many other cable
companies and DirecTV Japan.

Set-top box manufacturers may have developed their own operating systems, or they may simply license a system from one of
the above list. As an indicator to the spread of digital broadcasting,
one has only to look at two set-top box-makers, one British, one
French and some of their international contracts, to see how diverse
digital broadcasting now is.

Pace Micro Technology supplies:

Arab Radio & Television/1st Net	Middle East
BSkyB	UK
Canal+	France
Galaxy	Australia
Indovision	Indonesia
M-NET/Multichoice	Africa
NetSat	Brazil
Shinawatra	Thailand
Stream (Cable)	Italy
Televisa	Latin America
Tele+/Telepiu	Italy

Thomson supplies:

ARD/ZDF	Germany
Canal+	France
DirecTV	United States
Galaxy	Latin America
Indovision	Indonesia
TeleDanmark	Denmark
Deutsche Telekom (Cable)	Germany
Television Par Satellite	France

Television receivers

All the leading television set manufacturers are introducing so-called integrated digital TV sets during 1999–2000. A few examples include:

- LG (formerly known as Lucky Goldstar), a chip manufacturer, confirmed 5 November 1997 it had developed what it called the world's first commercial prototype integrated circuit chip-set for digital television.
- Motorola announced in November 1997 it would begin mass-manufacturing high definition chip-sets for televisions.
- Thomson launched a range of 27 in–33 in digital television sets at the January 1998 Consumer Electronics Show in Las Vegas.
- Hitachi had wide-screen televisions on the market in 1998.
- *Communications Daily*, a trade news magazine, reported on 7 November 1998, 'Virtually every major TV set maker will exhibit HDTV [digital] sets at the CES convention in Las Vegas'.

Having new digital television sets available is only the beginning. Television sets have a long life in the home, and while some markets (the United States, for example) tend to invest in a new television set at a faster rate than European viewers, the average replacement cycle is taken at about twelve years. Televisions are not simply thrown away, they tend to be cascaded through the house – a new set going into the main living room while the existing set is placed in a bedroom or child's room.

However, larger and wider screen digital television sets, with the additional benefit of near CD-quality sound, as well as the possibility of Surround Sound, in the expected US$1000–1500 price range, represent significantly better value than the 17–21 in sets commonly available ten to fifteen years ago. Prices of high-definition sets will be much higher than these figures, though, until volume production reduces the unit price.

The major television retail groups (for example, Dixons in the UK, Sears in the USA, Fnac in Benelux) have all expressed confidence in the consumer buying new digitally-equipped television sets once they are available. Meanwhile set-top boxes, which will carry out the digital conversion to analogue, will be around for some time; they are tumbling down in price and by the end of 2000 are predicted to be the size of a 'flash' memory card (a PCM/CIA card) common on laptop computers.

Electronic Programme Guides

One of the benefits of a digital data-stream is the extra information that can be carried, in addition to the broadcast image and audio. Electronic Programme Guides (EPGs) are perhaps the most tangible advantage to the viewer.

An EPG is simply the electronic equivalent of a television listings guide, but the embedded software in any EPG system has considerable advantages over the printed page. In its minimum format an EPG will show two classes of information, described as 'Now–Next'. The programme currently on air is listed, together with the programme immediately following. Even at this rudimentary level, viewers can examine, channel by channel, what is being broadcast. They can also delve deeper for programme synopsis, cast details, plot background, for example.

Second-generation EPGs (now generally available) can automatically select favourite channels, set a connected VCR to switch on and record a programme, instruct the television set to automatically switch to a channel when a desired programme starts.

Broadcasters recognize that EPGs are their 'shop window', the interface between viewer and programme. As well as providing the facility for viewers to choose which channel or programme to watch, the EPG will also be the entry point for 'on-demand' services. Broadcasters, and platform owners like DirecTV, BSkyB and Canal+, recognize the need for a guide to a listing of possibly 200–500 or more channels, which can be grouped by category or personal interest. EPGs can also offer a personalized message to the viewer, and may even include an e-mail messaging system.

On-demand technology

Digital transmission permits broadcasters and third-party suppliers to create special services for television viewing. While the usual catch-all labels of pay-per-view (PPV) and 'interactivity' are normally applied to on-demand technology, the reality is much wider. Indeed almost any software owner could supply data down the digital pipe for terrestrial, cable or satellite viewing. Video, movies or any number of other services, from banking to home shopping, recipes to medical services, could all be created on an 'on-demand' basis. These topics are covered in Chapter 6.

Cable, satellite or digital television?

Digital television was a relative latecomer to the UK; it was already a reality or scheduled in most other European countries and further afield. Satellite viewers in the USA had, via DirecTV, a digital satellite service as early as 1994. Ahead of the USA, and the rightful title-holder for the world's first digital pay-TV bouquet, was Orbit, the Middle East system, which started early in 1994 but with a non DVB-compliant system (dubbed MPEG1.5).

Digital via satellite

Digital satellite television broadcasts already cover the globe. These broadcasts fulfil two quite separate objectives:

- transmissions direct-to-home (DTH), by means of a satellite dish and receiver
- transmissions from cable head-ends, re-distributed to subscribers' homes

Table 4.1   Digital broadcasting start dates

Country	Satellite	Cable	Terrestrial
Australia	1997	1998	2002
Belgium	1996	1999	-
Canada	1994[1]	1998	1999[2]
Netherlands	1996	1998	-
Finland	1997	1998	2000
France	1996	1998	2002
Germany	1997	negl	2001
Hong Kong	1997	negl	-
Italy	1997	negl	-
Japan	1997	negl	2003[3]
Spain	1997	1998	1999
Sweden	1996	1998	1999
United Kingdom	1998	1998/9	1998
USA	1994	1997	1998

[1]Canadians are not officially permitted to view satellite digital transmissions from the USA, but it has been estimated that upwards of 250 000 DBS systems have been sold to Canadians.

[2]Canada's DTH ExpressVu digital system commenced in late 1997. Canada is adopting the same terrestrial high-definition system as the USA and transmissions were scheduled to start in 1999.

[3]Japan started testing digital terrestrial during 1998, but has delayed implementation until 2003.

Notes:

A report by Allied Business Intelligence Inc., published in November 1997, stated that by 2001 some 63 per cent or over 80 000 miles of US cable television plant mileage, will be equipped with Hybrid Fiber-Coax networks. Additionally, America's largest Multiple System Operator (MSO), Tele-Communications Inc., on 17 December 1997 ordered between 6.5 million and 11.9 million digital set-top boxes from General Instrument, to be installed by 2001.

The USA was committed to introduce digital terrestrial television during 1998, with 1 November 1998 as a voluntary date for commencement of transmissions. The Federal Communications Commission has mandated that the top ten largest markets should have completed their transition to digital by 1999. The end of December 2006 has been legislated for as the switch-off date for analogue. Those dates have all slipped.

Originally, communication satellites were designed to achieve two-way traffic between far distant communities for example, the USA and Europe, or Japan and the USA. All the early satellites (from the mid-1960s until the early 1980s) worked to this concept, for example Telstar, Early Bird/INTELSAT 1.

Few observers envisaged that the size or complexity of the huge Earth Stations then required to receive satellite transmissions could be reduced to the 40 cm or 60 cm dish, able to be casually fixed by relatively unskilled technicians to the side of a house. Another indication of the dramatic change in satellite broadcasting is that the Early Bird satellite weighed just 38 kg. The latest Hughes 702 satellite weighs 5200 kg.

Because of these dramatic changes, television today takes by far the largest share of the available satellite capacity. In 1982 there were only about 50 television stations in the whole of Europe, mostly publicly owned. Today there are well over one thousand, the greater proportion delivered by satellite. An authoritative report from Screen Digest (August 1999) states that European television channels have been growing 'at over 40 per cent per year since 1995'.

The advantage of satellite transmission is straightforward. A satellite signal can be received on a relatively low-cost home receiver – below US$150 in analogue, around US$300–500 currently in unsubsidized digital, depending on specification. The ex-works prices of digital Integrated Receiver Decoders (IRDs) are steadily falling as production volumes increase and component prices fall. In addition, economies are being achieved by the consolidation of internal components, improved design functionality of chip-sets and new suppliers coming into the market helping reduce the cost of such products.

Satellite transmission can also span thousands of miles within its footprint, delivering signals at a lower cost per household passed than any other method. While broadcasters have to deliver their signals to the orbiting satellite (uplinking) and lease transponder space from satellite operators such as Astra or EUTELSAT, the remainder of the investment required to view those signals is generally paid by the subscriber, firstly in the purchase of the receiver and dish, and secondly, in subscription fees which are of more direct benefit to the broadcaster.

There is also another payment model, drawn from experience in the cellular telephone business. Receiver/decoder box prices are increasingly being lowered by broadcasters subsidizing, in one form or another, the direct cost of the box. Examples are Canal+'s lease-payment plan, DirecTV and EchoStar's established subsidized box schemes and the BSkyB/British Interactive Broadcasting system to directly subsidize box prices.

Moreover, in the same way that some countries have embraced cellular telephone technology as a means of leap-frogging an inadequate hard wire system, so satellite transmission can enable countries to completely by-pass cable, whatever cable's merits. Such actions can effectively deliver 'free' television to huge areas with little or no infrastructure investment needed by local companies, municipalities or governments.

A recent study by PricewaterhouseCoopers explained how Mongolia has been connected to the US Internet using satellite. A Korean broadcaster is said to be contemplating delivering a television channel to Korean expatriates working in and visiting the Caribbean region. Arab Radio & Television, a broadcasting company operating out of Cairo and Jeddah, is beaming its signals to the USA, South America and Asia, via satellite.

Satellite television broadcasts can also be received via a Satellite Master Antenna system (SMATV), usually by a group of homes or apartment block. The system receives its signals by satellite and redistributes those signals to individual households either in one building or many adjacent buildings through cable.

Satellite television is now beginning to pose real competitive threats to cable. During 1997 the growth of the digital satellite television market considerably affected the stock price of cable companies in the USA, depressing already sluggish system prices downward – a situation not to be reversed until Microsoft invested US$ 1 billion in the US multiple system operator ComCast in June

1997. Companies backing digital satellites are unequivocal about satellite's potential to change radically the way people in the USA view television. EchoStar's founder Charlie Ergen recently stated, 'Our goal is not to be complementary to cable, we want to eliminate cable'.

Much has been stated of cable's ability to deliver near-limitless data over cable-specific modems. However, satellite is beginning to offer very similar capability. DirecTV has an associated company DirecPC that, via a proprietary system, can deliver Internet services to businesses and home office or small office users. EUTELSAT also introduced a DVB-compliant system in early 1998 which enables all computer users (domestic and commercial) to access Internet services, 'watch' real-time full-motion video broadcast over its satellites and access the web, at a planned cost of around US$200 per personal computer. SES/Astra is also enabling Internet-to-PC connectivity through its Astra-Net system, launched in October 1999.

The advantages of satellite over cable are:

■ immediate access to a large audience of potential viewers
■ very low cost-per-thousand to reach that audience
■ larger number of potential channels than cable
■ delivery to regions not adequately covered by existing TV signals: mountainous regions, thinly populated areas etc.
■ investment in receiving equipment borne generally by the viewer
■ instant coverage over a country or region without the need to invest in costly infrastructure
■ access to distant markets where the number of viewers, of those who can access the signal, may be low, but country or region-wide coverage can still make economic sense.

Satellite shares the following attributes with cable and digital terrestrial:

■ platform owners can encrypt signals to generate income
■ platform owners can limit access to signals to limit viewing to language or region-specific transmissions.

Satellite's weaknesses and risks may be defined as:

■ the risk of catastrophic loss either of the satellite upon launch or during orbit, damaging a broadcaster's business plan
■ a potential disadvantage to broadband cable in terms of interactivity.

Digital via cable

In-ground cable represents a future-proof investment in an architecture that is capable of being refined and adapted to whatever technology may throw at it in years to come. Older (in some cases pre-war) coaxial infrastructure – with its limited channel bandwidth – is being upgraded to wide bandwidth (referred to as broadband) fibre-optic linked circuits that can carry multi-media services including video, audio, data/Internet and voice in virtually unlimited quantity; either direct to homes or to 'nodes' of 250–1000 homes and then by coaxial into viewers' homes and business premises.

In some parts of the world, cable is ubiquitous and treated very much as a utility with national penetration levels close to 100 per cent. Some European countries are taking their first steps with cable (Italy, Spain) while others (The Netherlands, Belgium, Germany) are rebuilding their systems with Fibre Optic and Hybrid Fibre-Coax to more efficiently exploit broadcasting and multi-media opportunities.

A much-quoted illustration that is intended to extol the advantages of advanced fixed networks is that one single pair of glass optical fibre, about the thickness of a human hair could carry all of America's telephone calls on Mother's Day, allegedly the busiest day of the year for telephone traffic. That may or may not be an exaggeration; but it is a fact that fibre-optic can carry more than 10 terabits of information per second. Such capacity would translate into a half a million simultaneous two-way high-definition television channels – more than enough for even the most avid TV viewer!

Fibre is completely immune to electromagnetic interference, is lightweight (but more fragile than copper) and relatively inexpensive. Telephone and cable companies are using fibre as the backbone of their trunk networks, while keeping copper for what the industry calls 'the last mile' to the consumer's home.

Coaxial cable has two metal conduits separated and sheathed from one another by plastic. A single cable run can carry very high bandwidths of up to 1 GHz (or 1 Gbps), although cable amplifiers are needed to boost the signal every few hundred metres or so. Analogue cable systems can suffer from distortion because of this need to continually re-amplify the signal.

A Hybrid Fibre-Coax (HFC) network uses both fibre-optic and coaxial cable. Fibre is used from the cable company's head-end or main centre to a fibre-optic node or switch box in a neighbourhood. From this node, coaxial cable will be used to connect to the home. A neighbourhood might be a single apartment block of 100 dwellings or a suburban estate of 500 homes. Cable companies in the UK typically use nodes of 525 homes, while Spain's new build is using 1000-home nodes. HFC and its technical stablemate Fibre To The Curb (FTTC), which delivers a fibre-optic connection to within 1000 feet of the premises, tends to eliminate the need for most if not all amplification because only a short coaxial cable run is needed.

It is difficult to be precise as to the cost of establishing cable's network architecture but PricewaterhouseCoopers estimates the typical investment per site (which can be many dwellings) as US$850 for HFC compared with US$ 1200 for FTTC. Equity research from Bear Stearns places the cost at nearer US$ 500–600 per UK home passed (excluding the cost of the converter/decoder box).

Cable industry research consultancy Paul Kagan Associates estimated that by the end of 1997 only about 1 million USA cable homes had benefited from converting from coaxial to 750 MHz HFC systems. Kagan suggests that this number will rise to around 15 million homes during 1998, 25 million during 1999 and 32 million in 2000.

Tele-Communications Inc., the giant Denver-based cable operator now part of AT&T, announced in mid-December 1997 that it had entered an agreement with General Instrument Corporation to buy between 6.5 million and 11.9 million digital set-top boxes during the 1998–2001 period.

The investment needed to complete this work and the infrastructure projects underway in the UK, mainland Europe, Australia and the Far East is enormous. The UK's Cable Communications Association places the collective investment figure as more than £6 million per day in the UK alone. Spain's Cableuropa is investing US$3.5 billion in its cable build.

Cable modems

One important benefit claimed for cable is the improved connection speeds permitted by high-speed cable modems. The industry, particularly companies such as Scientific Atlanta and General Instrument, has developed modems specifically for cable which have speeds said to be up to 1000 times faster than the typical 28.8 Kbps standard in use today. The actual data-rate is measured by the length of time it would take to transfer a 10 Mb file. GI/Next Level's SURFBoard(r) cable modem products can deliver data at up to 27 Mbps.

Table 4.2 Modem speeds

Modem Type	Transfer Time for 10 Mb file
28.2 kbps phone modem	46 mins
128 kbps ISDN modem	24 mins
1.54 Mbs T-1 device	52 seconds
4 Mbps cable modem	20 seconds
10 Mbps cable modem	8 seconds

Source: Convergence Systems, 1997

There are two potential downsides to this development. The first is one of cost, as depending on specification and volumes ordered, these high-speed devices are relatively expensive. Graham

Wallace, at the time chief executive of the UK's Cable & Wireless Communications (CWC), said in October 1997 that such costs ruled out his company placing high-speed modems in all users' homes. Deployment, at least for Cable & Wireless, would be limited to business users and probably small office/home office applications. Since then, CWC has been absorbed by NTL, which has a different philosophy on the roll-out of high-speed modems.

The second problem concerns the perceived data-speeds of these devices. In essence, high-speed modems are giant ring-mains, similar to an Ethernet Local Area Network (LAN) where the available bandwidth is shared by everyone who is accessing the system at any given time. It is likely that a system supporting around 200 users would slow down delivered speeds to 1 or 2 Mbps, although this is still significantly faster than speeds currently experienced.

Cable's advantages and disadvantages

Advantages

- It is one of the most efficient ways of reaching apartment blocks and other high-density urban populations. This is also true of digital terrestrial transmission.
- It takes signals to viewers in distant regions or areas not adequately covered by existing TV signals. This is especially true of the USA and Canada.
- Its high bandwidth capacity can offer an immense choice of services, marrying telephony with television, interactivity with other multimedia services and higher-speed Internet access.
- New, tightly regionalized services can be created, incorporating local or community television and dedicated cable-exclusive channels.
- Cable companies in some parts of the world are seen as local utility services, often with excellent ties to the local community.
- High-speed cable modems, if deployed, could bring Internet-type services into the home, school or business at spectacular speeds.

Other advantages are also applicable to satellite or digital terrestrial television, or indeed telco-provided ADSL (Asymmetrical Digital Subscriber Line) services:

- The ability, through encryption, to generate income.
- The ability, through Conditional Access, to limit viewing to paying subscribers only.

Disadvantages

Cable also has some obstacles to overcome:

- high investment and start-up costs;
- usually cable companies have low or minimal expertise in broadcasting;
- cable companies are usually wholly dependent on broadcasters for product;
- competitive pressure from the number and choice of satellite channels available;
- pressure on cable television operating margins;
- frequently cable companies have a poor record in customer service;
- in new-build areas, customer service problems can be aggravated by negative publicity from environmentalists (tree damage, for example);
- continued further investment is necessary if high-speed cable modems are introduced;
- in the USA, with digital satellite getting Federal permission to offer local market signals, cable's unique selling point will be further eroded.

Digital via microwave

Specialists often use the phrase 'wireless cable', which can be divided into two sub-sets. Multichannel Multipoint Distribution Service (MMDS) is the term generally used within the industry for wireless delivery systems that use frequencies below 10 GHz. Over 10 GHz, systems tend to be referred to as Local Multipoint

Distribution Systems (LMDS) or Microwave Video Distribution Systems (MVDS). The concept and technology, if not the frequencies, are similar in each case. In very simple terms these MMDS/MVDS systems work like cellular telephony, beaming out dozens of channels to a town or city.

The main difference between sub-10 GHz MMDS installations and LMDS and other technologies operating over 12 GHz is one of broadcast area and broadcast conditions. Essentially, the higher frequencies have a limited radius of operation. Broadcasts in the 27.5–29.25 GHz band typically will have a guaranteed effective range of only about 2 km (although potentially larger in drier regions), and require frequent 'repeaters', each operating like a cellular telephony system. Hewlett Packard suggests using a hub broadcast system containing four 90-degree sector antennas to give omnidirectional coverage; even these relatively small cells can quite adequately cover a small town of 4000 to 16 000 homes.

The concept behind microwave delivery is straightforward: a low-power transmitter is erected specifically to target a town or city with television (or other) signals. Its advantage is simplicity: no expensive copper cables, no costly glass-fibre investment, no digging up streets, low maintenance, wide-scale immediate deployment.

Compared with hard-wired cable, MMDS deployment involves considerably less environmental disturbance. Buried cable also involves a slow, street-by-street, roll-out of the video or telephony service. MMDS is immediate. Once the tower is erected, signals can be sent within days, with the whole catchment area open to a sales effort and immediate 'connections'. MMDS and LMDS can offer telephony/data as well as television, so Internet and interactivity-based revenue streams are perfectly possible.

In some high-density European cities, a case in favour of cable can be made largely because of cable's greater capacity. When it comes to low-density suburban areas, however, the argument is less clear, and in semi-rural areas, the MMDS case becomes unarguable. This is especially true of the Middle East, where housing density is low, high-rise buildings are rare and terrain generally flat. A wide area can be covered using a mixture of omni-directional and repeater directional parabolic or cardioid antennas. General Instrument have installed a 40-tower all-digital system in Saudi Arabia.

MMDS systems have one major drawback: they are susceptible to water/rain attenuation (or rain-fade), especially at frequencies above 10 GHz. For this reason, most engineers strongly encourage broadcasters to adopt frequencies in the 2.5–4.5 GHz band range. The Middle East (especially the Gulf areas) tends to be considered as dry for most of the year, but it experiences high humidity, which can seriously interfere with signal coverage. Great care is needed with the installation of the local transmitters and the receiving antenna, at all times observing the 'line of sight' rule.

Propagation loss at higher MMDS frequencies can be severe. Detailed studies are now available from many sources, including manufacturers and end-users, which show the sort of broadcast efficiencies possible during different weather conditions. The Saudi Arabian and neighbouring Qatari systems, though, show what can be achieved with MMDS.

For example, Telekom Switzerland has coped with the most complex problems in MMDS deployment, ranging from high mountains, heavy rain and extreme snow cover. The Swiss system uses the 40 GHz band for its MediaSpot MVDS system, carrying 32 television channels to locations not served by broadband cable. Telekom Switzerland says that even low cloud and fog can cause a 0.9 dB/km signal attenuation; and even modest humidity levels can result in losses of around 0.16 dB/km for water vapour measured at 12 g/cubic meter at 15 °C. The end result is that engineers have to build in a safety margin equivalent to 3 to 4 dB per kilometre, or else limit coverage to a range of one to two kilometres only.

Typical MMDS frequencies are:

2.4–2.5 GHz
2.5–2.7 GHz
12 Ghz

27.5–28.35 GHz
29.1–29.5 GHz
31.0–31.75 GHz
40.5–42.5 GHz

Table 4.3   Countries where MMDS has been authorized

USA	2 GHz band
Ireland	2 GHz band
Eastern Europe	2 GHz band
Australia	2 GHz band
Hungary	10–12 GHz band
Romania	10–12 GHz band
Sweden	17 GHz band
EEC	40 GHz band

Source: Nokia, 1998

There are certain regions in the world where MMDS is being enthusiastically welcomed; the Middle East has already been mentioned, but Africa represents a real opportunity, largely because the MMDS broadcasting spectrum is still available for use. Most of the African services are currently analogue, and frequently limited to a handful of six channels, although new services are planned.

African countries using MMDS include:

Gabon
Madagascar
Mali
Togo
Benin
Burkina Faso
Cote d'Ivoire
Maurice
Niger
Senegal
Cameroun
Djibouti

Guinea Bissau
Guinea Equitoriale
Mauritania
Nigeria
Chad

Data: PanAfNet, 1997, France (analogue systems)

The (USA) Wireless Cable Association in 1997 claimed 4.5 million MMDS/LMDS subscribers in 59 countries worldwide. One study at that time forecast an installed subscriber base for MMDS of 13 million by 2000. Kagan Associates forecast 4.5 million US subscribers to MMDS by 2000, with a split of one third analogue and two-thirds digital.

One Canadian company (LookTV), building on extensive national experience in analogue MMDS, is planning a 23-tower system for Toronto and southern Ontario, offering 150 digital MMDS channels. LookTV's business plan forecasts 250 000 subscribers or 8 per cent of the market by 2005.

MMDS advantages and disadvantages

Advantages

MMDS advantages are best summed up as follows:

- immediate service over a tightly defined area with minimal infrastructure investment;
- low cost per home passed;
- telephony can be offered, allowing Internet and interactive services;
- an economic argument for service provision can even be made for rural areas;
- improved picture quality (with digital transmission);
- higher-value pay-television services and encryption can be easily incorporated;
- most digital MMDS systems allow for a wireless 'return path.'

Disadvantages

MMDS disadvantages are:

- high investment and start-up costs, although they are claimed to be significantly less than hard-wire cable;
- spectrum may not be adequate to offer more than 60 or so channels;
- operators generally have low or minimal expertise of broadcasting, consequently MMDS is very much a re-broadcasting exercise;
- usually wholly dependent on broadcasters for product;
- rural systems can be slow to financially break-even.

Digital television from the telephone companies

Now there's a new kid on the digital broadcasting block, with two opportunities for digital television to be delivered via the telephone. One is for telephone companies themselves, thanks to techno-logical improvements, to start providing entertainment services. The second opportunity depends on further software refinements, which will enable existing web-casters to deliver moving images via the Internet (of which more later).

Telephone companies have developed various engineering methodologies to help them squeeze more data down their wires. Already widely deployed are ISDN-based (Integrated Services Digital Network) services. ISDN digital telephone service was orig-inally designed over existing copper wire, but can also be offered by cable systems and fibre-delivered technology. ISDN (basic rate) provides 2 x 64 Kbps channels, enabling modem speeds up to five times faster than that achieved on a 28.8 Kbps modem and allowing the line to carry a conventional telephone call at the same time.

Even more radical is HDSL/ADSL (High-speed and Asymmetrical Digital Subscriber Line) technology, which allows video transmis-sions at speeds of 1.5 Mbps to 6 Mbps over copper wires. HDSL is two-way and needs two copper pairs; ADSL is also two-way, needing one pair but with a higher-capacity (up to ten times faster) in one direction.

ADSL: a broadcasting revolution in the making

... where POTS (Plain Old Telephone System) and PANS (Pretty Amazing New Stuff) will change our lives.

Revolution means overthrow, and the normal means of viewing entertainment in the home could be about to change. Consider these two statements from leading UK companies:

> The notion that TV and/or the Internet will mean anything to somebody in two years is irrelevant. It is my belief that currently the term television doesn't even have the same common meaning that it did even two or three years ago. It is totally changing.
>
> Steve Billinger, head of BSkyB's interactive division, September 1999

> IP networks are removing distance from the equation. So I can easily see the Hong Kong community in London having all the Hong Kong channels and services available out there available to them over an IP network of some kind in the London area, or indeed anywhere in the UK. The same would apply to the Japanese or any other ethnic group. The same could apply to Brits who want to hook into the Los Angeles area or elsewhere in the world. It will mean TV is available anywhere, anytime.
>
> Graham Mills, British Telecom's head of Internet and new media, September 1999

Steve Billinger comes from BSkyB, which currently takes a highly aggressive view of how viewers will use their interactive and home-shopping 'broadcasts', but which nevertheless is wedded to a 'conventional' pattern of television delivery – mostly via satellite and cable – to consumers in the home. Additionally, BSkyB is preparing for the day when the whole of the UK is viewing digital television, now virtually guaranteed by about 2006.

Graham Mills from BT takes the opposite view, suggesting that most UK homes already have a telephone, and for the majority of them, that telephone line is in reality the 'fat pipe'. The humble phone line is already a versatile technology, delivering voice, faxes, data and even rudimentary images without much help from the technologists.

ADSL has the potential to convert these sleeping dinosaurs, the telephone companies, into media companies at the push of a button. Forget digging up streets or rigging wires, or having limitations of bandwidth or even economic censorship – of which more in a moment – ADSL is a revolution in the making.

To say 'ADSL uses digital technology' is too simplistic, as all the xDSL's use digital. It is the asymmetrical part which is the important difference, in that while ADSL can carry ordinary voice-based calls at the same time as data, it can cope with massive surges downstream. In the splitting of voice from data, the telephone companies technically divide the line into at least two parts, transmitting voice at a lower frequency (voice is usually in 0–4 KHz band, while data is carried at 50 KHz–1.1 MHz band), although different operators/countries might vary these bandwidths slightly.

ADSL also has two defined methods of transmission: upstream to the exchange or downstream to the user. While the balance between the two might change in the future, it is generally accepted that the downstream link is the more demanding in terms of volume content. In practice, little pressure is placed on the uplink burst, or request for data to be sent. Over time, and with the growth of video conferencing, these elements may become more balanced, more symmetrical, in their use.

ADSL is limited, however, in the customers it can handle. While any number can be served, it is generally accepted that users have to be within 18 000 feet (approximately 5 km) of a telephone exchange. Tests and trials are currently underway to see how far this envelope can be pushed, and the results are encouraging. However, it is not foreseen that rural dwellers will enjoy much by the way of an ADSL service, as ADSL is urban and suburban in its concept.

For those lucky millions of town-dwellers, the results are breathtaking. Speeds of up to 1000 times an 'ordinary' modem line are quite possible, without the need to replace or significantly adapt existing telephone lines. In terms of capacity, ADSL can deliver up to 8 Mbps downstream and around 800 Kbps–1 Mbps upstream.

Most operators plan on installing in the home a 'POTS splitter'; this divides the voice element and sends it to the telephone handset, while the data component can be directed to a personal computer or set-top box for viewing. With ADSL installed, users at home are able to enjoy what has been described as a 'two-way tidal wave of data'. ADSL is always 'on'; there is no need to seek a dial tone for data connection, allowing viewers/users (or the increasingly common 'viewsers') to access whatever they want. As Graham Mills suggests, it might be they want to tune into webcasts from around the other side of the planet, or watch a sporting event on the same basis, or just to video-chat to friends or family.

Viewsers will no longer be limited to tiny, clunky, windows with slow-to-change images (as is typical today on modem-supported delivery). Instead, they will enjoy full-screen images just as good as those currently 'broadcast'. However, while we might want to view a transmission from Hong Kong, Los Angeles or Sydney, there are other, non-technical elements, to be considered. The most serious is the ownership, or 'rights', to a broadcast.

For example, viewing the local 6 p.m. news is not going to cause anyone any anxiety wherever the transmission emanates, be it Hong Kong, Los Angeles or Sydney. The moment we start receiving an episode of *Friends* or a live soccer match via a webcast from a distant country, however, then we have problems. The sit-com and the sports game will have had their national broadcast rights sold on an exclusive basis, and these rights will be zealously guarded.

There is another problem, more practical than technical, and often referred to as 'economic censorship'. A satellite broadcaster or cable television company operating in a digital environment have the ability to 'broadcast' almost any amount of programming to viewers. In reality, what they offer is a limited bouquet of popular choices. They might like to offer more, but suggest that to offer minority channels would be a waste of broadcast bandwidth. The key word here is 'broadcast'. By its very definition, we are talking about a 'one point to many receivers' (point to multipoint) economic model. Cable companies can hardly cope with the pressure on them for broadcast bandwidth and choose those channels and services that are more likely than not to be successful commercially. Other, limited interest services have to fall by the wayside, thus effecting an 'economic censorship'.

With ADSL that limitation vanishes. These are point-to-point services, from one source to one recipient, although the telephone companies also have the ability to 'broadcast' services/programming if they so choose. This brings us to the final technical limitation, again relating to distant suppliers. The Hong Kong to London, or Sydney to Los Angeles links each could easily be expected to have to get through half-a-dozen points of presence in the daisy-chain of links to the viewer. If any of these points create a typical web-style bottleneck, the system will fail or at best fall back to a rudimentary on-screen image. In other words the images have to be transferred to a local cache, minimizing the potential for bottlenecks, for guaranteed delivery to the viewer. Only if this happens will images be full screen, broadcast quality. This hurdle might be the most challenging for the telephone companies to overcome, and it will be interesting to see if they can meet not only the technical and pricing challenges of ADSL, but also the delivery obstacles. If they fail on any of these three elements, then viewers will, at best, be disappointed.

ATM – not getting cash

An ATM may be well-known as an automated (cash) teller machine, but as far as this book is concerned, our ATM stands for Asynchronous Transfer Mode. This two-way technology enables many different data types (data, voice or video) to be carried on a common circuit. The information is broken down into packets of just 53 bytes each (five 'header' bytes and 48 data bytes), leading to very high capacity. Indeed ATM packets can travel at between 22 and 622 Mbps, permitting full-motion video.

While most large telephone companies have tested variations of over-the-air 'broadcasting' on their wires, it is the programming-on-demand and interactive models that have created most interest. Most major telephone companies have been testing interactive delivery for some time. Some of the earlier tests going back to the mid-1990s.

Table 4.4   Programming on-demand trials

PTT/Region	Date	Homes in trial	Technology
British Telecom/Ipswich	1995	2500	ADSL/ATM
France Telecom/Rennes	1996	20 000	ADSL/ATM
Finland/Helsinki Telephone	1995	30	ATM
Israel Telecom/Tel Aviv	1996	100	ADSL/ATM
Swiss PTT/Grenchen	1995	400	ADSL
Telecom Italia/Rome+Milan	1994	1000	ADSL
Telenor/Oslo	1996	200	ADSL/ATM
Nynex, Manhattan, USA	1994	2500	ADSL
Time Warner, Orlando, USA	1994	4000	ADSL
Hong Kong Telecom	1997*	30 000	ADSL/HFC
Singapore Telecom	1996	300	ADSL/ATM

*Commercial implementation, commenced Sept 1997

All these tests are widely accepted to have proved inconclusive. While each met their technical targets, actual programming-on-demand needs have elicited some consumer interest but not on a scale that appears to justify the very considerable investment required to make the service commercially available. Time Warner's Orlando, Florida Full Service Network, was suspended in May 1997, with Time Warner, according to most reports, not keen to continue funding the experiment (reportedly having spent US$100 million) with such poor take-up rates. Time Warner chairman Gerald Levin stated in 1997 that development of the Internet had 'overtaken the need for the Time Warner degree of TV sophistication'.

The web – the true telephone delivery revolution

The delivery of real-time audio over ordinary telephone wires (normally referred to as Plain Old Telephony System or POTS) is well-accepted. Dolby Laboratories, the noise reduction specialists, can even enhance the normally mono-signal and create a real-time Dolby Pro-Logic surround sound version for the PC user. Video is moving in the same direction. Today it is perfectly possible to 'broadcast' moving images from point to multipoint via the Internet. Even with a rudimentary 28.8 K modem, users can see quite acceptable moving images (remembering the limited bandwidth of the modem).

Perhaps the most important advantage of this method of video delivery is that on the world wide web there are no channel restrictions. While the technologies that enable web-casting may still be considered somewhat embryonic, it is nevertheless true that they are operating to a completely different set of 'rules' and standards than their older-established radio and television counterparts. There is no allocation of channels in cyberspace.

No government has to allocate precious bandwidth to would-be broadcasters. Moreover, though this is certainly also seen in a negative light, there are no formal limitations on what these 'channels' may or may not 'transmit'. Government and industry officials often talk about restriction or limitations but generally there are no specifically drafted laws to cover web-casting other than regulations already in national use on decency and content. There are also no formal rules yet relating to the likely age or sensitivity of the viewer. No system has yet emerged which categorizes by age the content of a web site.

Singapore, the USA, the United Arab Emirates and Saudi Arabia are all examining how access to Internet material can be regulated. The USA has already passed a Communications Decency Act, designed to protect minors from unsavoury broadcasting over the web. The Act is, however, being challenged in the US Supreme Court by a free speech lobby group.

Anyone, whether established conventional broadcaster or rabid anarchist, can provide a site on the web, and while the large broadcaster is likely to place significant resources behind their web site, it is also true that anyone with a rudimentary electronic camera and video-streaming technology can just as easily place a 'channel' or programme on to the web and start their own radio or television show. There is no requirement for large capital investment in broadcast towers, no uplinking to satellites, no microwave links or fibre-optic connections.

Many of the so-called digital super-highway forecasts suggested that we would all soon be enjoying a world where 500 channels were commonplace. Then some predictions were made that perhaps a 5000 channel universe was likely to be the norm. Those estimates are both wrong and out of date. Today we have niche 'channels' by the hundred, indeed by the thousand, and they exist on the world wide web.

One outfit (www.broadcast.com) has proved to be rocket-like in the way the Dallas-based Internet company has shot to be one of Wall Street's hottest technology stocks over the past year. In April 1999 Broadcast.com was bought by web portal Yahoo! in a US$5.6 billion acquisition, which was not bad for a fledgling company that in 1998 had revenues of US$ 22.4m and just US$9.1 million in 1997. (Yahoo! is not dissimilar an outfit; its revenues in 1998 were US$203m, but it remains a hot favourite to emerge as the web's favourite search engine.)

Without doubt, Broadcast.com is now the largest and most sophisticated Internet broadcaster, currently streaming daily audio transmissions from over 300 US radio stations, and 40 television stations directly. Many more use Broadcast.com on an occasional basis, with regular clients including music companies and concert promoters as well as business to business users.

Broadcast.com has also just made its first major venture in sports transmission, by tying up the US Major League baseball clubs to an exclusive deal which allows it to web-stream the League's baseball games live on to the web. These games, together with the rest of Broadcast.com's content, have helped deliver more than 1 million users a day to its site, making the company a significant threat to US television screens.

Most conventional multi-channel broadcasters count themselves lucky to capture 250 000 viewers, or even less for some niche channels. Then, suddenly, along comes this web-based upstart and steals away another million pairs of eyeballs. It was Broadcast.com which handled the Victoria's Secrets lingerie airing in February 1999, and almost brought the whole world wide web to a standstill.

Broadcast.com is not alone. In 1998 RealNetworks, which supplies its RealVideo streaming technology to companies like broadcast.com, was happy to be a systems supplier to broadcasters and users alike. Indeed, its RealVideo is close to becoming the industry standard. One can find dozens of other stations on RealVideo (at www.real.com), and links to similar sites, each streaming television and radio stations to viewers.

Suddenly it seems there is a convergence of broadcasting technologies. Also available is NBCi, a competitor to broadcast.com (yahoobroadcast).

Highlighting the threat faced by the networks are the laws in the USA which forbid cable subscribers from switching to satellite during a 90-day period after they have cancelled their cable contract! Additionally, satellite broadcasters are not allowed to offer local stations to a wider market.

Yet, via the web, viewers can more or less watch what they want from hundreds of stations spread over the USA. It's a crazy business, and one that's bound to get worse once a larger number of digitally equipped homes, whether satellite or cable, start using high-speed modems to deliver web-based content at speeds sufficient to fill a television screen – and not the somewhat clunky and visually inadequate images that a limited telephone can currently handle.

Many readers will know how important music is to web-based retailers. Launch.com now offers more than 1000 music videos, along with news, reviews and the sales of CDs. Web-streamed content is vital to the company's business plan. Tunes.com offers a similar service.

One web-based outfit is even beating the studios and traditional networks. It is streaming online video clips (although not yet the complete programmes) of new shows that have yet to air.

Pilots (the name given to an outline first episode) of two shows, *Creepy Camera* and a show from the public who are invited to make their own video comedy/horror films is being 'aired' (at www.cameraplanet.com). These come from Broadcast News Network, another fledgling web-caster (found at www.broadcast-news.com) which already carries Citizencam, another variation on the broadcast theme.

Most of the USA's leading broadcast networks already web-stream much of their key material. ESPN and CNN are two of the best. CNNfn, its financial news station, already gets a huge number of hits a day (cnnfn.com), and has offered a full-time web-based 'live' financial news service since the summer of 1999, and is targeting to double the current 2 billion 'page-views' a year.

More humble stations can also reach around the globe. One innovative station (www.wpri.com) is a CBS-affiliate in East Providence, Rhode Island. With a self-admitted staff of just one technician, this friendly station is streaming all its daily newscasts (EST at 6 a.m., 5 p.m./6 p.m./11 p.m.) live and provides links to its big-brother CBS network. As well as local clips it is always neat to see what the weather is like, especially in hurricane season. And WPRI's page views, an impressive 500 000 a month, according to web-master Tim Reynolds.

To put all this news in context, it is only necessary to remember that most of these broadcasters are businesses keen to capture viewer loyalty. Anyone who suspects that we will not be using/ viewing web-based material in the future is way out of date with reality.

The costs for entrepreneurs to present their own 'channel' are minuscule. RealNetworks, formerly known as Progressive Networks, is the company behind RealAudio and RealVideo, probably the market-leader in web-based broadcasting technology. RealNetworks' own high-end software is available to users for under US$40 and has been bought by millions of users. It can be downloaded over the Internet direct from RealNetworks' web site and has the ability to use a base-standard 28.8 K modem for delivering what the company calls 'newscast quality' video.

RealNetworks pioneered Internet broadcasting when it launched the RealAudio Player in 1995. RealAudio quickly established market leadership and currently maintains a 90 per cent share of the Internet streaming audio market. Thousands of broadcasters, both large and small, have used RealAudio to establish their Internet broadcast presence.

In February 1997, RealNetworks brought Internet video to the mass market with the launch of version 4.0 of its RealVideo file format. RealPlayer has emerged as the leading streaming video application on the web with more than 20 million clients. RealNetworks claim more than 2 million of their web players are downloaded every month. RealNetworks customers include CBS, ABC, MCA, Warner Bros, FOX, ESPN SportsZone, Atlantic Records, MSNBC, MGM, Geffen, Sony, Intel, Merrill Lynch, AudioNet, and Bloomberg.

The 'broadcasting' end of the RealVideo operation is provided by Real Broadcasting Networks (RBN). RBN has its broadcast operations centre in Seattle, from where it incorporates the various incoming video streams. RBN and MCI then deliver content along the closest, least congested routes worldwide. These have included live concerts by pop groups the Rolling Stones and U2, as well as hundreds of radio and TV channels.

RealNetworks admit the scale of Internet broadcasting has been restricted by operating costs and technical challenges. These challenges are inherent in owning and operating the software, hardware and managing the Internet connectivity necessary to reach an audience of any appreciable size from a single location. The key factor in these costs is Internet connectivity, which, until now, has limited the growth of the Internet as a large-scale broadcast medium. RBN say they have solved this problem by distributing access to their 'broadcasts' throughout the Internet backbone and passing the resulting efficiencies in scale and reach to RBN customers and users.

There are other complications to consider, which in themselves are not very different from running a conventional broadcast operation; they include the technical and broadcasting skills of available staff, including advertisement insertion, managing access authentication and security, experience in content and programming, advertising and advertising sales as well as branding and marketing. However, these can be weighed against the benefits. RealNetworks claims that up to 50 000 users can access a single site at the same time, roughly the same reach as a US big city radio station, but of course these 'listeners' and viewers will be scattered across the globe. This technology can be viewed from sites like www.broadcast.com.

Web-casting as a viable business has gained extra credibility now that Microsoft has invested in almost all the available web-streaming software houses. It bought California-based VXtreme in August 1997 and has investments in VDOnet as well as RealNetworks.

Microsoft's purchase of Vxtreme in August 1997 prompted the US Department of Justice to request information from Microsoft as to its intention within the market sector. Microsoft stated that it was simply seeking to promote compatibility to benefit customers. Microsoft has incorporated RealNetworks audio and video streaming into the latest versions of Microsoft *Internet Explorer*.

Telephone delivery: advantages and disadvantages

Advantages

The main benefits of telephone-delivered content include:

- no limit on number of channels/themes/interest groups available;
- highly personal 'narrowcasting';
- considerable opportunities for closed-user groups with significant revenue potential;
- web-delivered information has the possibility to boost sales of some products, with book and music publishing already seeing sales and even everyday items to isolated communities;
- it can be wholly interactive.

Disadvantages

Its disadvantages are:

- potentially expensive for the consumer to 'view' on-line because of line costs;
- some web sites have little expertise in broadcasting, although some users consider this to be a positive advantage;
- telecommunication companies have little or no expertise of managing content;
- perceived risks over financial security, credit cards/bank and financial statements (although web-based security is now considered robust by most specialists);
- risks over content, e.g. pornography being viewed by minors;
- considerable risks over copyright issues and illegal distribution.

Digital terrestrial

The progress made in digital compression has proved vital for the emergence of digital terrestrial television. However, other developments have also spurred on this concept, not least the scarcity and consequent high value of the broadcast spectrum itself.

Since the mid-1990s two separate digital terrestrial trends have emerged. While in 1995 Europe established its MPEG-2 DVB broadcasting standards – with the suffix /C for cable, /S for satellite and /T for terrestrial – the USA has followed a different path under the generic term 'Advanced Television' using a standard commonly referred to as the 'Grand Alliance'.

The four regions where plans for digital terrestrial television are most advanced are Europe, Japan, Australia and in particular the USA. In Europe all broadcasters have now adopted the MPEG-2 DVB/T transmission standard. The UK is already broadcasting in MPEG-2 DVB/T (since November 1998) and amongst other European countries Scandinavia and Spain are furthest advanced.

In July 1999 India also selected the DVB/T European standard following 18 months of comparative testing. A pilot scheme was promised for Delhi before the end of 1999 followed by a national roll-out.

Europe

- The UK has licensed six DTT multiplexes and broadcasts commenced in late 1998.
- In Germany experimental licenses were granted for the Lower Saxony region in mid-summer 1999. DTT is expected to be gradually introduced from 2001 onwards.
- Finland has created two DTT commercial multiplexes, each with eight channels as well as a multiplex ceded to the public broadcaster. Testing and initial construction was taking place during 1997–8. Broadcasts are scheduled to start in the autumn of 2000. Licences will run for 10 years (from 1 September) and licence-holders are required to guarantee coverage of 70 per cent of Finland's population by 2001, with the whole country covered by 2006, when analogue is scheduled to be switched off.
- Sweden continued testing DTT during 1997–9 and has given specific approval to DVB/T's introduction, with a spectrum auction of eight digital terrestrial channels taking place early in 1998. The Swedish government will reserve at least two channels for local programming, and although it set January 1999 'at the latest' as the start dates for DTT, actual implementation was delayed until the summer of 1999. However, the most recent data available (October 1999) states that only 250 subscribers have signed up. In October it emerged that a radical re-think was underway, with services being supplied free to viewers until there are 100 000 'subscribers'.
- The French audiovisual authority, the Conseil Superieur de l'Audiovisuel (CSA) has expressed support for DTT although a technical deployment is not expected before 2000. Trials have been taking place in the Brittany region and the city of Rennes since June 1999.

■ Spain's Retevision has plans to commence national DTT transmissions during 1999–2000 in the Catalonia and Madrid regions, rolling the system out to other population centres during 2000–2001. The Catalonia regional government sees new digital terrestrial channels being used for region-specific cultural and educational broadcasting as well as entertainment services. The Commercial licence-holder is ONDA and broadcasts started on 15 November 1999.

■ The Netherlands is testing DTT. With cable so widely available it is likely that DTT will be implemented more slowly.

■ Italy has been conducting a DTT trial in the southern city of Santa Agata since June 1999. The place was chosen because of its difficult local terrain. Telecom Italia says projects will be introduced which provide DTT to all towns by 2006, when analogue is to be switched off.

Japan

Japan is generally considered far ahead of other countries in the region in terms of plans for digital terrestrial television. Certainly it has a head start in having already launched higher definition television and having already built up a wide portfolio of programming. Its hosting of the winter Olympics at Nagano in 1998 also gave digital HDTV a boost. Furthermore, many Japanese viewers are familiar with the advantages of HDTV and there are a growing number of wide-screen sets in their homes.

The Japanese Ministry of Post and Telecommunications stated that it wanted digital terrestrial broadcasting to commence by 2000, although that date has in practice slipped very badly. In mid-1999 the Ministry said it would delay for 30 months the setting of frequencies for DTT, that is nominally until 2003.

At the same time, state broadcaster NHK has moved away from support of the analogue-based HiVision High-Def system. The decision was not altogether voluntary, as NHK's hand was largely forced by various chip-set makers themselves deciding to withdraw from the HiVision market. In December 1996 Fujitsu said it was going to switch research and development from HiVision to digital, a move echoing Toshiba and Oki's earlier announcements that they were to turn their energies into the more lucrative digital market.

Japan's largest commercial television company, Nippon Television Network (NTV), working with telecommunications company Nippon Tsushinki, is already looking at the opportunities to transmit signals digitally for cable subscribers, taking the technology already available from the two major satellite platforms into viewers' homes.

Australia

In December 1997 the European DVB/T system was tested in Australia, in its HDTV mode, as part of a 7 MHz channel bandwidth. Australia has already tested the 'normal' MPEG-2 DVB compression standards for multiplexed terrestrial television. The earlier tests were designed to provide practical experience of a digital multiplex and occupied the channel 8, normally unused in the Sydney area. Australia decided in 1998 that it will adopt the European paradigm of multiplexed channels, with the possibility of wide screen.

Australia's DTT-day is 1 January 2001, although the broadcast standards that have now emerged (see www.standards.com.au) show a hybrid system that is compliant with DVB/T but with local modifications which enable a 'fast track' for high definition.

USA

The USA is the only country so far to have legislated for a specific closure date for analogue transmission – December 2006. Much of the discussion between government and industry has revolved around the introduction of high definition television (HDTV).

The 'Grand Alliance' is a consortium of US broadcasting companies (and certain European companies like Philips and Thomson, both working through their US operations), manufacturers and engineers, who were working initially on various competing HDTV systems. In May 1993 the FCC invited the competing groups to come together and create a common 1250 line all-digital 'standard' for the introduction of HDTV in the USA. The competing groups were:

- AT&T and Zenith
- General Instrument and MIT
- Philips, Thomson and Sarnoff.

These groups went on to work as the Digital HDTV Grand Alliance and, with the David Sarnoff Research Centre as the co-ordinating body, its standard has been approved by the FCC and adopted by the US industry. Although still using MPEG-2 compression, the US standards are slightly different from those developed in Europe – but digital standards conversion equipment will make any such differences marginal.

Yet the US television industry currently faces a dilemma. The FCC exerted pressure on US network broadcasters to adopt not the European multi-channel digital model but a high definition model of – at best – two channels per station and the rapid roll-out of high-definition, wide-screen broadcasting. The FCC has set an aggressive timetable to complete the conversion from analogue to digital, with 31 December 2006 as the 'switch off' date, now considered by some observers to be far too optimistic.

There is another significant difference between the USA and Europe. The US broadcasts will be free-to-air at no charge to the consumer. Each (terrestrial) network currently transmitting gets a 'free' slice of bandwidth for the new HDTV services, which can be a simulcasted existing broadcast or a combination of current and new material. The reaction of American broadcasters to supplying a 'free' HDTV channel to viewers has not been philanthropic. However, they are enthusiastic about advertisers exploiting this new technology, offering new services to viewers and thus funding the HDTV channels.

The USA's road to high definition television has not been easy. In August 1996 the FCC issued its 100-page 'master plan' which called for each of the 1600 existing American stations to be given new digital frequencies, sufficient, using digital compression, to enable each station to broadcast two signals. The FCC stated that stations could use the new frequency allocation for a full wide bandwidth high definition channel, plus a second digital (but not HDTV) channel.

The FCC offered one other option. Television stations could, if they wished, use the bandwidth for a greater number of channels at standard definition, but these would have to be digital and the same timetable would apply. On 24 December 1996 the FCC saw its proposals enacted as law.

In return for the commission's largesse, the FCC would require the eventual return of the station's existing – and much wider – slice of valuable bandwidth. Senator Bob Dole, during his election campaign, stated that the returned bandwidth to be worth at least US$34 billion, although the FCC gave the spectrum an even higher value of between US$40–100 billion. President Bill Clinton stated that the first batch of returned frequencies (due to be auctioned off in 2002) will bring in US$14.8 billion. Then, year-by-year, analogue spectrum will be returned until the whole country is, hopefully, fully digital by 2006.

The FCC's announcement has created a dilemma for most US television stations, forcing them to assess in detail their current equipment levels, to ask how far the new digital transmissions will extend, with many operators worried about audience shrinkage leading to an inevitable reduction in advertising revenue. Early technical tests also showed that digital signals will frequently not achieve the area coverage that a current high-power analogue antenna delivers. In New York, a tightly defined geographical area consisting of the five city and suburban boroughs, digital coverage will be between 97.9 and 99.9 per cent, almost perfectly matching the existing analogue signals (although with vastly improved images). In Los Angeles, however, a sprawling city spreading over a huge and largely ill-defined area, there will be significant coverage problems. According to the FCC the local CBS station in Los Angeles (KCBS) will only achieve about 81.1 per cent of its existing coverage area. With broadcasters having to spend large capital sums re-equipping their facilities for high definition, the last problem they want to face is to lose up to 20 per cent of an existing audience. One Oregon station (KOTI in Klamath Falls) has discovered that its HDTV signals would only reach some 54 per cent of its existing population.

Nevertheless, it seems the networks, many advertisers and the government are firmly behind the plan to convert all of the USA to digital by 2006. Indeed, the FCC in April 1997 told broadcasters it expected the major cities to be served by HDTV by Christmas 1998 and this target was met. Critics of the FCC's timetable have said it is foolish to expect viewers to replace all their television sets including those in children's bedrooms and in kitchens as well as portable sets.

Technology may provide some solutions. Some modern analogue sets might be convertible by means of a replacement card, or a 'plug-in' or 'behind-set' device placed in-line between roof-top antenna and aerial input. Such PCM/CIA card-type modular options have additional benefits. Set-top boxes today are far larger than they need to be. They contain a tuner and printed-circuit board (increasingly being reduced thanks to silicon-chip efficiencies), but their size is greatly influenced by space requirements for the dissipation of heat from the built-in transformer. If the power were to be drawn from the television set chassis, it would allow for smaller set-top boxes.

Table 4.5   The USA's original HDTV timetable

Nov 1998	First HDTV stations on air
1999	10 largest cities must have HDTV channels
2003	At least 50% of programmes must be digitally simulcast
2004	At least 75% of programmes must be digitally simulcast
2005	100% digital simulcasting
2006	Analogue frequencies handed back

Manufacturers have welcomed HDTV, and are anticipating a huge volume of sales of television sets. Viewers will benefit not simply from additional programming and improved picture quality but from Electronic Programme Guides (EPGs) which will be essential for the consumer to navigate through the dozens of channels and services.

Besides the obvious increase in demand for new transmitters, it is probable that many studios and transmission centres will use HDTV as the springboard for a wholesale studio re-equipping exercise. The expenditure involved is huge. LIN Television, which owns just six stations scattered across the USA, stated recently that it has already spent US$15.4 million, and expects to spend another US$40 million in converting to HDTV. Victor Tawel of the Association for Maximum Service Television predicts the typical costs of conversion per television station to be in the US$7–12 million range.

Wide-screen high-definition images are seen as desirable by the creative community (and this includes the Hollywood studios) as well as some key broadcasters, not least of which are channels like Discovery (who transmit documentary and natural history programming) and Home Box Office (HBO) (which depends on movies for its income).

The US government policies are likely to greatly influence planning by other governments worldwide:

- In December 1997, the Canadian Federal Industry Ministry stated that Canada will adopt the ATSC A/53 standard for HDTV digital television – the same standard that the USA has adopted. The ministry stated that Canadians can expect to see the first digital television broadcasts some time in 1999, but that analogue broadcasting is likely to persist for 10 years or so before being fully replaced by the digital technology.
- In May 1997 the Australian Broadcasting Authority chairman stated that he wanted to see HDTV included in Australia's digital plans, saying 'I remain unshaken in my belief that Australian audiences should be given the same opportunity to see network TV in high-definition.' Nevertheless, Australia

eventually adopted Europe's DVB/T format but with local provision for the early introduction of HDTV.

While not directly relevant to the DTT position in the USA, satellite operator DirecTV launched its first HFTV channel 'HBO on HDTV' in August 1999. This channel promised at least 60% of its output would be HDTV in the 1080 Interlaced (1080i) format. HBO has subsequently added a second HDTV channel.

The challenge

The question now is whether the USA's adoption of 'true' digital high definition means the rest of the world will follow suit. Currently (end of 1999) the situation is clouded by two 'standards' emerging.

Abe Peled, CEO of News Corp's technology arm NDS (since October 1999 part of Tandberg) described the USA's move into HDTV as 'a big yawn.' Peled says:

In North America HDTV is a quiet disaster, and a non-event. Stations continue to introduce HDTV equipment, but many of them are going for the cheapest possible option. They are waiting for something to happen, and as for consumers, they greeted it with a huge yawn. At NAB (Spring 1999) I gave a talk which said that simply broadcasting the same event in HDTV is not going to be enough. And that concept has resonated elsewhere. DirecTV will start showing HDTV but it's more of a flag-waving exercise.

Peled says the biggest interest they have seen is for data carriage from broadcasters, of value-added services on top of the HDTV signal for which they can charge extra.

Where is digital today?

In this chapter we take a global tour and look at where digital broadcasting is today. We shall examine the early trials and tribulations of a few specific broadcasters to see what lessons, if any, may be learnt.

As with so many other technology innovations, North America was the first major region to adopt digital broadcasting. In Chapter 4 we outlined some of the problems facing terrestrial broadcasters with their HDTV obligations, but in one area digital is already a huge success – satellite DTH broadcasting.

North America

In North America there were, until recently, four different satellite platforms transmitting digital television channels. Their signals cover the whole of the USA and much of Canada and are all intended specifically for DTH reception. In both countries, cable is the main means of television distribution and these satellite platforms are considered a direct threat to cable companies. Primestar was the exception as it was owned by a consortium of cable companies who used the platform as a means of delivering their programming to potential clients outside their cable franchise areas.

The four platforms were:

- DirecTV
- DiSH (EchoStar)
- United States Satellite Broadcasting (USSB)
- Primestar.

A fifth DTH satellite broadcaster, Alphastar, went bankrupt in August 1997 with assets of US$72 million and liabilities of US$105 million. In late December 1997, the assets were purchased by Champion Holdings Inc. for US$4.6 million, the intention being to re-commence broadcasting during 1999 from its Earth Station, which the company claims has capacity for 200 channels. Initially, the company says it will target the Caribbean region.

However, at the end of 1999, consolidation had reduced the four active broadcasters to just two: DirecTV (including USSB and PrimeStar) and EchoStar.

Table 5.1   US Satellite market share forecasts ('000)

	1999	*2000*	*2001*	*2002*	*2003*
DirecTV*	6320	8418	9314	9953	10520
USSB*	2653	3167	3581	3910	5260
EchoStar	3066	4376	5264	5902	6469
Primestar	1230	-	-	-	-
Total**	10 616	12 802	14 578	15 855	16 989

*DirecTV and USSB are now merged.

**Totals do not add up as some viewers subscribe to more than one service.

Data: Bear, Stearns & Co., 1999

DirecTV

DirecTV is owned by a consortium led by Hughes Space & Communications, and at September 1999 had more than seven million subscribers. On 9 October 1999, DirecTV 1-R, its fourth satellite, was launched, becoming the first commercial satellite to be launched from the ocean-based Sea Launch platform.

The new satellite added extra capacity to DirecTV's overall mission, and to deliver local broadcast network channels. The satellite will operate from 101 degrees West longitude, which is DirecTV's main orbital slot. DirecTV 1-R is an HS 601HP model, with 16 high-power Ku-band transponders. It will deliver 30 per cent more capacity than DBS-1, an HS 601 spacecraft that currently serves DirecTV subscribers from 101 degrees West longitude, but that will move to 110 degrees West to serve as back-up capacity. DirecTV 1-R began service around 1 December 1999.

On 29 November 1999, DirecTV announced it had started transmitting local broadcast network channels via satellite for its customers in New York and Los Angeles. These transmissions mean DirecTV's customers in the New York and Los Angeles areas can receive their local broadcast network channels via satellite.

It costs a little, but it means viewers in these two regions can watch all the local channels, from the large networks like NBC, ABC, CBS and Fox for US$5.99 per month. In addition to local broadcast network channels, a national PBS feed is included in each local channel package at no additional charge. DirecTV say they will continue to add additional regions which can receive local television throughout 2000.

A statement in 1999 from DirecTV's president, Eddy W. Hartenstein, summed up the appeal of adding local channels to a satellite bouquet.

By offering local channels on DirecTV, our customers can access entertainment and information that's most relevant to their lives and they can watch their local channels with digital picture and CD-quality sound. Now is as good a time as any for consumers in New York and Los Angeles to cut cable and choose DirecTV as their source for home entertainment.

Local channels are delivered to DirecTV's subscribers in New York and Los Angeles from its primary orbital slot at 101 degrees West longitude. A few days after this statement DirecTV added the Denver and Washington regions to the local line-up.

At the same time, DirecTV said it had 7.8 million customers, including old Primestar customers. The addition of local television channels, approved by the US congress in November 1999, removed the last attraction for some viewers for staying connected to cable.

EchoStar's DiSH network

EchoStar is majority-owned by one of the earliest pioneers in satellite television, Charlie Ergen, co-founder of EchoStar. Ergen is without doubt responsible for the early growth of satellite television in North America, as his company supplied the mini-Earth stations to enthusiasts that enabled them to eavesdrop on transmissions emitted by the early 'Telstar' satellites of their day. This grew into a lucrative and sophisticated business with branch offices all over the world. EchoStar for example has the contract to supply Spain's Via Digital service with set-top boxes.

While Ergen's company could supply any amount of kit to receive satellite signals he had no control or influence over the actual broadcasts, nor in the satellites themselves. He cured that by launching his first satellite, EchoStar 1, atop a Chinese 'Long March' rocket at the end of 1995. The second was launched in September 1996, and the company now has a fleet of five satellites. Owning his own satellites was an enormous gamble for Ergen, and hugely expensive. However, few would argue that Ergen had a thorough understanding of the market, and whether it is described as a gamble, a risk or simply a shrewd investment, the project is paying off.

Although he launched his Digital Sky Highway (DiSH) service almost three years after DirecTV, it is catching up on subscriber numbers. His prices are highly competitive, and the DiSH system seems to go 'the extra mile' in creative packages for subscribers.

On 7 October 1999, EchoStar Communications Corp. said it had hit the three million subscriber mark, with 132 000 net new subscribers in September. In the third quarter of 1999 the service added 375 000 subscribers. On 10 November 1999, EchoStar announced it had added approximately 141 000 net new DiSH subscribers during October 1999, the largest monthly gain in its history and a 41 per cent increase over the number of net new customers in October 1998. The additions brought DiSH's total customer base up to approximately 3 113 000.

The gain of October 1999 marked the thirteenth consecutive month that DiSH's network achieved customer growth of over 100 000 net subscribers and represented an increase of 75 per cent over the first ten months of 1998.

Like DirecTV, EchoStar, who in fact had pushed very hard for the ability to add local channels to its bouquet, added its first channels in November 1999; but unlike DirecTV which limited itself initially to just two major markets, EchoStar, not untypically, went the extra mile, offering local channels to some 30 per cent of North America. On 24 November 1999, Echostar began beaming local channels by satellite and by noon on Monday 29 November it was beaming to 13 of the nation's largest markets just as President Bill Clinton signed the satellite television legislation into law.

EchoStar's DiSH Network, in the words of the company, 'can now offer true competition to cable TV by providing ABC, CBS, NBC and FOX local network channels in these 13 selected cities covering approximately 33 per cent of the total US households'. EchoStar's DiSH Network introduced local channel service to seven additional cities before the end of 1999. They are also aiming to introduce local channel service to 13 additional cities during the first quarter of 2000, bringing local channels to over 30 of the nation's largest markets which reach approximately 60 per cent of the US households. The cost? Thirteen cities for only US$4.99 per month, and the initial cities covered: New York; Los Angeles; Chicago; San Francisco; Boston; Washington, D.C.; Dallas/Ft.

Worth; Atlanta; Miami; Phoenix; Denver; Pittsburgh and Salt Lake City.

EchoStar intends adding local channel service in approximately 20 of the following 30 cities, by the end of 1999, depending upon favourable retransmission consent agreements with network broadcasters in these cities: Philadelphia; Detroit; Houston; Seattle/Tacoma; Cleveland; Minneapolis; Tampa/St. Petersburg, Fla.; Sacramento, Calif.; St. Louis; Orlando, Fla.; Baltimore; Portland, Ore.; Indianapolis; San Diego; Hartford, Conn.; Charlotte, N.C.; Raleigh/Durham, N.C.; Cincinnati; Nashville, Tenn.; Milwaukee, Wis.; Columbus, Ohio; Kansas City, Mo.; Roanoke, Va.; Oklahoma City, Okla.; Albuquerque, N.M.; Las Vegas; Memphis, Tenn.; New Orleans; Jacksonville, Fla.; and San Antonio.

EchoStar V, EchoStar's newest high-power direct broadcast satellite, was launched on a Lockheed Martin Atlas IIAS rocket on 23 September 1999, to the 110 degrees West orbital location.

Latin America

There are two main digital satellite broadcasters operating over Latin America, with Brazil and Mexico as primary markets: Galaxy Latin America (GLA) and Sky Latin America (SLA). In Brazil, both GLA and SLA have approximately equal penetration. In Mexico, Sky Latin America, despite having lower subscriber numbers, is considered to have the marketing edge. One other satellite broadcaster operates specifically over Argentina: Television Directa al Hogar (TDH). TDH is the officially licensed digital satellite service for Argentina, thereby in that country effectively closing out the two other rival services.

GLA is a consortium of Hughes Electronics (DirecTV, 60 per cent), MVS Multivision (Mexico, 10 per cent), Televisao Abril (Brazil, 10 per cent) and Cisneros Group (Venezuela, 20 per cent). GLA broadcasts a digital bouquet from its Hughes-owned Galaxy 3R satellite at 95 degrees west and Galaxy 8-I (co-located at 95 degrees West since December 1997), with footprints covering the whole of Latin America. The service broadcasts two beams: an

East beam that provides mainly Portuguese-language channels targeted at Brazil and a West beam that supplies Spanish-language channels to the rest of the continent.

Both Latin American satellite outfits have formed local commercial partnerships, and the activities recently in Mexico show the challenges they have to overcome. Latin America's two satellite television groups are now seeing subscriber numbers grow as they both invest heavily in Mexico, but analysts suggest it will be a long time before they see profits. Sky TV, the country's leading satellite television company, claims 75 per cent of the market and said its customer base would grow 40 per cent year-on-year by the end of 1999. DirecTV lags amid tough competition for those Mexican consumers who can afford 140 TV channels.

Sky Mexico is owned by top Mexican broadcaster Grupo Televisa, Rupert Murdoch's News Corporation and Liberty Media International Inc., a unit of AT&T Corp. It says that its subscriber base grew 42 per cent during 1999 to 379 000 as of 30 September, from 266 000 at the end of 1998. News Corporation and Liberty Media are part owners of other Sky satellite television endeavours in Latin America. 'We project we will reach during 2000 our break-even point for operating profit,' Jorge Alvarez, director general of Sky in Mexico, said in 1999.

Chris Recouso, a telecommunications analyst with Bear, Stearns & Co. in New York, said he did not doubt Sky would break even during 2000. However 'the issue is when they would break even in terms of "free cash flow",' a figure he said would take into account working capital and capital expenditures. Recouso calculated the company would reach that point in 2003, which he said was a long wait for investors.

'I don't know what internal projections are for payoff of investment, but I can bet it's a very long-term horizon,' agreed Carlos Diaz, vice president of Atlanta-based Latin American Pay Television Service, which sells movie programming to Sky and DirecTV throughout the region. 'The things they've done to compete – entering into exclusive programming deals and giving heavy discounts on installation – impose a heavy financial burden,' he said.

Observers said DirecTV and Sky, both launched in 1996, were subsidizing subscribers in a price war for clients. 'What's the use of having all these subscribers if none are profitable?' Recouso said. Executives for DirecTV, managed by Galaxy Latin America, which is held by a unit of Hughes Electronics Corp. and the Venezuelan media group Cisneros Group of Companies, declined to give subscriber numbers for Mexico, although industry sources put DirecTV's subscribers at somewhere near 150 000. Galaxy says it has more than 660 000 subscribers throughout Latin America.

Industry insiders say Sky's big edge is that it offers the broadcast channels of both of Mexico's major broadcasters, TV Azteca and Televisa, while DirecTV has a deal only with Azteca. Diaz also said Sky has had a more solid sales organization, and it has not had management upheavals like DirecTV, which changed management a year ago from Mexican microwave television company Multivision de Mexico, to Galaxy. DirecTV is still majority-owned by Multivision, through a holding company called Grupo Galaxy Mexico.

DirecTV director Arturo Sardaneta admits growth had been more difficult than anticipated. 'Our competition is very well consolidated,' he says. He projected 44.5 per cent subscriber growth for DirecTV in 1999. Sardaneta declined to provide investment figures for DirecTV but Alvarez said Sky's investment in Mexico so far included US$375 million raised through high-yield bonds.

Diaz said there is demand for satellite television in Mexico, where the penetration of pay television, including cable and microwave and satellite, is about 12 per cent of television households, compared with 55 per cent in the more developed Argentine market. Diaz said DirecTV and Sky could grow by a combined total of 10–15 000 subscribers a month during 2000.

However, despite demand, it is unclear whether the two companies can prosper in a region where poverty is widespread. Diaz said the conventional wisdom was that there was not room in Latin America for two satellite television companies. Recouso said it would be very difficult to mass market satellite television to lower income sectors in Mexico. 'The perennial question is will there be a combination ... there have been from time to time conversations about combinations and my sense is that the financial pressure is sufficient to keep bringing that to the table,' Diaz said.

Europe

Europe has three principal satellite television broadcasting platforms operated by:

- Society Europeenne des Satellites S.A., which owns the Astra system
- EUTELSAT, owned by a consortium of Europe's PTT's
- Telenor AS, owned by Norway's PTT and Sweden's Telia.

There are other players, not least HispaSat (Spain), TurkSat (Turkey), Sirius (Scandinavia) plus Loral, Arabsat, Nilesat, PanAmSat. They all have some influence on European broadcasting, but are placed into the shade by the 'big three' listed above.

All these satellites are themselves home to broadcast platforms, from BSkyB (in analogue and digital) to European operators like Canal+ and Leo Kirch's Premiere World. In other words, the satellites are acting simply as giant transmission towers in the sky and are carrying the signals generated by the various broadcasters.

Most of Europe's digital television platforms have emerged from analogue platforms. Europe is now dominated (at least as far as subscriber numbers are concerned) by two broadcasting groups, Canal+, which launched digital television across many European countries during the mid-to-late 1990s and BSkyB which launched a digital platform in October 1998 from Astra's second orbital position at 28.3 degrees East.

In total, by mid-1999, there were 15 different pay-TV platforms (not all in digital) offering some 700 channels. Some of these channels were near identical (Discovery or MTV, for example).

Canal+

Canal+ is many things. First, it is the holding company; then it is a single channel broadcast in France terrestrially and encrypted, and on satellite in analogue and digital. Copy-cat Canal+ channels exist in many European countries (Poland, Spain, the Benelux, Scandinavia). These Canal+ channels have four core elements: movies, sport and documentary with the 'flagship' nightly show a live one-hour studio broadcast.

Canal+'s French digital services are carried within a bouquet called Canal Satellite Numerique. Some of the channels within the Canal Satellite bouquet have different minority shareholders, but Canal+ holds this digital system together. Canal Satellite launched in April 1996, and finished 1997 with 700 000 subscribers, well ahead of its own predicted total of 500 000 subscribers. Canal Satellite transmits from the Astra satellite system.

Canal+, describing itself as 'Europe's leading pay-television group', reported its half-year results on 22 September 1999. Chairman Pierre Lescure said the full year results, due in six months, would show an improvement in the aggregate contribution from overseas earnings, but that Italian and Polish investments would continue to mean lower than expected net earnings. Canal+ has television investments throughout Europe, in France, Spain, Italy, Belgium, Scandinavia and Poland, and in addition its 'MediaGuard' encryption system is in use as far afield as the USA (MediaOne) and UK (ONdigital).

Lescure's mid-1999 highlights for Canal+ were:

- consolidated revenues up 12 per cent to Euro 1.3 billion
- EBITDA rose 54 per cent to Euro 282 million
- operating income tripled to Euro 127 million
- half-year loss of Euro 36 million

At the time of writing (mid-2000) Canal+'s largest shareholder is the Vivendi group, a French conglomerate with considerable interests in water and electricity. Press reports during late 1999 suggested that News Corporation is working with British Telecom

Table 5.2   Canal+ financials*

	1H/99	1H/98
Revenues	1308	1172
Operating income	127	46
EBITDA	282	183

*(Euro millions)
Source: Company accounts, 1999

Table 5.3   Canal+ at a glance

Subscriptions	30 June 1999
France	6 318 270
Belgium (Wallonia)	187 911
Belgium (Flanders)	179 598
Spain	2 396 502
Italy	1 720 576
Netherlands	271 797
Nordic region	635 095
Africa	139 157
Total	12 301 320

Source: Morgan Stanley, 1999

Table 5.4   Canal+ headline income*

	1996	1997	1998	1999E	2000E	2001E
Subs revenue	8 901	9 947	12 598	13 885	14 656	15 458
Advertising and sponsorship	440	483	538	560	575	591
Other activities	2 287	3 160	3 089	3 319	3 548	3 779
Total	11 628	13 590	16 234	17 764	18 779	19 848

*All in millions of French Francs
Data: Morgan Stanley, Dean Witter, Company reports 1999

(BT) to mount an aggressive bid for French utilities-to-TV conglomerate Vivendi S.A. The theory seems to be that Vivendi, claimed to be the world's largest water company, will be broken up, with Rupert Murdoch taking its television interests, which currently include a 49 per cent stake in Canal+, and BT taking Vivendi's telephony operations Cegetel (France's second-largest telco) and cellular outfit SFR. Vivendi has a market capitalization of some US$40 billion, and owns 24.5 per cent of BSkyB.

Spokesmen for Vivendi and BT both declined to comment on market speculation. However, it's worth noting that News Corp. and Vivendi are already working together with the Japanese e-commerce venture capital outfit Softbank. Up until now any talk of further co-operation, at least between Canal+ and BSkyB, although favoured by Vivendi's CEO Jean-Marie Messier, has been firmly ruled out by Murdoch. A Paris-based analyst said in early 2000 that if such a deal was to happen it would at least make 'Murdoch captain of BSkyB again'. However, Vivendi is on record as seeking a fresh injection of funds by selling off its unneeded 9 per cent of its 49 per cent stake in Canal+.

As to sales and subscriptions, figures published in November 1999 from Canal+ reveal a total of 12.789 million pay-TV subscribers in Europe as of September 30, an increase of 17 per cent over the previous year, while international subscriptions grew 28 per cent. Some 3.4 million of them are for digital services, an increase of 65 per cent. The Canal+ premium channel in France now has 4.5 million subscribers. Canal Satellite recorded growth of 285 000 over the past 12 months, possibly helped by an expanded football offer.

Internationally, demand was boosted in French-speaking Belgium by an August 'cash and carry' offer in shopping centres. In Spain, Canal Satellite passed the three quarter million mark while the premium channel subscriptions increased by 27 per cent over the previous year.

Canal+ reported an improved performance in the Nordic countries, with close to 90 000 new subscriptions in the first nine months, compared with 30 000 for the year before. Canal+ (its single channel) also claimed good results in Poland, with a 39 per cent increase in subscriptions to the premium channel. However, the total for Cyfra+ (the digital bouquet of channels) just edged up to 169 698 from the previous year's 151 916.

Although subscriptions in North Africa had declined since January, owing to what Canal+ calls 'the highly seasonal nature of the business in this region', Canal reported that subscriptions were 11 per cent up on the figure for September 1998. Canal+ Horizons (the Canal+ 'overseas' channel) is to be marketed as a premium channel on the Canal Satellite Madagascar package, which launched in October.

British Sky Broadcasting (BSkyB)

BSkyB launched its digital satellite service in October 1998. The Sky digital service includes PPV/NVOD channels and multiplexed versions of the existing premium channels at no extra cost. (Sky services, which for the sake of simplicity, also include separate companies like Viacom's MTV and Nickelodeon bundle of channels, Turner Broadcasting's CNN, Cartoon Network and TCM, Flextech's bundle which includes Bravo and UK Gold, as well as channels from the BBC, Channels 4 and 5 and other independents).

BSkyB is owned 40 per cent by News Corporation. Investment bankers Morgan Stanley expected BSkyB to achieve 2.4m total digital sales by the end of December 1999. Sky's net additions in their first quarter in 1999 were 122 000 and this number 'should be even better in Q2' (three months to 31 December) says Morgan Stanley.

But in an otherwise favourable report Morgan Stanley exercise some reservations about BSkyB's involvement in Leo Kirch's Premiere World digital platform (see Germany/DF-1 below). Their reservation centres on the strength of the free TV market in Germany and what would appear to be BSkyB's 25 per cent minority stake, leading to limited influence. 'We think there is also a risk that management's time and resources are diverted. . .' The report also says that News Corporation involvement in Deutsche Telekom's cable sell-off 'further complicates the picture'.

Nevertheless, at the end of 1999, BSkyB remained an 'outperform' stock for Morgan Stanley and they see continued subscriber growth as well as the benefits of the interactive service 'Open . . .' and other new media activities 'creating further momentum'. Morgan Stanley predict an overall improvement in Sky's DTH status, growing from 3.582 million (end September 1999), less churn estimated at 9 per cent (46 000), less some 345 000 analogue-to-digital subscribers, plus new and migrated digital subs of 584 000 taking the overall DTH total to 3.775 m.

On the question of digital churn, Morgan Stanley say (late 1999) current rates are running less than 1 per cent, 'although we expect a rise to about 5 per cent in the second quarter.' The report says so far the quality of digital subscribers provides us with comfort on BSkyB recouping its heavy investment.

Table 5.5   BSkyB magic 8 million subs

	30 Sept 98	30 June 99	30 Sept 99
DTH	3 404 000	3 460 000	3 582 000
Cable	2 913 000	3 189 000	3 252 000
ONdigital	-	204 000	363 000
Eire	565 000	589 000	591 000
Total	6 882 000	7 442 000	7 861 000

In mid-1999 investment bankers ABN-Amro issued a bullish report (ABN-Amro, 1999) on the UK's digital take-up, saying 83 per cent of all UK television homes will access digital television within the next ten years, with 60 per cent of all homes 'subscribing to digital pay-TV'. Non subscribers will view free-to-air networks. ABN estimate that more than US$3 billion will be invested in digital services over the next two years, aggregated between the three competing digital systems, BSkyB, cable, and terrestrial outfit ONdigital. ABN issued an investment 'buy' note on both ONdigital partners Carlton Communications and Granada Media Group, and also on

UK box-maker Pace Micro Technology, which 'will be a key bene-
ficiary of accelerated demand'.

BSkyB have also raised the stakes, by suggesting it may want
to bring forward its analogue direct-to-home switch-off date –
already promised for 31 Dec 2002 – because of its buoyant digital
sales. At the time, a spokeswoman for Pace said the box-maker
could supply one million digital boxes a year from its own UK
facility, plus almost limitless imported stocks. With Philips, Nokia,
Grundig, Panasonic and others also supplying the market, it could
be that Sky's analogue switch-off could advance by around a year.
Indeed, most observers now expect BSkyB to cease analogue
transmissions early in 2001.

Nevertheless, ABN media analyst Patrick Kirby says he does
not see the UK as a 'zero sum game with only one winner
. . . [because] a large proportion of premium content [is] common
to all three platforms' (ABN-Amro, 1999). However, he also says
UK cable is under 'increased pressure . . . with Sky's reduced price
telephony offer eroding the competitive advantage historically
enjoyed by cable operators . . . [and] . . . the competitive dilemma
exacerbated by cable's position as third entrant into the market.'

It seems this anxiety about being third to market is behind
ABN's cable pessimism, which place Sky's DTH universe (including
Ireland) as topping 6.3 million homes by mid-2009. Cable manages
a perfectly respectable 5.6 m base by 2009 while ONdigital comes
in definite third place with 3.2 million homes, and the highest churn
rates of the trio [forecasted churn: ONdigital 15 per cent, cable
13–15 per cent, BSkyB 6–8 per cent]. Interestingly, ABN suggests
the bulk of ONdigital subscriptions will come from owners of integrated television sets (so called idTV's with built-in conditional
access and decoders).

ABN expects the number of homes passed by cable to reach
72 per cent of the country by 2009. The report also states that
by 2009 BSkyB-backed online service Open . . . will be generating
annual revenues of some US$560, or US$88 per subscriber. This
equates to US$470 million profit per annum, of which BSkyB's
share will be US$150 m.

Table 5.6 UK digital TV forecasts*

	1999	2000	2001	2002	2003	2004	2005	2006	2007	2008	2009
UK TVHHs	24 102	24 222	24 344	24 465	24 558	24 711	24 834	24 958	25 033	25 108	25 184
DTH analogue	2673	865	79	0	0	0	0	0	0	0	0
DTH digital	670	3023	4381	4810	5125	5415	5652	5850	6032	6199	6303
DTH Total	3343	3888	4460	4810	5125	5415	5652	5850	6032	6199	6303
Cable: Sky Analogue	3231	2558	2065	1404	796	451	256	0	0	0	0
Cable: Sky Digital	0	438	1032	1889	2822	3552	4183	4814	5140	5421	5616
Cable: Digital misc.	39	40	42	43	44	46	47	48	50	51	53
Cable Total	3270	3037	3139	3336	3662	4049	4485	4863	5190	5472	5669
DTT											
STB subs	160	632	1073	1187	1069	944	873	559	251	54	16
id-TV subs	0	88	285	653	998	1388	1707	2170	2555	2917	3213
DTT Total	160	720	1358	1840	2066	2332	2580	2729	2806	2971	3229

*Year to June (000s)
Source: ABN-Amro 1999

ONdigital

The United Kingdom's second digital operator is ONdigital, a company owned jointly by Carlton Communications and Granada Media Group. ONdigital is the world's first digital terrestrial (DTT) pay-television operator.

It is worth remembering how ONdigital won the licence to operate its 25-year franchise. Two consortia bid for the broadcast rights. British Digital Broadcasting (BDB) originally included three equal partners: BSkyB, Carlton TV and Granada TV. Rival Digital Television Network (DTN) was led by International CableTel, a UK cable franchise which also owns NTL, the UK-wide transmitter network.

The DTN bid has 15 mostly unnamed programme 'partners', although Turner Broadcasting was known to be involved. The BBC seemed to have promised programming to both parties, although the BBC Worldwide/Flextech joint venture said at the time it had agreed to give first option support to the BDB bid.

In essence, the two rival bidders were seeking the non-allocated shares of the six multiplexes, or frequencies, available. Some multiplexes were 'protected' and already allocated to existing network providers like the BBC, ITV and Channels 4 and 5, and S4C. The British government split the available frequencies into six parcels, or multiplexes. Each multiplex, with MPEG-2 compression, can carry around five channels although DTN say they will offer a 7:1 compression, building to 9:1 by 2001. They are also testing movie services at 2 Mbps.

The proposals, although at the time widely expected, caused more than a few surprises, especially in regard to the International CableTel bid, which had been expected to include Canal+ and British media tycoon Lord Hollick's United News and Media group, owners of the Central and Meridian commercial television franchises. Canal+ and UN&M reportedly withdrew at the eleventh hour, although DTN chief executive Jeremy Thorpe later said the Canal+ involvement was no more than a rumour.

International CableTel said, if successful, it would develop new data services using what it calls 'The Infobarn', with an interactive search-engine operated via an Electronic Programme Guide, leading to a virtual shopping mall. Within the 'mall', users will be able to access by telephone banking services, train and bus timetables, buy theatre tickets and gain consumer advice from the Consumers' Association. DTN have seventy data 'partners' in place.

Thorpe said DTN had submitted multiple applications 'based on every possible permutation' including single multiplexes, although the full multi-channel offering was based on them winning all three multiplexes. Thorpe promised their marketing campaign 'would be one of the biggest product launches the UK had ever seen'. NTL, in fact was going to win either way, either as a part of the International CableTel bid, or as the likely transmission provider to BDB.

There was a third applicant for a 'half-multiplex' currently secured by Welsh-language broadcaster C4C, a joint venture between the BBC and Channel 4. This half-service has been applied for by ITN, the British national news provider, which will supply a national motoring/travel channel and an information channel.

Both BDB and DTN said they would subsidize set-top boxes, although DTN insisted their box would be 'highly specified' and capable of coping with cable or DTH feeds. DTN refused to be drawn on the cost of their proposal, but said their prices – for boxes and subscriptions – would be highly competitive.

At the time, the applications caused a degree of panic in financial markets, sending cable stocks tumbling. Roy Payne, spokesman for the Cable Communications Association, said he wondered whether the application by BSkyB wasn't an admission that there isn't a future in direct-to-home satellites.

Most cable stocks suffered, Nynex lost 12 per cent on the day. TeleWest fell 11p to 117p and General Cable fell 13p to 176p. By contrast, all the bidders rose, some sharply. Carlton rose 39p to 558.5p and BSkyB 8.5p to 599p. Besides marking BSkyB shares up, the market responded well to the BDB proposal, taking the view that with its 200+ digital satellite launch later this year, plus domination of the programming sector on cable and now terrestrial, the company cannot lose.

The CCA seemed to share the same view, and immediately warned that it might be objecting to the various fair trading bodies on the grounds that BSkyB was offering its channels in such a way that discriminated unfairly against cable television companies.

BDB predicted up to one million subscribers in its first three years. In 1999 BDB's chairman Nigel Walmsley (director of broadcasting at Carlton) said 'Our plans are based on the three-quarters of British homes that do not have subscription TV. That's 16 million homes which means an enormous number of people who could be drawn to multi-channel viewing by digital terrestrial TV.' BDB estimated the total costs would be around £300 million (US$450 million).

The DTN senior management team included James Gatward as chairman. Gatward founded TVS, a regional commercial television station, in 1979. Steve Wagner, of CableTel, will act as director of marketing and subscriber management. Wagner said 'We've always believed in digital terrestrial. We know UK consumers through CableTel and we know they aren't just looking for 200 more channels. They want quality programming and interactive services which have real value for them.' DTN chief Jeremy Thorpe agrees, saying 'We believe DTT will be more attractive than cable'.

The rivals

British Digital Broadcasting
Three equal shareholders comprising:
BSkyB, Carlton Communications, Granada Group

Programming line-up:

Basic tier

Carlton Select
Granada Plus
BBC Horizon

Carlton Films
Granada Good Life
Sky 1
BBC Style/BBC Showcase
Public Eye
Granada TV Shopping
Carlton Entertainment
BBC 1 TV
Granada Sports Club

Premium

Sky Movies
The Movie Channel
Sky Sports

+ PPV

Digital Television Network

backed by International CableTel/NTL
Programming line up:
The Money Channel
Discovery's Animal Planet
ITN Living History
Travel TV
The Box
Turner Classic Movies
Cartoon Network
MGM Gold
British Sports Channel
Knowledge Network
Digital Box Office (PPV)
Metro TV/Hindi Channel
Shopping Square
BBC Horizons
BBC Style/Showcase
BBC Arena/Learning
Data services including Banking from 70+ data partners

The result

The result of the digital terrestrial auction sent BSkyB into a tail-spin, and created a very bad week for BSkyB. It all started on Friday, 13 June 1997. That morning British Interactive Broadcasting (now better known as BSkyB's Open ... interactive service) put out a press notification that Peter van Gelder would be its new managing director. 'And by the way' the release seemed to say, 'BIB welcomes the appointment of Sam Chisholm as first chairman of BIB.' Up until that moment Chisholm was the hard-talking boss of BSkyB, the man who had famously turned Sky from a financial disaster to one of the top companies in the UK, and an absolute jewel in Rupert Murdoch's glittering crown. Rumours about Chisholm's health had circulated for some time.

The press release seemed to set the BSkyB house of cards wobbling. The financial markets were again swept with rumours about Chisholm's health and long-term future with Sky. A firm denial that anything was amiss was issued on Monday June 16, but the damage had been done. Somewhere in the smoke-free atmosphere of Sky's Isleworth headquarters – or was it at Murdoch's St James's flat, or at Fox's Century City offices in Los Angeles – a decision had been made. The news broke on Tuesday, issued by PR guru Sir Tim Bell (now Lord Bell) so everyone knew this simply *had* to be important: Sam would retire to his Australian ranch, comfortable from his accumulated earnings and a 0.5 per cent share of Sky's profits, at least for this year.

From then on, the share price told the whole story. From being a near £10 billion capitalized company at the start of the week, by the following Friday it had lost £1.5 billion, finishing its nightmare week with a capitalization of £8.5 billion. Monday was certainly 'wobble' day, with the shares losing a few pence and closing at 588p. Tuesday was 'worry' day and a loss of 22p. A relatively low 5.2 million shares changed hands, but there was worse to come.

Losing Sam Chisholm was a bad enough call; but then the news emerged that his trusted lieutenant David Chance would also go. This was a loss too far, and it seemed to many that the news had been deliberately kept quiet. There was no statement from Tim Bell on this one, just a few well-placed words to Fleet Street, almost as an afterthought.

On Wednesday the markets found the David Chance explanation difficult to swallow and various theories were floated: 'Sam and Dave had made a pact' said one; 'David and his ulcer have had enough of 80-hour weeks' said another; and 'He's done well, now he wants to take it easy'. Where did this leave Sky? And who was this Mark Booth? Five minutes at embryonic JapanSkyBroadcasting, another five at FoxTel and various stints at UIH Programming and with Robert Maxwell, seemed a somewhat lightweight CV to run BSkyB, especially with Sky about to take another great leap forward with digital terrestrial television.

Then, still on Wednesday, the problems really started to bite. On top of the David Chance news came more rumours, this time concerning the ITC, and their all-important decision which required the British Digital Broadcasting consortium to get rid of its one-third partner, Sky, or else lose the bid. The shares went into free-fall, being battered 45p on the day. 22.3 million shares were traded, closing at 521.5p and well below £9 billion capitalization.

There was a sort of consolation prize from an increasingly muddled and confused ITC: Sky could still supply programming to BDB. The markets loved this, only marking the shares down Thursday a thumping 13.5p, knocking another £200 million off Sky's capitalization. Too much good news like this and Sky could soon be in bankruptcy court.

More than one analyst asked much the same question: If Sky were still supplying programmes where was the separation between them and Granada/Carlton? Was there any real benefit to viewers? Wasn't there still a programming monopoly? Would even this be acceptable to Brussels? Without doubt, the crunch question came from DTN, the almost forgotten bidder in this apparent walkover for BDB. 'Who would supply conditional access? Who would take care of subscriber management? Who would look after billing and card issuing and pay-per-view and' . . . the list went on.

The questions were timely, and, with the benefit of a few years hindsight, it is now clear that ONdigital, while a technical success, has had to work hard at the other elements questioned. Despite signing an agreement with Canal+ to supply its MediaGuard conditional access and MediaHighway broadcast technology, ONdigital has struggled to get some of its core services on air, not least the important digital text services from the BBC and Teletext. At the end of 1999, some 14 months after launch, these technologies were only in 'test' mode.

Under the terms of the ITC ruling, it was determined that Sky would receive £50 million and gain a 5-year contract to supply programmes. It was also said, almost with a sigh of relief, that Sky would now not have to 'invest' £100 million in BDB's initial losses expected to amount to a total of £300 million. One report at the time (1999) said: 'Phew, that was a close one. No investment means no windfall for Sky when BDB eventually comes good, as it surely will, but at least we've saved £100 million. Hardly the spirit of Rupert Murdoch, who has gained his reputation for being the bravest of the brave when it comes to investing the bank in a concept that he believed in.'

The markets agreed. They didn't care for the prognosis either, and on Friday, normally a quiet trading day, marked BSkyB's shares down another £200 million, 10.5p, closing at just 497.5 and a capitalization of barely £8.5 billion.

British Digital Broadcasting, without BSkyB, and now trading as ONdigital was duly licensed to operate three out of the four commercial digital multiplexes (Multiplexes B, C, D). NTL had some compensation, as it was granted the right to operate commercial Multiplex 'A', the one with the best overall coverage of the UK. (The BBC automatically received Multiplex 1, and ITV/Channel 4 automatically received Multiplex 2).

ONdigital was expected to deliver some 550 000 subscribers by year-end 1999. However, the company has been beset with problems, not least wholesale management defections including CEO Stephen Grabiner. His departure, and others, forced the joint-venture partners Carlton and Granada to look again at how

ONdigital was being managed, and the end result was a change in the corporate hierarchy, with Carlton giving up day-to-day control and Granada's director of channels and interactive media, Stuart Prebble, being appointed to run ONdigital.

As a footnote to this history, ONdigital did hit their 550 000 target at the end of 1999, while BSkyB declared 2.3 million digital subscribers, and say they are confident they will reach 5 million 'digi-subs' by June 2001. Their share price has also more than recovered to around £20 per share.

France

Television Par Satellite

Competing with Canal+ within France is Television Par Satellite (TPS), a rival digital bouquet which launched in December 1996, backed by France's national television channel, France Telecom. By year-end 1997 it had achieved 320 000 subscribers, again well ahead of its target of 175 000. TPS transmits from the EUTELSAT satellite system. By November 1988, TPS had achieved sales of more than 500 000 subscribers.

In October 1999, public broadcaster France Television confirmed it would sell its 8 per cent stake in TPS to France Telecom, leaving France Telecom with 25 per cent of TPS. France Television would use the proceeds (US$72 million) to help fund its new programming on the suggested French digital terrestrial system. The deal values TPS at about US$890 million.

AB Sat

A third French digital bouquet is AB Sat, owned by AB Productions, and initially broadcasting from the EUTELSAT Hot Bird satellites and designed to be available either as a stand-alone mini-bouquet or as additional channels to the TPS bundle. However, AB Sat has also negotiated digital capacity on Astra, and as a result is now available to viewers of the Canal Satellite Numerique bouquet.

The result of this activity is that AB Sat is now seen as an independent channel provider, more than as a stand-alone bouquet.

AB Sat said (June 1999) that it had a total of 325 000 subscribers (288 000 from satellite and 37 000 from cable), up from 284 000 in March 1999.

Spain

Canal Satellite Digital

Canal Satellite Digital (CSD), backed by media group Prisa and Canal+, is the acknowledged digital television market leader in Spain, helped by a 1.5 million subscriber base from its existing terrestrial (analogue) film and sports channel. On 31 January 1997 it launched a package of 30 television channels delivered via the Astra satellite system. At the end of 1997 Canal Satellite had over 150 000 subscribers, growing to 575 000 by the end of 1998.

Via Digital

Via Digital, backed by a consortium of Telefonica, Televisa, state-broadcaster TVE and with a 17 per cent equity stake reserved for DirecTV, launched via the Hispasat satellite system on 15 September 1997. Via Digital offered a digital bouquet of 50 channels: 35 channels on the basic package, plus 15 other channels free of charge until December 1997 as a promotion to encourage subscriptions. The number of Via Digital subscribers was reported at around 130 000 at the end of 1997, and 348 000 at the end of 1998.

Italy

Telepiu/Tele/D+

Until three years ago Telepiu had the following shareholders: NetHold/Canal+ 45 per cent, Leo Kirch 45 per cent and Mediaset 10 per cent. It is now 90 per cent owned by Canal+.

After disappointing market growth, major changes were made to management and to the channel line-up. By October 1997 D+, the generic name now given to Telepiu's digital service, was reported as having reached 180 000 subscribers (*Cable & Satellite*

Europe, March 1998). At the end of December 1997, Canal+ Italy claimed its number of digital subscribers had reached 200 000 and 312 000 by October 1998.

D+ have a number of development plans for new channels. Already added to the D+ line-up are three new movie channels (Cine Cinema 1, 2 and Cine Classica) in parallel with the Canal+ French and Spanish digital channel line-up.

Germany

Premiere World

On 6 December 1999, BSkyB confirmed its long-expected involvement with Leo Kirch's Premiere World pay-TV platform in Germany, taking a 24 per cent share in KirchPayTV Gmbh. The deal is subject to regulatory approval. In return Kirch gets 4.3 per cent of Sky, with Kirch Group vice chairman Dieter Hahn joining the BSkyB board on completion. In a joint statement it was also confirmed that KirchPayTV would seek an IPO during 2003. Sky get two seats on the KirchPayTV six-person supervisory board.

This is the second attempt by BSkyB to involve itself in Kirch's activities; the first, an attempt to gain a stake in Kirch's DF-1 platform, failed to get off the ground in March 1997. DF-1, and all-digital bouquet, launched in July 1996 and had gained around 230 000 by year-end 1998. DF-1 had a rival, Premiere (that broadcast in analogue and digital), which at one stage had been part owned by Canal+. Early in 1999 Kirch's DF-1 and Premiere merged to form Premiere World. Prior to the merger, Premiere claimed 500 000 subscribers (May 1999).

The details saw BSkyB investing DM1 billion (about £320 m) in cash in KirchPayTV to be funded by the issue of new BSkyB shares, with News Corporation and Vivendi taking up their allocation in full in order to maintain their current percentage share-holdings. Kirch then was allocated 78 million in new shares, which at market closing on 3 December 1999 stood at £7.97 a share, representing 4.3 per cent of the enlarged share capital, worth £622 m.

Germany is Europe's largest television market with some 33 million television households, and with 29 million of these receiving signals either by cable or DTH satellite television. As at 6 October 1999, KirchPayTV had some 2 million subscribers, split between cable and DTH, representing 6 per cent of the market. Premiere World says it has sold 200 000 new subscribers in its first two months of operation. Operational break-even is expected at 11 per cent penetration or some 4 million homes. Besides its Premiere World operation, KirchPayTV also has a 40 per cent ownership interest in Teleclub AG, operating in Switzerland.

In a statement at the time BSkyB says it did not expect 'any synergies in conditional access technology or sports and movie programming rights to arise from the transaction', which seems to rule out, at least in the immediate future, any switch to NDS encryption or joint-venture activity over sports rights, one of Kirch's strong points. However, BSkyB owns the German rights to the English soccer Premiership and it is likely that Premiere World will benefit from these showings.

Premiere World re-launched itself in September 1999 and official data from the company stated the new combined bouquet had 1.01 million subscribers at the end of October 1999.

Africa, Asia and the Far East

There are digital platforms operating over three regions within Africa, Asia and the Far East:

Africa

Africa has MPEG-2 DVB digital transmissions from PanAmSat's Indian Ocean satellite (PAS-4) for South African-based M-NET and MIH-owned Multichoice. In addition, transmissions from two ArabSat craft deliver digital signals to what is best described as 'greater Arabia' as far south as Tanzania and west to Morocco. A third satellite (NileSat) delivers digital channels to the Middle East.

India

India is under the digital footprints of many orbiting satellites, some country-specific and others operating pan-regionally, for example. Panamsat PAS-4, AsiaSat, Satelindo, MeaSat, Thaicom, Insat.

Japan

Prior to 1998, there were three Japanese digital platforms: DirecTV Japan, Japan Sky Broadcasting and PerfecTV. The first, DirecTV Japan has DirecTV as its major shareholder. However, the two other digital platforms merged in 1998. Japan Sky Broadcasting and PerfecTV merged in time for combined broadcasts of between 140–60 channels to commence 1 May 1998. A formal agreement was signed in March 1998 and the new company is called SkyPerfecTV. Shareholders (with equal 11.375 per cent holdings) comprise News Corporation, Sony, Softbank, Fuji TV and Itochu. The new group claims it will have achieved 1 million subscribers by March 1999.

Australia

Australia, until recently, had four digital platforms operating:

- Australis Media (which trades as Galaxy)
- Austar/East Coast
- Foxtel
- Optus Vision

All four digital broadcasting platforms had made commitments to migrate their analogue services to digital. However, Australian digital platforms have had to face major problems, both regulatory and financial. Despite encouraging take-up figures, churn amongst all Australian broadcasting platforms is very high, reportedly over 50 per cent (ABN AMRO report on Telstra, September 1997). This stems from the fact that Australian households traditionally disconnect their pay-TV systems during the summer months.

Australis Media ultimately failed, going bankrupt in 1998. At its collapse, it had some 50 000 subscribers (to its Galaxy service). Its assets were largely acquired by Foxtel.

It is generally accepted that establishing pay television from 1992 in Australia has cost the various parties more than Aus$3.1 billion in losses in the period to 1996–7, and at the time there seemed little prospect for any of the parties moving forward into profit under the split and divided structure then in place.

In February 1998 it was estimated that the (analogue and digital) pay-TV penetration amounted to a total of some 13 per cent of Australia's 6.3 million television homes. The pay-TV market share (analogue and digital) in Australia is shown in Table 5.7.

Table 5.7   Pay-TV market share in Australia

Operator	Subscribers (Sept 1999)	Potential Homes
Optus Vision	210 000	2.2 m
Foxtel	540 000	2.5 m
Austar	360 000	2.1 m

Source: Company reports

Platform	Coverage
Foxtel	Cable, in Sydney, Melbourne, Brisbane, Gold Coast, Adelaide
Optus	Cable, in Sydney: Northern & Western suburbs
	Melbourne: Northern and Eastern Suburbs
	Brisbane
Austar	DTH national 72%, MMDS regional 25%, cable in Darwin 3%

Source: Telstra company data, August 1999

Austar

By the end of 1997, Pace Micro Technology had delivered more than 230 000 digital set-top boxes. At end of 1997 Austar surpassed Optus as Australia's second largest pay platform with some 343 000 subscribers. Optus, at the same time, had some 215 000 subscribers and Foxtel had 500 000.

Austar is in the main a DTH satellite platform (using the Optus B-3 satellite at 158 degrees East) and 72 per cent of its 325 000 (May 1999) subscribers receive signals from satellite. Some 25 per cent receive signals via the company's MMDS re-transmission systems, and 3 per cent via cable in and around Darwin.

Austar's losses (1996–1998) were huge, placed at Aus$420 million. Austar is now owned by UnitedGlobalCom, the Denver-based cable operator. On 20 July 1999 Austar had an IPO raising Aus$486.5m (US$312m), leaving United retaining a 74 per cent stake and the balance in public hands. The losses continued through 1999, losing Aus$175.36 million for the first 9 months of the year, although sales reached Aus$186.82 million. However, Austar has unfettered access to Australia's bush and inland regions; while Foxtel and Optus might slug it out in the cities, Austar has the rural regions all to itself.

Foxtel

Foxtel is owned 50 per cent by Telstra, 25 per cent by News Corporation and 25 per cent by Kerry Packer. Rupert Murdoch has publicly stated (November 1999) that he sought to buy out Telstra's 50 per cent share of Foxtel, or else see the shareholding equalized to 33 per cent each. However, Foxtel does not own its cable delivery system, which is 100 per cent owned by Telstra. Telstra's cable system is duplicated to about 75 per cent of homes by Optus' system. In effect, both companies have cable running – if not along the same poles, then certainly along the same roads. Foxtel has stated it is on track, after accumulating losses of Aus$500 million, to move into profit in 2001.

Optus

Optus is Australia's second telephony company; Cable & Wireless is a shareholder which in 1997 increased its stake from 24.5 per cent to 49 per cent. In May 1998, Austar and Optus set up a 50/50 satellite distribution joint venture to lease four high-power

Ku-band transponders on an Optus-owned satellite. Each transponder delivers up to 12 channels. The joint venture, in December 1998, struck a deal with Foxtel to supply satellite channels.

DTT

The Australian Broadcasting Authority has determined that it will start a digital terrestrial television system on 1 January 2001, using the European developed DVT-T standard, but with local provisions for high definition television.

In addition, a new Australian company, Television and Radio Broadcasting Services (TARBS) in July 1999 bought for Aus$12m the wireless assets of bankrupt Australis Media and launched a package of 17 channels. The system has focused on so-called ethnic channels (Mandarin, Vietnamese, Greek, Spanish and Arabic) in an attempt to carve out a special audience for itself.

Middle East

The Middle East has four competing digital platforms fighting for viewer loyalty:

- Arab Radio & Television (ART)
- Orbit Television and Radio Network
- Star Select
- Showtime

Six years ago there was no subscription television in the Middle East. The few direct-to-home (DTH) satellite channels were initially all free-to-air and largely replicas of the monopoly state-run national television channels. However, over the past few years the Middle East has become a fascinating region, where free-to-air satellite channels have captured a major portion of the market. Also since the mid-1990s four different digital satellite pay-TV platforms have emerged.

The first two Arab pay-TV platforms have Rome as their operational base: Orbit and Arab Radio and Television (ART). Both have substantial new facilities, including studios and playout centres. Both ventures are backed by substantial capital investment. Based on claimed viewers, Orbit is the market-leader of all the competing platforms, thanks to the seemingly bottomless pockets of the Saudi Arabian Al Mawared group. Orbit (at November 1999) claimed 400 000 'viewing points', its description of its installed receiver/ decoder base including hotel rooms.

ART is funded by two billionaire Saudis, Prince Al Waleed bin Talal (an investor in News Corporation and Netscape) and Sheikh Saleh Kamel. Arab Radio & Television (ART) in some six years has gone from a single free-to-air analogue DTH channel to a 5 pay-channel platform with plans for further expansion. ART transmits digitally from ArabSat and NileSat.

Orbit claims market-leadership in Middle East digital television broadcasting. It currently transmits 15 television channels and some 25 audio channels uplinked from Rome. Orbit's DTH platform launched in May 1994, making it the world's first digital broadcast platform although as at December 1999 it still uses the so-called MPEG-1.5 non-compliant version of the MPEG standard. It means Orbit subscribers cannot view digital transmissions from other broadcasters. Orbit transmits digitally from ArabSat.

The third platform is News Corporation's Star Select package, which in 1996 placed itself firmly in alliance with Orbit. Star Select and Orbit share the same decoder and can be bought together but remain separate packages. Star Select transmits about 12 channels targeting western and Asian expatriates in the Gulf states. StarSelect transmits digitally from ArabSat.

The fourth pay-platform comes from Gulf-DTH, which trades as Showtime, backed with English-language programming by Viacom Inc. and financed by Kuwait Investment Projects Co. (KIPCO), a Kuwaiti conglomerate. Showtime broadcasts digitally from NileSat.

Multichannel packages

Digital television can be delivered as stand-alone channels. For example, a national broadcaster (either public or commercially funded) could digitize their existing network and simulcast it on satellite, cable or terrestrial in digital form, without charge. The BBC and Italy's RAI have adopted this model, and will deliver their existing channels in digital format free of charge to viewers (the BBC will use digital terrestrial, while RAI are using digital satellite).

It is possible for a broadcaster to keep certain of its channels (analogue as well as digital) in-the-clear in some geographical regions, while the exact same channels can also be part of a pay-TV platform or bouquet in another region. A good example is the Cartoon Network owned by Turner Broadcasting (now part of Time Warner) in Europe. Until recently it was available free of charge (in analogue) from Astra, but at the same time is part of the Canal Satellite Digital bouquet in France from Astra. In this case Turner Broadcasting would receive a fee from Canal Satellite Digital based on the number of subscribers delivered.

Most digital channels will be included within bouquets organized or packaged by a single company. Table 5.8 shows examples of digital bouquets.

Bouquet Providers make their bouquets available principally via satellite DTH. Additionally they may make them available on cable or MMDS. Cable operators and MMDS Operators create their own bouquets of channels, usually comprising a large number of channels from the predominant satellite or cable broadcaster (BSkyB, Canal+ etc.) but adding a number of independent channels, perhaps international channels or channels from third-party suppliers, or even channels generated by the cable company itself.

In the mature cable industry in North America, cable channels are theoretically available on a stand-alone basis, that is, cable operators are free to choose whichever channel they think will be attractive to their local subscribers. However, the owners of popular channels often have considerable muscle in pushing another less popular channel in their portfolio on to cable operators. The same dilemma faces cable companies elsewhere in the world where there is a dominant supplier of such programming (BSkyB, Canal+, for example). This issue is now becoming prominent and has led

Table 5.8   Digital bouquets

Bouquet provider	Country
AB Sat	France
Arabesque	France
Astro	Malaysia
Austar	Australia
ONdigital	UK
BSkyB	UK
Canal Satellite Digital	Spain
Canal Satellite Digital	France
DBS Asia	Taiwan
Premiere World	Germany
DirecTV	USA
DirecTV Japan	Japan
DiSH	USA
Foxtel	Australia
Galaxy Latin America	Latin America
Indovision	Indonesia
ART	Middle East
M-NET	South Africa
MIH Multichoice	South Africa
Optus Vision	Australia
Orbit	Middle East
Star Select	Middle East
Showtime	Middle East
Sky New Zealand	New Zealand
Sky PerfecTV Japan	Japan
Sky Latin America	Latin America
Star Select Pakistan	Pakistan
Telepiu/Tele+	Italy
Television par Satellite	France
Wizja TV	Poland
Via Digital	Spain
Wharf Cable	Hong Kong

in some countries to considerable lobbying of regulators on fairness and competition grounds.

On satellite or cable/MMDS systems, bouquets are usually split into various tiers or levels of purchase. This will generally consist of a large basic package that the viewer has to buy in order to move to the higher/more expensive tiers, which usually include the premium sports, movies and specialist channels (adult, games, for example).

Just as in the analogue domain, new services and sales techniques are being tested in digital. These include smaller, basic tiers, often grouped thematically (youngsters, music, family, for example) to satisfy subscribers who in some studies have indicated a reluctance to buy channels that they see as being superfluous to their own needs.

In some markets, channels can also be sold on an 'a la carte' (individual) basis, with viewers deciding which specific channels they wish to watch. Two Middle East broadcasters (Orbit and 1st Net) sell their channels in this way. This is a major issue, especially in Europe, and is covered in detail in Chapter 8.

PPV/NVOD channels

Pay-per-view (PPV) channels are rapidly becoming available on all digital platforms. Viewers are able to pay for a single movie, event or television programme at fees commonly ranging from US$2 for a limited interest film to US$50 or more for a world-championship boxing match. Near-Video on Demand (NVOD) services, pioneered in the USA by DirecTV, are now becoming more widespread for movie transmissions. In NVOD, broadcasters dedicate a number of digital channels to the same film, transmitted at 10, 15, 20 or 30-minute intervals. The appeal of this service is that the viewer is never more than a few minutes from the start of the movie.

Other PPV systems are also now available in the USA and Europe, where 'season tickets' are sold to specific series of events (American football, NBA basketball, ice hockey, soccer, motor racing, rugby, cricket etc.). Such schemes are already in operation in France (for Formula 1 Racing) and Italy (football).

Other variations on the 'season ticket' theme include '24 Hour Movie' or 'All Weekend' tickets, where viewers have access to a specific movie as often as they wish over a 24 hour or weekend period.

Other transactional services

New advanced transactional digital services/channels are being rapidly introduced. It is important to understand that future trans-actional services will be more wide-ranging than the often-quoted 'home-shopping/home banking' type.

Claimed to be the most advanced is Open. . ., the BSkyB joint venture with British Telecom, HSBC and Panasonic. Open. . . has offered interactive and transactional services since the summer of 1999 and promises interactive advertising. Available now or shortly to be added are services such as downloadable games, information services, e-mail, competitions, banking, TV voting, lottery ticket-buying, 'extended' retail, complex travel, online betting/gaming, education services.

On the Canal Satellite Numerique system, viewers can watch 'TV Boutique', a retail channel which also promotes concerts, music, theatre and cinema. The Canal Satellite digital receiver has two slots, one for the 'smart card' to decode the signals, the other for a credit card. Viewers can instruct the system to deduct cash from the credit card to buy concert tickets, CDs, video or music cassettes, etc. The system has two levels:

- At the broadcast level, which 'service' viewers see when they switch to the channel, a non-stop opportunity is offered not only to buy, but to learn more about the product on offer. This might be an interview with a recording artist whose CD is on sale, or the director of a play or concert which is offering tickets.
- At the second level, viewers can enter a site-specific 'shop' where products that are currently being promoted can be purchased.

European digital television viewers in France, Spain, Italy, Germany and throughout Scandinavia can download computer games. In France users pay an additional FFr50 (about US$7) a month to download a specific number of 'free' games a month. But addi-tionally they can download branded software direct from the satellite, usually at a discount of at least 20 per cent off the normal retail price.

An increasing number of broadcasting bouquets are including home shopping/banking and other related services (including tele-gambling) within their broadcasting plans.

Canal+ in France claims its low churn (annual cancellation) rates, typically 9.3 per cent and the lowest in Europe, are in part due to their transactional services. Additionally, it intends using some of its normal transponder 'downtime' for new services. For example, the Internet-to-the-home satellite service will occupy the evening and weekend hours when its broadcast service to doctors, Medicine Plus, is not active. This makes for efficient use of the available bandwidth helping to keep costs low and charges attractive. Canal+ believes that transactional services represent a valuable additional income stream that will be appreciated by consumers and quickly become part and parcel of the broadcasting mix. Much the same sentiments come from most broadcasters, all of whom see 'interactivity' and home shopping-type services playing an increasingly lucrative role in their overall broadcasting mix.

We examine these options in Chapter 6.

Is new content still king?

As with most things in life, entertainment was once a much less complex product, especially for television broadcasters. There were movies, a variety show, a quiz, the news, and a sports match. That was television. The accepted mantra, whether from Hollywood or Wembley, is still that 'content is king'; if broadcasters package up the very best array of on-screen talent, then the audience will follow. Now in an age where the Internet and talk of inter-activity and tele-shopping is seemingly on every broadcaster's lips, the 'content' rule is getting a little frayed at the edges.

Content for broadcasting has tradition-ally come from a well-established number of sources, broadly conforming to the following categories:

- movie rights-holders ('Hollywood' and the other film studios)
- sports rights-holders

- mainstream broadcasters, who by means of generating original material (product) are creating fresh rights to be exploited
- thematic broadcasters
- programme producers, packagers and independents.

And more recently:

- narrowcast services
- data services.

The United States Federal Copyright Act of 1909 covered all published works in the USA, and provides the basis for the contracts of most studios. A major revision (Copyright Act of 1976) widens the scope of copyright to include unpublished works, and further refines the categories and scope of the earlier legislation to include (under section 102):

- literary works
- musical works, and their accompanying words
- dramatic works, and their accompanying music
- pantomimes and choreographic works
- pictorial, graphic and sculptural works
- motion pictures and other audiovisual works
- sound recordings.

There is no mention here of anything remotely connected to the Internet. But the narrowcast and data services mentioned above are generally seen as representing huge opportunities for broadcasters and those controlling the transmission pipes into people's homes. These pipes, the so-called digital super-highways, are in the hands of broadcasters, cable companies and telephone operators. What sort of content traditionally goes down these pipes?

Movies are a primary driver for all subscription television platforms. In some markets (notably the Middle East and in particular Saudi Arabia), cinemas simply do not exist. In traditional markets, having the rights to broadcast the latest Hollywood blockbuster is very important to the television station. For the sake of brevity, the term 'Hollywood' here includes film studios wherever they may be based, but only where they conform to the Hollywood release pattern.

Some ten to fifteen years ago, the local channel or publicly-funded television network would broadcast a Hollywood film generally around three years after its theatrical appearance, perhaps holding back a special movie for Christmas, or another key date in the viewing year. There were no other choices available. The consumer either saw a movie in a cinema or waited three years for it to percolate down to television.

Now it is very different. Hollywood firmly controls the television market, and dictates when a movie is seen. The studios are bound by a set of customs and practices as regards restrictions on film release 'windows', and it is to Hollywood that one must look for an explanation on movie release patterns.

The key term involved in a discussion of release patterns is release 'window'. A release window is that period of time when a licence is granted for commercial exploitation of the copyright. Some windows may be open-ended (such as theatrical or home video release), or highly restricted (subscription or pay-per-view television). For US-produced films, theatrical release is the first window, with a prompt follow-up for airline, video rental and PPV. The following list is a guide only, and many variations do occur.

Typical Release Window

Month 1	Cinema release
Month 3–6	Airline release
Month 6	Video/DVD rental
Month 6–9	Pay Per View
Month 6–12	DVD/Laser release for sell-through
Month 6–9	Hotel Pay Systems
Month 9–18	Video sell-through
Month 18	Subscription TV
Month 18–36	Network (free to air) TV
Thereafter	Syndication

In general, Hollywood films are released according to a highly efficient plan, designed to maximize revenue for the studios. The studios' goal is straightforward: to maximize the number of people who will pay to view the movie. Notice the key word here is 'pay'. Simply releasing the latest Hollywood blockbuster after a few weeks in the cinema directly on to television would gain millions of viewers, but the revenue for the studio would be modest.

Hollywood maximizes the income prospects of a movie through the constant manipulation of the release windows in a continuous effort to maximize revenue in all markets. This means the length of the windows is frequently changing.

There are exceptions to this general rule. Commonly in North America and Europe there exist certain co-financing deals that may give the participant broadcaster certain release benefits, leaving the other partner(s) to gain corresponding benefits elsewhere in the world. For example, a broadcaster like Canal+ (which is obligated under national regulations to plough cash into French movie production) might jointly finance a movie with one of the large Hollywood studios. This deal would allow Canal+ to release the movie in French cinemas, and to show the film itself on its own channel after a reasonable interval, usually about 18 months. The 'partner' studio would be responsible for releasing the film in other non-French parts of the world.

These distribution deals might be quite separate from any profit-sharing agreements. Consequently, a broadcaster (like UK-based Channel 4) might financially benefit from a blockbuster movie like *Four Weddings and a Funeral*, although the broadcaster's key aim in producing the movie was to attract viewers and therefore advertisers to the channel. The broadcaster also tries to balance the financial risk of investing during the initial development or production-financing stages, against the risk of paying far higher sums to acquire the broadcast rights once a film was a success.

The complexity is increased by other exceptions to the rule, including:

■ US made-for-television films that might even be shown in cinemas in Europe (for example many Home Box Office

(HBO) and other television movies are given theatrical release outside the USA)

■ Hollywood films that box-office experience has demonstrated are so unappealing that they miss a cinema release, going instead straight to video

■ made-for-television movies that miss video and go straight to subscription television.

Every player in the financial partnership required to get a movie made has its own vested interest to be considered, making some release patterns highly complex. This 'controlled availability', when combined with country-by-country distribution agreements and pre-sale commitments, will also help determine a film's release pattern.

With the exception of movies that are heavily dependent on computer-generated graphics, digital technology is shortening the period from principal photography to cinema release, and this new phenomenon is altering quite dramatically the release patterns world-wide, especially for blockbuster movies. Until the mid-1990s, the key date in Europe that determined television screening was the release date of the video. Now subscription television plays a major role in this respect. Movies are generally available to be shown on subscription television (Sky's movie channels, HBO, Canal+, Premiere, for example) 12 months after their video rental release, or some 18 months after cinema release.

The release pattern of Hollywood films is gradually standard-izing, as Hollywood adopts a world-wide simultaneous release pattern. In the movie business, though, even a few weeks may carry a significant financial value. Releasing a film at the Cannes Film Festival in the spring is often enough to trigger the French video release date within a few months. Other film fans in Europe might still be waiting until the autumn for the movie even to be at the cinema, meaning a video rental the following spring. This pattern could mean a movie being shown on Canal+ six or twelve months sooner than on Sky, and well ahead of an Arab broad-cast date, for instance.

Economic value

The early release of a Hollywood movie in the Dutch or Nordic markets is usually sufficient to guarantee a movie an early airing on one of the Scandinavian movie channels. The same applies in France with Canal+. There is another element in the equation, though, which is the economic or cash value of a country/market. In simple terms, it is the difference between, say, the UK and Germany, or Spain and the Middle East. The UK and Germany are simply more important markets for Hollywood films and will usually be higher on the list for distribution deals and release.

In addition to the normal movie 'first window' rights, other rights are classified linguistically. The 'German-language rights', which might cover the whole of Europe, would certainly include Austria and the German-speaking cantons of Switzerland (unless expressed otherwise).

Licensing and merchandising

Licensing and merchandising of products associated with movies and television series is today a highly profitable sector, and has led to some programming being marketed at less than its conventional value in a particular country or region because its exposure on television was expected to lead to higher revenues from ancillary rights. This is particularly true of some animation programming where the merchandising revenue potential from toys, foodstuffs, books and video sales far exceeds the income likely to be derived from a local broadcast.

Sports

Sports are generally recognized as a main driver of subscription television. The rights to broadcast a sporting event 'live' are again classified by market in much the same way the film rights are distributed. However, there is a significant difference in that 'live' sports events have a much greater value than recorded material. Spectrum Strategy Consulting, a London-based consultancy, stated in a 1996 report that live events tend to get some 30 per cent of the audience while a (first show) event recording will achieve less than 5 per cent of the audience. Consequently, significant sums are paid for sports rights to key events. Some significant examples include:

■ In 1948, the BBC paid £1500 (equivalent to £27 000 in 1996 prices) for the rights to telecast the Olympic Games to UK viewers.

■ In 1996, broadcasters from around the world paid a total of US$900 million for the rights to transmit the Atlanta Olympic Games.

■ IN 1996, NBC, a US network, paid US$3.6 billion for the broadcast rights to the Olympics up to and including the 2008 Olympiad.

■ In 1994, Rupert Murdoch's News Corporation paid US$1.6 billion (outbidding CBS) for the television rights to cover four years of (American) National Football League. When, in 1998, the contract came up for renewal (for the 1999 and ongoing seasons) News Corporation paid a world record sum of US$17.6 billion to cover a seven-year period, or US$2.5 billion per season.

■ In July 1996 Kirch Group, a Munich-based broadcasting conglomerate, paid US$2.36 billion for the rights to show the soccer World Cup competitions in 2002 and 2006. While Kirch has the exclusive rights for the competition, they will assign sub-leases of their rights to individual broadcasters around the globe. Indeed, it is quite probable they will make a profit from exploitation of those rights. Nevertheless, the sum paid represents a six-fold increase over the sums paid for the rights to the World Cup tournaments during 1990–98 (which achieved, in total, US$344 million).

■ London Economics, a UK consultancy, stated in 1996 that sport accounts for around 15 per cent of all television spending. During its 1996 financial year, BSkyB spent some £100 million on sports – one third of its programming budget. The BBC typically spends 4 per cent of its programme budget on sports in non-Olympic years.

Table 6.1 shows other recent key sports deals of note.

Table 6.1   Sports broadcasting deals

Event	Rights dates	Buyer	Cost
Olympic Games	1996–2008	NBC	$4 bn
Olympic Games (EBU)	1996–2008	EBU	$1.44 bn
World Cup soccer	2002–2006	Kirch	$2.36 bn
NCAA basketball	1995–2002	CBS	$1.73 bn
National Football League	1995–1998	Fox	$1.58 bn
National Football League	1999–2006	Fox	$17.6 bn
English Premier League	1997–2001	BSkyB	$0.96 bn
English Premier League	2001–2004	BSkyB	$1.65 bn

Note: Cost in US$

In some cases sports broadcasters seem to have recognized the inherent value of by-passing the normal round of negotiations and instead are themselves acquiring ownership of the sport, or at least some of the key clubs. For example, Rupert Murdoch in early March 1998 totally acquired the Los Angeles Dodgers baseball team for US$311 million (in other words, News Corporation owns 100 per cent of the club). Two weeks later News Corporation acquired a significant share (10 per cent for US$150 m) of the Los Angeles Lakers basketball club.

As a guide to the economic value of sports rights, it is worth looking at BSkyB's cash-flow position, as examined by Dresdner Kleinwort Benson in August 1997, with regard to their sports coverage. The data stop at 2001 with the end of the current English Premier League soccer rights.

Other events

Some events lend themselves to special exploitation, in particular for pay-per-view (PPV) income. In the sports area this is especially true of boxing and wrestling, in particular in North America where boxing and wrestling bouts consistently do well. In the non-sports area concerts of popular music (and in North America country music events) and to a lesser extent of classical music

Table 6.2   Sky Sports Revenues, at June each year

	1996	1997	1998	1999	2000	2001
Average BSkyB Subscribers	5m	5.8m	7.1m	8.3m	9.6m	10.7m
% taking Sky Sports	62.5%	63.9%	62.6%	61.4%	58.7%	56.9%
Average Sky Sports subscribers	3.1m	3.7m	4.4m	5.1m	5.6m	6.1m
	(£m)	(£m)	(£m)	(£m)	(£m)	(£m)
Sports Subs Revenues	171.5	206.5	254.7	309.3	341.2	382.3
Sports Adverts Rev's	30.7	39.6	48.8	59.3	71.3	83.6
Total Revenues	202.1	246.1	303.6	368.6	412.5	465.9
Total Sky Sports Costs*	134.8	215.8	275.8	306.8	341.5	383.5

*Includes Premier League costs
Source: Dresdner Kleinwort Benson

can also generate appeal. In 1997, events drawn from the list below counted for nearly 70 per cent of US PPV revenues.

- World championship boxing
- Wrestling
- Martial arts contests
- Pop-music concerts
- Classical music concerts.

UK-based boxing promoter, Frank Warren in June 1997 described championship boxing as:

the most honest form of TV, you cannot cheat the ratings, the figures are there to be seen, the revenues being split between the rights holders and [broadcasters]. Our first match (Bruno v Tyson) created a 14 per cent buy-rate (660 000 subs) even at

5 a.m. 'Judgement Night' got 420 000 subs (9 per cent). The 'Night of Champions' 720 000 buys or 15.5 per cent and the 'Brit Pack' on May 3 [1997] achieved a 6 per cent buy rate largely because Tyson vs Holyfield was postponed.

Canal+ have been selling between eight and twelve channels of PPV soccer on their digital platform since 1996, although it has been reluctant to publicly announce the results to date. The attraction of PPV sports was perfectly described in 1997 by Swiss-based ISL, partners in the Leo Kirch deal to acquire television rights to the 2002/2006 World Cup tournament: 'PPV is exciting, and is for the ultimate fan, the ultimate grass-roots supporter prepared to hand over some of his income to the TV turnstile, and the viewer who religiously enjoys every single split-second of the match. It also delivers some of the very best production values around.'

Charging PPV prices (usually at rates between US$10–50) for sports and event programming is simply exploiting the greatest value at the top of a multi-tiered pyramid of rights values, whose base is free-to-air television.

Mainstream free-to-air networks

It is part of broadcasting folklore and often repeated that in the early days of video-recording, some public broadcasters struggling to meet budgetary constraints wiped the video recordings of their programmes to re-use the tape in order to save money on buying new tape stock. They thereby destroyed any prospects for the original item to be shown again.

Such an action would now be seen as wilful destruction of the broadcaster's main asset: the content. Today's public and commercial mainstream broadcasters are as shrewd as the Hollywood studios in exploiting and re-showing their material. They invest in new programming with two objectives. The first, naturally, is to satisfy their viewing audiences. The second is to allow them to re-broadcast the material or sell on the rights in the form of licensed windows to other broadcasters, either in the originating country or in foreign markets.

A network might originate its own show and repeat the transmission later that week or some time later. It might air the programme on a subsidiary network that it owns, or sell the rights to a rival station once the unique merit of the show has faded. It might also sell the show overseas.

The USA is the most aggressive seller of its broadcasting content, arguably proving to generation after generation of viewers that its output is the most popular on the planet. Whether it is in shows like *Wagon Train* (1957–65), *Peyton Place* (1964–9), *Dallas* (1978–91) or *Baywatch* (1989 to date), the world's television stations have bought US television shows above all other productions. It is arguable as to the real merits of some content, but the 'typical' viewer loves them.

However, the USA has also had to operate under some very strange regulations. The US terrestrial networks operate under Federal Communications Commission (FCC) restrictions as to the number of broadcast hours they may produce for their own transmissions. These regulations (or licence obligations) were strengthened in 1971 by the Prime Time Access Rules (PTAR), which limit network affiliates in the top 50 (USA) markets to three hours of network programming from their own production resources.

The FCC rule was intended 'to make available for competition among existing and potential program producers, both at the local and national levels, an arena of more adequate competition for the custom and favour of broadcasters and advertisers' (FCC, 1971). The result of the ruling was to open up the 7–8 p.m. EST time block (and post-11 p.m. time slot) for non-network producers to gain access to the network.

The rule was allied to the 1972 introduction of the Financial Interest and Syndication Ruling ('fin-syn') designed to limit the financial involvement of the main networks in the programming produced for them. The networks were restricted from wholly owning the show purchased or commissioned by them. While a network's main objective was always to secure what it saw as top programming for its audiences, the result, prior to the fin-syn act, was to limit severely what the originating producer could subsequently do with the show once its main network showing was completed.

The fin-syn rules, although significantly eased in 1991, had the result of creating a strong independent production sector in North America. Most of the cinema studios set up television divisions, first to work with the networks but then to exploit the syndication, overseas and other re-transmission rights permitted them under the ruling. The main networks also sold off their own production divisions: CBS sold its division to an emerging company called Viacom and ABC sold its production to Worldvision.

Those regulations have now been relaxed, but as an example of the complexities involved, the 1996–8 US television ratings-winning programme *Seinfeld* is produced by Time Warner-owned Castle Rock Television studios. The show is 'first run' contracted to the NBC network, although it is offered for sale by Columbia TriStar Television Distribution for the syndication market.

Outside the USA, the television value chain has evolved more conventionally, with public-service broadcasters taking the lead in national production. Even the entry of commercially funded broadcasting has not altered this picture; the commercial stations (though more likely buyers of material imported from the USA) have still heavily invested in studios and original programming, initially for their own use but increasingly for overseas sale.

Thematic or niche broadcasters

Thematic broadcasting differs from mainstream broadcast programming in that it focuses on niche or special interest material, with the explicit intention of attracting viewers to that niche. Channels devoted wholly to movies and sport are examples of thematic channels. Movie channels, by and large, are acquirers of existing product, and while some US movie channels (in particular HBO) invest considerable sums in producing or commissioning new films (for television showing in the USA), the majority of film channels do little more than provide interstitial programming links between movies.

However, even within the generic 'movie' classification, there are now channels themed into sub-classifications: action, romance, comedy, for example. One such themed movie channel, American Movie Classics, owned by Rainbow Media Holdings, in May 1998 launched 'American Pop', showing archive films, newsreels, promotional films designed to 'tap into popular culture'. While the use of 'classic' and 'cult' material may not create original (and thereby newly licensable) programming, in many cases the channel brand itself becomes a valuable asset. Cartoon Network is a perfect example of this, with the checkerboard logo licensed in many countries.

The Disney Channel, which mixes animation with live action programming, launched 'Toon Disney' in early 1998, a self-contained digital channel designed to appeal to younger viewers. This is also fast becoming a licensable device.

C-SPAN, an analogue and digital television service in the USA, which broadcasts 'gavel to gavel' coverage of the House of Representatives (and C-Span 2 which covers the Senate chamber) launched in March 1998 a new audio channel, C-Span Radio, as part of a digital audio bouquet offered by CDRadio, a 50-channel direct-to-car satellite service scheduled for launch over North America in 1999. The radio service demonstrates that extra revenues can be achieved from lateral spin-off services, where core material can be re-used to create income and reach wider audiences.

There are growing numbers of thematic channels available as part of subscription television bouquets which increasingly create their own exploitable programming copyrights:

- **Discovery**, a documentary channel founded in 1988, originally bought in all its material from existing film and video libraries, drawing heavily on the archives of public broadcasters around the world, not least the BBC. Today it is the leading commissioner of documentary programming in the world. In March 1998, it entered into various joint-ventures with the BBC to co-produce and finance new channels. The first three channels, Animal Planet, People &

Arts and BBC America, have proved remarkably popular, and others are planned.

- **Arts & Entertainment** (A&E), a thematic channel owned in part by the US network NBC, has spun off another channel, The History Channel, devoted to factual documentary programming. One of its constituent parts, a nightly *Biography* programme is also under consideration to be spun off as a stand-alone channel. A&E has followed the Discovery example, and while initially only exploiting existing archive material, is now increasingly involved in commissioning new material specifically for the channel.
- The **BBC,** through its commercial arm BBC World-wide, has entered into a joint-venture with Flextech plc, a company owned in part by Tele-Communications Inc. to launch new factual thematic channels under the UKTV brand (Horizons, Arena, Style etc.). Initially, the channels will exploit the BBC library, but the agreement is already leading to the origination of 'new' programming for the channels as well as new versions of existing programming, for instance, a 50 minute version of a 30-minute motoring programme *Top Gear.*
- **Canal+** has invested (along with TCI, Havas and other companies) in 'Multithematiques', a group of documentary channels (Seasons, Jimmy, Cine Cinema, Planete etc.) which are being rolled out to other European platforms in which Canal+ has an interest. Multithematiques is committed to increase local production, especially for its Seasons channels (described as a thematic channel for those interested in hunting, shooting and fishing).
- **CNN**, perhaps the best known of all niche broadcasters, launched its all-news network in June 1980. Since then, it has launched sub-niche versions of the channel: CNN Headline News, CNN International, CNN fn (Financial News), CNN:SI (Sports Illustrated), CNN Airport Network and CNN Interactive, plus stand-alone services for Latin America, and is a 49 per cent share-holder in ntv, a German-language news channel. Moreover, the CNN brand is now seen on language-specific local news channels (CNN+ in Spain, CNN-Turk in Turkey) and more of these are planned.

■ **Cartoon Network**, created by Ted Turner but now owned
  by Time Warner, initially depended on its vast library of
  MGM cartoons, but some five years ago realized that to
  keep the library growing it had to invest in new
  programming. As a result of that decision, new animated
  programming has been commissioned, including material
  from European creative houses (which has helped overcome
  some of the regulatory quota problems within Europe), and
  such new programmes have been among the most popular
  shows aired on the channel.

Some other better-known American thematic channels include:

■ Black Entertainment Television (BET)
■ Playboy TV
■ Nickelodeon
■ ESPN
■ Disney Channel
■ E! Entertainment TV
■ Family Channel
■ Lifetime
■ Nashville Network.

All of these channels are investing in new programming, so
that they own at least some of the broadcast as well as ancillary
rights.

Producers and packagers

The role of programme producers who create programming for
the main broadcasters has already been examined. There are
numerous other producers who are less well known, even though
their shows may be very familiar. A good example is Carsey Werner
Inc., who currently 'handle' shows such as *The Cosby Show*, *Grace
Under Fire* and *Third Rock From the Sun*.

Often it is difficult to differentiate between programme
producers and channel or programme providers. For example, does
Hallmark Entertainment Network qualify as a studio? It produces

'made-for-TV movies' of the calibre of *Gulliver's Travels* and *Moby Dick*, which it sells to mainstream broadcasters around the world. However, Hallmark also packages product for its own channels around the world, especially for those regions where its own product is not available (because rights have been assigned to other broadcasters).

The same analysis could be applied to a channel like National Geographic Television which, when launched in 1997, reportedly owned only some 180 hours of its own exclusive material, not all of which was exploitable in certain key markets (again because rights had been assigned elsewhere). Consequently, it had to acquire and package suitable natural history and similar documentary material to show under its brand. National Geographic Television also works with Canal+ and Turner Original Productions in DocStar, the packager (with Explore International) of the trio's documentary programming.

Discovery Communications is clearly a major producer (and co-producer) of factual programming. It has also entered into joint venture, co-production deals to make new programming with organizations such as the BBC, Canal+, German public broadcaster ZDF and others. It licenses its product to other broadcasters, but also has to acquire programming from third-party producers for some of its own spin-off channels, such as The Learning Channel (TLC, also known as Discovery Home & Leisure in some regions of the world) and newly announced channels like Discovery Kids and Discovery Civilisations. In some cases Discovery will act as a packager of third-party produced programming for certain of its channels, especially where its own archive is not complete enough to provide sufficient high-quality material to sustain a channel.

Discovery is also moving into radio, packaging a weekly audio service (from May 1998) in a joint venture with a division of London-based Television Corporation. The service is designed to offer 'half-a-dozen topics per program,' according to the company, which will mirror Discovery's usual video content.

Narrowcast television

Digital television presents a much greater opportunity for highly specific narrowcast services. For example, Canal Satellite Numerique is already transmitting:

- Medicine Plus, a closed-circuit channel for doctors
- Demain! (Tomorrow), a 'self-improvement' channel
- France Courses, a horse-racing channel
- f. Fashion TV (a fashion channel, and see below).

Other tightly-targeted thematic channels include: CNN's group of sub-niche news channels (CNN Headline News, CNNI, CNNfn, ntv etc.); Bloomberg Television, a spin-off of Michael Bloomberg's stock-exchange data service; and NBC's global news channel CNBC, also designed to serve business-viewers.

Narrowcasting can be even more finely tuned than these sub-niche examples. For example, f.Fashion TV is a Paris-based, thematic channel broadcasting in digital from EUTELSAT and Astra, but it has announced the following narrowcast services:

- f-1, the current channel comprising advertising-free, non-stop catwalk show video-clips with the original backing music, featuring more than 100 of the world's leading couture houses;
- f-2 will broadcast interviews with the designers, backstage scenes and advertising;
- f-3 will be a PPV channel, broadcasting full fashion shows;
- f-4 is described as comprising programmes for 'fashion-conscious viewers';
- f-5 is a shopping channel.

Proposed extensions to this package include f-g, a proposed 'gay' channel, f-s for sports-wear, and f-j a 'jeans and junior' channel. These channels could not possibly be financially viable without the transmission savings brought about by digital television.

Elsewhere there are broadcasters using digital television to narrowcast educational services. Sheikh Saleh Kamel, the Saudi

Arabian television entrepreneur, has launched one channel devoted to students of the Koran. India, Pakistan and China have variously announced plans to adopt digital television for distance learning projects. Within Europe, Denmark has been using digital television for many years to transmit educational and other programming to isolated communities in Greenland.

Satellite operators, SES/Astra, EUTELSAT, Orion, Galaxy and PanAmSat have all spoken of plans to encourage narrowcast services to businesses. Some companies already have Very Small Aperture Terminal (V-SAT) installations (closed circuit transmissions) often in analogue, but increasingly switching to digital transmission, for moving image and data services to clients. A good example in Europe is the Ford Motor Company, which uses such services to talk to dealers.

Data services

However large and unexploited the digital business television market may be, the adoption of digital data-transmission services by the likes of DirecPC, Canal+ and others cannot be ignored. Chapter 10 covers the PC/TV convergence in some detail, including data transmission direct-to-home and to small office/home office users.

Business Television (BTV) can include moving image transmission as well as data. SES/Astra have formed a joint venture with Swiss-based The Fantastic Corporation to offer data services across greater Europe with minimum infrastructure investment. The Fantastic Corporation, claims the value of this sector to be worth US$400 billion a year. The company uses Astra's high-power transmissions to broadcast data to small dishes (about 60 cm diameter, depending on location). The small dishes and inexpensive digital decoder boxes have dramatically reduced the overall installation costs for such multiple installations. SES/Fantastic launched the service in early 1998, and are already supplying digital bandwidth to customers (which, they state, include many 'Fortune 500' companies) for the following applications:

- corporate announcements
- internal company communications
- distance learning programmes
- in-store customer viewing.

Almost without exception, satellite-transmission owners can offer similar services. Astra has its own proprietary data-casting system (Astra-Net) which launched in January 2000 (although it had some 50 clients already using Astra-Net by the end of 1999).

There are many companies offering similar services globally. In the USA, Convergent Media Systems (CMS) claims to serve 70 per cent of the business television market, initially in analogue, but rapidly switching to digital transmission. CMS estimates it delivers programming to more than 40 000 offices totalling some 5 million people in the private sector. It also serves 17 000 higher education schools with upwards of 10 million students. In government (local, state and federal) it claims to supply data services and video material to over 1000 locations serving more than 1 million people.

Walt Disney World, the Florida theme park, uses Business TV datacast services from satellite company Globecast North America to transmit and receive between the Disney/MGM studios (located at Disney World) and the Disney-owned ABC broadcast studios in Los Angeles and New York. In addition to having the ability to send and receive material, the circuits will also be used to transmit a 24-hour radio show for Disney (*Radio Disney*, ABC's 24-hour music programme).

Flextech – moving into interactivity

Flextech has now merged with Telewest and what is increasingly clear is Flextech's adoption of interactivity as a revenue-generating tool for its broadcast channel, as well as web-based access. As a case study, their entry into on-screen e-commerce is a near perfect example.

Adam Singer, Flextech's chairman (as at December 1999) is keen to see the end of analogue broadcasting, but also hints that Flextech's analogue service could be curtailed well before satellite subscriber numbers are down to the last 200 000 or 300 000 homes. 'It takes a lot of subs to pay a £4.5 million per annum transponder cost. This has not been thought of and it may be that the cut-off point on satellite is much higher than had previously been imagined and it's going to be interesting to see what happens.'

Setting aside the conversion to digital, Flextech's progress during 1999 was good. Its ad-revenues grew 30 per cent against market growth averages of 20 per cent. Its UKTV joint venture saw revenues boosted 52.9 per cent to £34.4 m, with flagship channel UK Gold's operating profits up 66.5 per cent to £9.1 million. Out went the loss-making Playboy TV (sold in March 1999) and in came a 25 per cent stake in Multimap, which provides online maps and guides.

Flextech's thrust is towards interactivity on most of its channels. In 1999 Singer said 'Our interactive division in the last six months made, excluding the travel side, £387 000 in ad revenue. That's starting from zero. We are staggered and delighted. I can tell you that is more ad revenue than some full channels are making in a full year – not Flextech channels I must stress – although it's more than the advertising revenue we took on some of our channels when they started up a few years ago. So clearly there is a lot of money out there and this, we believe, is a true indication of what is available from advertising without touching the e-commerce income possibilities. Look at Living Health where you have the channel together with drop-down diagnostic opportunities plus e-commerce and you have a whole range of advertising benefits.'

Flextech is looking to sell its Living/Bravo/Trouble channel formats into overseas markets, but Singer says the current priority is the Internet and interactivity. 'Part of the issue is that the Internet wave has hit all of us in television. We are the new kids on the block, and we had better find that fountain of youth.'

Of course, everyone is searching for the golden prize at the end of the broadcasting rainbow. Open . . . the digital interactive service from BSkyB, BT, bankers HSBC and Panasonic, started its trans-missions in basic form in mid-1998, with extra services added throughout 1999. During 1999 around £60 million was spent on advertising and promotion. Open. . .'s CEO is James Ackerman.

Open. . .'s technical director Colin McQuade said in 1999 that the Open. . . system was not like the Internet. 'It's designed for TV. It's designed for my mother who has never seen an error message on her TV set, or had to re-boot whenever she wants to watch the news.'

Referring to the spectacular growth of Dixons' Freeserve free-of-charge e-mail service, which very quickly racked up more than 1 million subscribers, McQuade predicted 'This time next year [that is in early 2000] Open . . . will be the biggest e-mail provider in the UK'. Sky digital subscribers will be able to send and receive e-mail anywhere in the world. Up to eight e-mail 'accounts' can be dedicated to each subscriber, allowing parents and children, for example, to each have a dedicated e-mail address.

'E-mail is going to be phenomenally important' said Open. . .'s chief executive James Ackerman. 'E-mail provides traffic, traffic means more people will come into the Mall and create more oppor-tunities to transact.' Users will also be able to pick up e-mail at their office, or via BT's High Street interactive terminals. 'It would be a disaster if it were just limited to fellow subscribers to Open. . . .' Sky is selling a wireless keyboard, styled to match the remote control, costing £39, although Ackerman also expects the device to be given away by some retailers as a branded premium.

Open . . . added Hasbro as a retail partner who will use the Sky digi-box to download games to consoles. Ackerman said the tech-nology was now in place to download any other commercial software direct to the PC, linked to the digi-box. Open . . . launched with 68 Mbps of satellite capacity (from Astra 2A, equivalent to about two transponders) and more is available as the system grows, says Ackerman. 'Then we'll start to learn. We'll see whether books sell better than CDs or CDs sell better than trainers and we'll start making some decisions as to which products our consumers want.'

'I know Sky is not putting any less emphasis on this venture,' said Ackerman. 'In fact they are putting more emphasis through the creation of their own interactive division. Sky One, Sky Movies, Sky Sports and the rest will all have brands developing interactive elements. Flextech have done the same with their interactive division so that we can start developing applications ahead of the game, beating a lot of people to the punch. It is absolute nonsense to suggest that Sky is emphasizing this venture any less. Further to that, one of the main differentiating factors between analogue and digital TV is interactivity, and interactivity is Open .... You will see this year a lot of emphasis from Sky Digital on interactivity on the Open ... services. What people have had up till now is emphasis on the launch of Sky Digital and the broadcast services because that's all there was.'

He argued that the Internet has developed portal sites to bring order from chaos. 'An interactive platform like Open ... is bringing things together, quality retail sites to the most commonly used device in the home, the TV set. No need to enter web addresses, no need to go through complex routes and the ability to promote your products through the broadcast stream. This has got to have a massive interest. I believe the Internet proves that the interest will be there and that this is going to take off big time.'

Datacasting: the PricewaterhouseCoopers view

In December 1999, management consultants Pricewaterhouse-Coopers (PwC), released a major report on what they called 'datacasting', the broadcast transmission of data, which is worth examining in some detail. According to PwC specialist Howard J. Postley, datacasting has been around for over 15 years. In many cases, data are incorporated alongside other media for 'free' transmission; for example, using the vertical blanking interval (VBI) in a television broadcast.

This is especially true in Europe, where the VBI portion of the analogue signal has been used for, among other things, so-called 'teletext' services. In addition to these text services, though, the VBI has also been used by broadcasters to 'piggy-back' other content, notably specialized slow-scan data and picture files for clients. In the UK, for example, British Rail uses the VBI on an analogue satellite channel to 'broadcast' its train timetables direct to its platform television displays.

The USA (in its analogue transmissions) uses the VBI not for messaging or teletext but for 'closed captioning' of broadcasts for deaf and visually impaired viewers.

Whether or not they are bundled with other signals, datacasts are frequently secondary content in support of primary broadcast content, as services like the Radio Data System (RDS) illustrate. Regardless of how the signals are transmitted, or with what other media they may be associated, datacasts usually consist of text-only information.

PwC's Postley stresses that 'mediacasting' is an altogether different concept. While mediacasts may include some of the same types of data, they go far beyond datacasts. Mediacasting is the broadcast delivery of rich-media content directly to storage in addressable receivers. Unlike traditional broadcasts, mediacast content is designed to be stored at the destination before it is presented.

PwC expect that mediacasting will not only supplant data-casting, it will effectively replace broadcasting as it is currently performed.

Market forces

Postley says that mediacasting is the result of a variety of forces but is, at the core, one of the many ways in which that conver-gence is changing the broadcasting industry. There have been many debates about whether broadcasting will be replaced by the Internet, whether all Internet content will be provided by television programmers, whether all Internet use will eventually be through television, and so on. These discussions, while interesting insofar as they serve to highlight the strengths and weaknesses of various media, are largely irrelevant.

PwC recognize that the single most significant force to shape mediacasting is the internet, and its standard yet flexible foundation. By breaking media and other data into small digital chunks, they can be moved over any kind of transport link, from a slow dial-up modem to a fast fibre-optic connection or wirelessly via terrestrial and satellite broadcasts. In fact, all of those mechanisms can be used in different parts of the route. Like shipping a package, the shipper does not care how a package gets to the destination, and the freight company does not care what is in the package.

The basis for all digital transmission is the breaking up of data and/or images into digital chunks, or packets. These packets can travel not only over a variety of transport media, but also they can travel different routes, depending on a variety of factors, and arrive in a different order from when they started – to be reordered back into the correct sequence at their destination.

The Internet, says Postley, allows the use of receiver processing power to reduce transport inefficiencies. While it is easy to discount the use of the Internet and its associated technologies for the delivery of media to the home, it is important to recognize the value that the flexible Internet protocols provide. As an example, PwC uses the delivery of a single US television signal. An analogue television channel in the USA uses 6 MHz of spectrum for 30 minutes to send 30 minutes of audio and video content. There is no practical way for time or bandwidth to be reduced while retaining compatibility with common receivers. In the digital world, the equivalent content can be transferred in approximately 1.25 MHz of spectrum for the same 30 minutes. While the amount of spectrum is reduced due to digital coding, current technology receivers are still designed to deliver and play the content in 'real time'; i.e. it is played as soon as it is delivered.

PwC accurately state that the evolving model for mediacasts is fundamentally different. Since mediacasts are designed to be stored at their destination before presentation, other options become available. A half-hour SDTV (a digital channel but of conventional, that is, non-HDTV format) programme requires approximately 720 Mb, (that is 30 minutes x 24 Mb/minute = 720 Mb) of disk if it is to be stored.

Unlike standard broadcasting, mediacasting allows burst delivery. Using a different kind of compression that benefits from having all of the content stored before it is decompressed, the 720 Mb can easily be reduced to less than 90 Mb. By mediacasting that content as data using all of a standard SDTV channel (that is, a standard higher-definition, but not HDTV, digital channel in the USA), 30 minutes of content could be delivered in well under one minute. To look at it another way, an entire day of television programming could be delivered in less than 45 minutes. The ratio of compression for countries outside the USA is slightly different, but the argument is just as valid.

New formats mean new opportunities

PwC say datacasting enables the role of the receiving devices to change into that of intelligent network peripherals. This, in turn, enables a dramatic increase in the variety of those peripherals and the diversity of media that they can use. There are already a number of peripherals which use mediacasting to create new opportunities, and others which do not currently utilize mediacasting but are clearly headed in that direction. An example that is easily recognizable is the new digital video recorders (DVR) now being offered by entrepreneurial companies such as TiVO and Replay Networks. While technically these devices are a new form of the traditional VCR for standard broadcasts, it is useful to look at them as mediacast receivers where the mediacast happens to be carried in the format of a standard television signal. It is not difficult to envisage similar devices receiving content that has been burst over cable or satellite, or trickled in through a DSL connection.

At least two US companies, Tranz-Send Broadcasting Network and Intertainer, are now attempting to establish themselves for video distribution using this method. Because mediacast content is played from local storage, it makes no difference how long or what route that content took to get to the receiver.

Additionally, says PwC, one should also look past the traditional television set, because there are a variety of new devices becoming available which also must be supplied with media content. Today, electronic books, such as the Rocket eBook and SoftBook, and digital music players such as the Diamond Rio and Saehan MPMan, are supplied on an individual basis via the world wide web. Likewise, the computer software industry is rapidly moving to electronic distribution. Video games, especially those that require some type of network connectivity for multiplayer gaming, are likely to follow this lead.

New viewing model

Mediacasting will support a new viewing model that allows the consumer to do the content aggregation. Traditionally, content is selected and scheduled for passive viewing by the networks or cable providers. The majority of consumers want a relatively small subset of the available content. We already see that large numbers of consumers have identical content delivered to them individually. Imagine if every song on the radio had to be delivered separately to each listener every time it was played. Current delivery mechanisms are much more expensive than they need to be. This situation is exacerbated by the ever-increasing costs and complexities associated with serving a growing audience.

An addressable broadcast solution, with receiver storage for an 'on-demand' capability, provides a much more efficient and scalable solution. Given that the DVRs are already shipping with enough storage to store more than a full day's worth of continuous viewing, and the ability to schedule its playout, and the availability of new types of media devices coupled with the capability of mediacast burst delivery, every broadcaster has to ask the question: 'What is the highest value use we can get from our bandwidth inventory?' Given the opportunities presented by these new technologies, 'commercial television' is not the only answer and, increasingly, may not be the most profitable.

Jockeying for position

PwC says the industry, and consumers are looking forward to a digital future, but there are a very few paths to get content to a destination. Historically, right-of-way issues have limited options for telephone and cable TV service providers. Ironically, similar types of issues are likely to limit wireless options from satellite, microwave and RF sources in the same ways. While the businesses of the companies that provide them continue to change, the primary ways of getting significant amounts of data to a destination will continue to be cable, telephone lines, broadcast RF and satellite. However, while the delivery channels may not change much, the ways in which they are used will change dramatically. Today, less than 25 per cent of the US population receives television solely 'off-air.' By the time the current FCC-mandated date for digital television cut-off in the USA rolls around, that number will be less than 10 per cent. The question is: will there be anyone watching a DTT signal?

As is evident from its penetration into US households, cable is the preferred channel for media delivery. There are myriad reasons for this but one of them is the sheer capacity. A digital cable system can provide up to 1 GHz of bandwidth, as much as 4 Gbps of data. Contrast that with the just under 20 Mbps of data that can be provided by a DTT channel or the puny 1.5 Mbps of ADSL and the advantage is clear. However, that advantage is also temporary. Estimates are that within five years, the average American household will receive 5 Gbps of data. For that to happen, given the estimates for digital cable roll-out, the majority of that bandwidth will have to be delivered via wireless means. While wireless broadcast systems lack cable's return path, telephone companies are already positioning themselves to solve that problem. A 1.5 Mbps inbound data channel may be nearly useless for media delivery; it is more than adequate as a private dedicated outbound channel.

Implications

PwC point out that in 1989, Nicholas Negroponte, Director of the MIT Media Lab, predicted what has come to be known as the 'Negroponte Switch'. He predicted that most forms of communication that had been carried on wires would move to wireless means and those that had been transported wirelessly would move to wired services. Due to the inherent complexities and costs of providing high-bandwidth via widespread deployment of any type of wiring, several effects appear likely.

- The majority of inbound data to consumers will arrive via wireless means.
- The majority of outbound data from consumers will depart via wired means.
- Transport mechanisms will be combined to provide the most optimal configuration for a given application.
- Internet Protocol (IP) will provide the common ground to allow bifurcation of inbound and outbound communication channels and the replacement of one-source solutions with open systems.

PwC define the 'broadcast crossover' axiom as their corollary to the 'Negroponte Switch'. This axiom states that the majority of media that have historically been presented under the control of the broadcasters, at the time they are transmitted, will be media-cast and presented under the control of the audience at times it finds convenient.

These changes present a variety of new business opportunities for broadcasters and many other businesses in the broadcast industry. While the growth of bandwidths to each home would tend to imply that bandwidths will become 'commoditized', limitations on available spectrum will continue to make broadcasting a business of resource management. Furthermore, the development of new devices and new types of media, coupled with the continual increase in the quantity of traditional broadcast media, will more than counterbalance the increased data density that can be achieved through improved coding and modulation techniques. For a variety of reasons, broadcasters have been limited to a specific media type for a given facility – television facilities do not transmit radio. While their essential asset has always been their ability to transmit any type of content, the facilities are optimized for a single type. Changes in the marketplace, however, will cause a re-evaluation of past practices. Mediacasting can allow broadcasters to become more focused on deriving the most value from their bandwidth and less on the content it carries. A mediacast of television, music, and interactive media require the same facilities.

A by-product of mediacasting and the 'broadcast crossover' axiom is that processes that have been implicit in the broadcast product can now be made into products of their own. For instance, the optimization of a broadcast schedule in order best to satisfy the target audience is a complex task. Mediacasting will enable schedules themselves to become content of their own and, due to the transactional nature of mediacasting, revenue generating products. This is exactly what TiVO is attempting to do; their hardware enables the sale of their scheduling service.

PwC say that since all mediacast content goes to storage before it is played out, users perceive that it is available on-demand. That demand can be generated directly by viewers, by schedules, by other content and any combination thereof. The same set of content can support everything from a mass-audience schedule to one for an individual viewer. Furthermore, the different sets of advertising spots can be inserted depending on the schedule. While these capabilities have been described in terms of television programmes, they also apply to music, video games, books, and any other content that can be mediacast.

New devices, new types of media and new services mean new types of customers for mediacasters and also new responsibilities. With the increased diversity of the content and its audience, mediacasters will need to cultivate that same kind of diversity in its sales force to approach and service a much broader range of customers and customer needs. The range of opportunities is likely to be so large that the most critical business issues will be those related to choosing and servicing the subset of opportunities that are most promising and put the mediacaster in the best strategic and competitive position.

Mediacasting will consolidate a variety of technologies into a system that will ultimately replace traditional broadcasting. Broadcasters are among the best positioned to take advantage of the new system. To the extent that the bandwidth is available, it is more efficient and more scalable to broadcast content and allow the decision to store it to be made at the receiver than to address data to individual receivers at the transmitter. However, adoption will require new business models, reformulation of corporate and operational strategies, new processes and new systems. The combination of more bandwidth and addressable receivers with local storage allows one-to-many broadcasts to behave like one-to-one narrowcasts. Broadcasters can apply traffic yield management and focused audience targeting to achieve zero marginal cost per receiver.

PricewaterhouseCoopers state simply that mediacasting will change the face of broadcasting and that broadcasters must adapt to remain competitive. They are right. Dr Abe Peled heads up News Data Systems, the News Corporation-owned company that develops broadcasting technologies, encryption and compression systems. Peled is also acknowledged as one of the industry's foremost thinkers. In January 2000, he described his views on television's digital future. Peled says:

> The biggest factor, I call it the sleeper of technology, is the growth in local storage. When the PC first came out, in the early 1980s, it came with 10 Mb of local storage. Today you would be hard pressed to find anything with less than 2 Gb of storage. That's an improvement factor of 200 times. The modem at that time was about 2400 bps, today the equivalent would be a 28.8 Kbps, another significant growth factor.
> As the prospects for a 10 Gb hard drive becomes interesting, when it is linked to compression and inserted into an STB it can expand the content window. In the UK the content window before Channel 5 and Sky was four, a four channel content window. With cable and Sky analogue, you have a 40 channel content window, more in the USA, perhaps 80 channels. With digital the content window expands to nearer 200. Today's improved compression could give us 400 channels of content without a problem. But if you add 10 Gb into the STB now, costing around $100 in the year 2000, that would add

another 50–80 virtual channels. But go just a little further, and add 100 Gb of hard drive would mean 800 virtual channels. And 100 Gb is suggested for within the next 5 years. So we think the biggest revolution as far as the consumer is concerned will be local storage, which will completely change the paradigm for viewers, which is currently based on time. We ask 'what's on now'. And local storage changes that, and we can start asking 'what would I like to watch'. It is going to be content-driven from your local disk, with maybe 1000 hours of choice, and not necessarily the 200 hours of broadcast channel choice.

Peled predicts viewers will dramatically change not so much what they view but how it is called up for viewing.

You can come home and view *Friends* or *Eastenders*, whether it is on the air or not. Because it will be a content-based paradigm, not a time-based paradigm. Programme schedulers get paid a lot of money to package together an interesting evening of material. They will vanish. And advertisers will need to look again, perhaps even paying us to view their ads. They will either have to be very entertaining or give us a reward, perhaps a prize, for watching them.

Asked whether these developments will change the way programming has traditionally been viewed, Peled is unequivocal.

The reason people want to watch TV is because they like to chat about it the next day around the coffee machine or water-cooler. And that is true, and big events, sports, news stories, and other key programming will still attract viewers. But the fact is that in the USA some 40 per cent of viewers don't bother to watch these big events. They tune away. My answer is 'yes', there will be a some boring people who want to talk about last night's big event. And my TV friends say they are still in the majority. But there will be another group of people who might see it an hour later, or the next day, or the following week. They want the content, not the time.

We began this chapter talking about content, and finished with much the same phrases. Content is king, and will always be king, whether it be a transmitted movie or a web-streamed movie that has been downloaded to our set-top box overnight. However, the concept of sitting down at 8 p.m. in the evening to view a network's prime content is fast dying. We might want to see the show at 7.45 p.m, or 8.15 p.m. – and we will get it. We might want it the next day, or the following week. The broadcaster will give it to us, or else they will go out of business. Whether movie, or news broadcast, or datacast or Internet access, the rule remains that content – in whatever form – is still king.

There is another theory which suggests that broadcasters might have to find another model to attract us to their key programmes. This is one that gets down to the fundamentals of what commercial television is all about: money. It may be that the network will start to pay viewers directly for watching the prime-time 8 p.m. show. They might not actually send us a cheque for what might be a very small amount of cash, but it's quite likely that they'll tempt us with prizes, or money-off coupons, or some other sort of reward that's directly linked to our viewing.

7

Selling digital television

Most marketing directors in entertainment companies feel they are seen as fluff, responsible only for making 'cool stuff'

Viewers and customers are important, but the Number One priority is advertisers

Some channels, they get so desperate for income and open the doors for anything, and then they wonder why advertisers don't come back

Ed Sullivan

It has been estimated that by 2003 there may be a five-fold increase in the number of digital channels available. If one includes web-cast services, the number could be measured in the tens of thousands. The perennial question asked by television marketing executives is: 'How do I differentiate my channel from my competitors?' The answers are complex and varied.

Ed Sullivan, co-founder and president of Pittard Sullivan, is probably the world's leading marketing communications outfit in the entertainment industry. He advises:

In my experience rarely is there an overall [marketing] plan. Our first step is to make that communication activity start inside the company through all the various presidents, vice-presidents and senior departmental staff. It's an organizational process at first. Then it becomes a tactical execution process further down the road.

Some channels have an easier time of it, in particular any niche channel that is clearly defined by its output and audience. For example, Sullivan said it's easy for MTV: 'A new employee on Day One will know exactly what MTV is all about. But someone joining Sky One, or TF-1 or RTL, will have a difficult time because they're the "department store" of TV, offering a bit of everything.' Sullivan says these 'general entertainment' channels, often with an audience for *Oprah* as well as a 'cops' show face immense challenges. 'There are exceptions, and maybe the cops show is delivering the exact demographic you want and that might become your strategy, but it's a tough one to sell to advertisers. How are you going to migrate the female audience for *Oprah* into cops? It's tough.'

Ed Sullivan is uncompromising in who he wants stations to attract:

Viewers and customers are important, but the Number One priority is advertisers. I don't care what anyone says but that's where the money is at. It's also vital that the advertiser is 'on side', besides they will be conducting the exact same process for their brand. Talk to them in terms of your own brand strategy, positioning and demographic targets, because they'll understand all that. It will fit with their own objectives, and in my experience, result in them buying a lot of what you've got, and stations should quit trying to be everything for everybody.

Pittard Sullivan is working with many of Europe's leading broadcasters, and in particular with Thomas Kirch and Pro Sieben Media

AG. 'Pro7 came to us and said they wanted to be seen as more than just a movie service. They already had young demographics in the 18–25 range, and they wanted to widen that envelope to the 18–49 age range, which is the hottest advertising target.'

Pro7 place a great deal of importance in outdoor events. Ed Sullivan states:

Persuading stations to invest heavily in an outdoor event is a challenge. First one needs to know how influential the people are at such an event. There is no such thing today as mass communications. Mass communications equals mass inefficiencies, and 100 000 influential people are worth far more than one million where the bulk of them are not influential.

Cartoon Network is a station that should have no problem identifying its audience, or its audience with it. But that's not always the case, according to Cartoon's Nicky Parkinson, VP-marketing. 'In Italy, for example, we are positioned as a kids' network, but in Holland we have a huge following among 14–18-year-olds.'

Parkinson says Cartoon Network invests heavily in non-traditional marketing, and that outdoor activity allows people to 'touch' the brand.

The more people can experience some element of the brand directly, the greater the chance of success. But you have to weigh up the cost of exposure to the quality of that exposure. We can promote a brand on air very effectively to our existing audience, but taking an event outside reinforces viewer loyalty because we are giving the public another way of experiencing our brand. They want the product, the brand to play a more important part in their lives.

Parkinson also says that an important part of the marketing mix is what she calls 'the goodies'. 'Our premiums, the brand-heavy merchandise, all help our message. But it is no more or less targeted than – say – posters. You might still get massive wastage, but it depends on what those marketing objectives are.'

Parkinson had another aspect to consider: 'In our European markets the challenge is often more about driving distribution, and supporting the platform. The advantage of events is that they're often a place where our distributor can also get a benefit.'

Cartoon Network's 'goodies' are vital, but it is also important to get the overall marketing strategy sold to every member of a station's staff, says Ed Sullivan: 'The problems for most marketing directors in entertainment companies is they feel they are seen as fluff, responsible only for making "cool stuff", and bosses want them only to make more "cool stuff" and most marketing directors know damn well that's not it at all.'

'Strategy is all important'

Sullivan says strategy is all-important, and should be a top priority, with marketing driving everything else the station does: buying programmes, making presentations to ad-buyers, having road-shows and deciding which media to focus on.

> Most often they need someone to come in from the outside to help them focus on this, or else they risk being drowned out by twenty other voices around a board-room table. It's hard, because most people expect the marketing head to talk about marketing, but often we find that general entertainment channels and sometimes also niche services are out there buying programming without a strategy behind it. They are buying for ratings, sometimes with little idea as to overall strategy.

The challenge for Pittard Sullivan at BSkyB was to turn what Ed Sullivan saw as a broadcasting 'sports star' into an all-round entertainment star. Pittard Sullivan completed Sky's new identity this summer, ready for its digital launch, and Elisabeth Murdoch was reportedly well pleased. 'In a multichannel environment, especially in niche programming, it is important to have a clear relationship with your audience,' she says. 'You have to remind people of the emotional value they are getting out of the service.'

Emotion is also running high at ZDTV, a new technology channel from the Ziff-Davies publishing empire which in barely 90 days (it launched 11 May 1999) reached hard distribution in 6 million US homes, and access to another 25 million. Its niche is clear, yet it has to try even harder in today's overcrowded marketplace. Tom Grams, ZDTV's head of world-wide sales: 'Satellite and cable love us because it gives them another genre of programming to offer, that doesn't exist anywhere else.' ZDTV is running a consumer campaign but wants to catch what Grams calls 'that wave of increased collective consciousness where the Internet is concerned'.

One of the ways ZDTV maintained contact with its viewers, and also created a unique point of content with its viewers, was to deliver around 1000 web 'net-cameras', which allows viewers to call in direct to the station as reporters, via their PCs, telling ZDTV what is happening in their neck of the woods. Grams says: 'The net-cams are simply wonderful. It's also a great form of promotion, in fact only days ago we had a TV executive in Australia call us up after he'd seen some of our web-streamed programming and said "Send me your show-reels; I am interested in taking your stuff".'

'Cool, upscale. . .'

There can still be problems, according to Ed Sullivan:

In the US, in Germany and the UK, if you've a young channel, skewing 18–34 year-olds, young people who are cool, upscale and aspirational, then you're not going to have much success selling Mercedes 600 series autos. Yet you can see this sort of ad appear, and the station must wonder if their advertiser has misunderstood the audience. Better to be promoting a smaller, hipper model like the 300. Mercedes are smart, they don't tie Rap music into their 600 series, but they could, on the right channel, with a 300. So it's also matching the channel to fit with the advertisers and then there's no stopping the income, if you can deliver on that. Indeed, more often than not, advertisers will help deliver that audience for you.

Sullivan had clear advice on where to start rebuilding efforts, especially when faced with seven days of schedules:

> If channels can get it right, if only on two nights a week, then they should focus on that, building up from that solid base. On the viewer side the channel has to focus on viewers, too. Rolling out the consistent message to viewers, production companies and everyone involved in the creative process. Remember, your advertisers are your viewers, your viewers are your production companies, and the production companies your advertisers. You have a very influential medium with a huge word of mouth.

'Word of mouth' can almost work miracles, especially amongst youngsters, but stations have to be careful to tailor campaigns to suit the local market. Cartoon Network deploys its furry characters as often as possible, but Nicky Parkinson warns about misjudging the market: 'There's the degree of "cuteness" in the market. For example, the furry characters we send out are hugely popular in Spain, France and Italy, but British kids are a bit more cynical about them. In India and the Middle East those self-same characters generated a enormous response with pictures in the national press.'

Asked how successfully campaigns transfer from one market to another, Parkinson said,

> In general anything that is a good idea IS a good idea. But there can be difficulties. For example, in the US we have 'dive in theatre' where Cartoon Network takes over an outdoor pool and the kids sit around in rubber rings and watch cartoons, eating ice-cream. We product-sampled our new cartoons, including *Dexter's Lab*, and it was a terrific concept. But for Europe, and especially Britain with our fickle weather, it's more of a problem. We had thought of indoor pools, but it doesn't seem to have the same appeal.

Cartoon Network, like MTV or Fox Kids, or even CNN, has a clear idea of its audience and its corporate mission statement would be easily understood by viewers and advertisers alike. But there's one group which is often forgotten – a station's own employees. The message has to be sold to them just as competently. Sullivan comments:

> Most people who just get a pay check every Friday or each month, they find it difficult to relate to a goal like 'we want to increase our rating by 2.5 per cent share this year', or 'we want to put DM300 m more in the bank this year'. They ask us 'How do we do that?' and it's great going into a management meeting and discussing something that is not expressed in vague mission statements but in highly specific marketing goals.

Sullivan says the station should set out to achieve this at every opportunity.

> We do it in our voice, our style, our feel, who we are, how we are going to position this property and how are we uniquely competitive in this marketplace with the assets we have. Everything starts – and it is sometimes eye-opening to senior staff who sometimes have a financial background – with this strategy. People need to know the 'why' as well as the 'how to'. If you want to use that most overused 'B' word, of brand marketing, it's really about become focused on what it means to clients, advertisers, other production companies supplying you, as well as staff and then viewers.

Getting a single channel talked about is hard enough, so what are the challenges that face broadcasters with a bouquet of channels to package and market? Some broadcasting organizations have had difficulties selling their new digital products to viewers, and the past five years have seen clear examples of failed, or failing, products that prove that very real challenges exist:

■ Leo Kirch's DF-1 all-digital platform was re-launched (having absorbed the rival and more successful Premiere platform) as Premiere World in September 1999;

- PrimeStar, AlphaStar and USSB, three American outfits have either failed or been bought out by more successful rivals;
- ART, Orbit/Star Select and Showtime. Four Middle East-based digital platforms, all still exist but with reported massive losses, and in ART and Orbit's cases little likelihood of repaying their investment to their owners;
- Australia's digital experience has been far from successful with millions in losses;
- Italy's experience in digital has been a near-disaster to date;
- in France, AB Sat, which launched as a stand-alone platform, is now little more than a channel provider to the two larger platforms;
- Spain's Via Digital, despite have the active backing of the public broadcaster is struggling to stay afloat.

There are plenty of other examples where pioneers have lost their investors millions. So what is it about digital television that distinguishes it from other electronic service offers to the consumer? There is unfortunately no easy answer to this deceptively simple question. We know there are some key elements that ought to make the sales proposition fairly straightforward:

- programme choices
- instant ordering of PPV services
- interactive or transactional services
- improved picture or sound quality.

Most digital television operators concentrate their marketing message in one or more of these areas. However, the 'mix' will be determined by a complex of different factors, the most important of which are the nature of the competition from rival platforms and – where they already own subscribers – the avoidance of 'cannibalization'.

BSkyB's digital satellite package in the UK provides a good example of the potential dilemmas faced by broadcasters marketing digital television. At the end of 1997 BSkyB had around 6.5 million subscribers in the UK and Eire on analogue DTH and cable, a lucrative franchise which it could ill-afford to abandon. In late 1997 BSkyB's chief executive Mark Booth was reported as believing that BSkyB's analogue subscribers fall into two main groups, and that they are representative of most broadcasters' main target audience: sport-loving males; and females and children, which Booth said BSkyB had neglected.

At the time it seemed Booth's comments suggested that BSkyB's strategy was initially to market digital television to its existing premium subscribers (film and sports enthusiasts); this would be done by emphasizing the appeal of NVOD movies and PPV sports, offers that may be expected to immediately appeal to this group.

BSkyB's second thrust would be to compensate for any loss of premium-channel revenues through cannibalization by expanding the remaining group of analogue subscribers – through emphasizing the attractions of the BSkyB 30-channel basic package at £11.99 per month.

In terms of differentiating its offering from digital cable and digital terrestrial, BSkyB has competitive advantages in each sector: it has exclusive sports to which cable does not have access (and which cable will have to buy wholesale from BSkyB); and it can legitimately argue that its analogue multi-channel package is cheaper to install, cheaper to subscribe to, and offers wider programming choice than digital terrestrial. These factors figured prominently in their subsequent marketing campaigns.

In addition to such competitive considerations, there are also national, cultural factors to be taken into account. In Italy, a country that is more obsessed with football than almost any other European nation, it was natural for Telepiu's digital service to seize on the idea of pay-per-view football matches as the principal consumer driver for its service. Indeed, this perception directly motivated the company's decision to acquire exclusive soccer rights.

In fact, pay-per-view has little or nothing to do with digital television as such, as PPV sports events can be offered on an analogue service (indeed, BSkyB has already done so). In the UK, meanwhile, the BDB digital terrestrial television consortium backed by

Carlton and Granada TV appears (as at mid-1999) to be basing its hopes partly on the potential appeal of drama, on the basis that the most popular programmes on UK television are soaps. Another example can be found in the USA, where DirecTV has actively exploited widespread resentment of cable pricing in order to promote its impulse PPV movie facility.

Generally speaking, outside the USA digital marketers may be wise not to dwell too much on the technology itself, despite the obvious attractions of doing so. As mentioned before, the mass market does not generally buy technology; it buys applications.

An interesting illustration of this phenomenon is provided by the fate of Philip's CD-I format, which attempted to turn the domestic television set into a focus for interactive multimedia in the home. CD-I's problem, essentially, was that it was a technology in search of a Unique Selling Proposition (USP): CD-I players could play audio CDs, films and games and could in principle be used to provide an interactive overlay to television programmes or to order items from a home shopping catalogue on disk when linked to a modem. Consumers, however, were confused by the idea of a convergent, interactive, multimedia platform, and the format is now all but defunct. Significantly, it has had some success in niche sectors, such as karaoke or professional training, where its ability to deliver an improvement with respect to a single application was emphasized.

Moreover, there are particular dangers associated with promoting technology-driven applications that may be difficult to deliver in practice. The most notorious case in recent memory was the Apple Newton, a hand-held personal digital assistant (PDA) which incorporated handwriting recognition software that purported to be able to decipher notes written on its touchpad with a small 'pen'. Put simply, the software didn't work. Newtons became the subject of consumer ridicule, and even though Apple subsequently changed the marketing focus to that of a general communications tool, and solved many of the technological problems, later versions never proved successful. The Newton saga soured the whole market for PDAs for a number of years, and early in 1998, Apple dropped the product-line.

The most tempting application to focus on in the case of digital television is the 'home cinema' experience. In theory, MPEG-2 is capable of delivering a high-quality, wide-screen (16:9) image with CD-quality surround sound. In practice, such is the quality of PAL and SECAM that, outside the USA, the quality improvement over analogue transmissions may be indiscernible; indeed, the quality could actually be worse. Moreover, except in those small (but growing) number of homes with wide-screen television sets and surround-sound equipment, much of this allegedly cinema-like experience will be unavailable (and most television set loud-speakers are not capable of reproducing sound to the level of fidelity present in the MPEG-2 transmission).

Hence, while the promotion to the consumer of such 'technology quality' aspects of digital television might well induce them to buy, the consumer may be disappointed. This may not matter if, after purchase, the consumer finds other potential benefits of digital television to be attractive (for instance, extended programme choice). However, the risk of an Apple Newton scenario cannot be completely discounted, and adopting such a strategy is clearly not without risk.

A marketing strategy based on other technology-led applications, such as impulse ordering and interactive or transactional services, should also be treated warily. Impulse ordering is a concept with which few outside the USA are familiar. It may prove more successful to downplay the impulse-ordering facility and simply tell consumers that they are able to view the movie they want, when they want it, at the touch of a button. (Even then, care needs to be taken not to over-emphasize the immediacy or range of the available experience, as the best any digital television service can offer to date is 15-minute start-times, and this generally only covers the top 20 or so titles.) For sports pay-per-view, again the point is not the technology; it is the ability to watch one particular game from within a range of simultaneous choices.

A similar caution must be expressed about interactive and transactional services. The one-way point-to-multipoint infrastructures used by most digital television operators will prevent them from offering advanced interactive services for the foreseeable future, and the provision of 'turbo-Internet' access, in particular, is fraught with danger, as the experience of DirecPC (DirecTV's Internet access service) has demonstrated. DirecPC's customers have complained that they are frequently unable to access the Internet at the advertised speeds (400 Kbps in the case of the fastest package), with some claiming access speeds are on occasion around a tenth of what they thought they were purchasing. Even though the technology may eventually be fixed, the initial word-of-mouth damage is often enough to condemn a perfectly decent product to the technological scrap-heap.

Transactional services such as home shopping require an extensive and effective fulfilment infrastructure to ensure that the right product at the right price reaches the right purchaser at the right time. It only takes one delivery going wrong for consumers new to this type of experience (and not everyone is used to shopping from catalogues) to decide not to use the service again.

Marketers have to be very certain that the new digital technology can deliver what they promise before they choose to promote their digital television offering on the basis of technology-dependent applications. The implication is that digital television operators should, rather, concentrate on the relatively low-risk strategy of emphasizing programme exclusivity and range. Here broadcasters know what programming rights they have and should be reasonably certain they can deliver. No-one can dispute that they are able to offer a greater choice of channels than are available on analogue systems, nor, where they have spent large sums on acquiring exclusive film and sports rights, that they have programming to show which is unavailable elsewhere.

This is certainly the approach adopted by Canal+, which gained over 850 000 subscribers to its digital satellite service after less than two years in operation. Although it possesses what is one of the most technologically sophisticated digital television packages in the world, its technical director, Henri Joubaud, in August 1999 explained that Canal+ chose to adopt what he described as a 'broadcasters' approach' for its digital platform. 'The prime concern,' he stated 'was to come up with a strong programming mix offering real choice and diversity from day one'.

On balance, digital television's 'unique selling proposition' (USP) must relate to television: more of it, packaged and made available in different ways, rather than any advanced applications, otherwise there is a substantial risk of incurring consumer disappointment.

There is, it should be noted, a countervailing argument to this proposition, based on the fact that the consumer market is segmented into a number of different categories, some of which are technophiles who will buy new products just because they are new. According to this line of reasoning, this segment of the population is much less sensitive to technological under-performance. Traditionally, one can divide electronic product purchasers into five groups.

- **Innovators**: keen to experiment and untroubled by perceptions of risk, they often act as trend-setters (in well-accepted studies they make up 2.5 per cent of the eventual total of purchasers).
- **Early adopters**: not as impulsive as innovators, they are often opinion leaders (13.5 per cent of the eventual total of purchasers).
- **Early majority**: cautious buyers who take time to make up their mind, they may be influenced by early adopters (34.0 per cent of the eventual total of purchasers).
- **Late majority**: sceptical about new products, they will only purchase when they perceive there is general acceptance of a particular product innovation by the rest of the population (34.0 per cent of the eventual total of purchasers).
- **Laggards**: suspicious of anything new, they are traditionalists who oppose new products on principle (16.0 per cent of the eventual total of purchasers).

A historical analysis of take-up rates for launches of new consumer electronics, such as colour television and VCR, shows that, although the categories overlap somewhat, it takes around three years for the innovators to be 'converted', around five or six for the early adopters, around 10 years for the early majority, and around 15 years for the late majority and laggards.

If this analysis can be applied to digital television (which is far from certain, as the accelerating pace of technological change may have compressed this sequence), it suggests that the risk of emphasizing technology-driven aspects of digital television in the early years of its introduction may not be quite as acute as has been suggested above, since it is mainly the innovators who are making the purchase. By the time early adopters and the early majority come to invest, many of the technological wrinkles will have been ironed out. However, the crucial group is the early adopters, who are opinion-formers. If they are disappointed, their disappointment is likely to 'cascade' through the population, which is exactly what happened with the Apple Newton.

Tier system

In the analogue domain, pay-TV packages have traditionally been structured into two tiers: basic and premium. Access to the premium tier was only possible if the subscriber was already paying for the basic tier. There were sound business reasons for this prac- tice: premium programming, such as exclusive films and sports, is much more expensive for the operator to buy than the general entertainment or re-transmitted terrestrial channels that make up most basic offerings, which are often made available on a non- exclusive basis. The margin on premium programming is therefore generally much lower, if not actually loss-making. Because of the relative cheapness to the operator of the content of the basic tier, therefore, such tiers are potentially much more profitable. The problem is that the content in the basic tier is not particularly attractive to consumers; they can frequently obtain it (or some of it) from another source.

The solution reached was to entice consumers to subscribe by emphasizing the attractions of the premium programming, but force them to 'buy through' basic in order to get it. Basic tiers, in general, were charged at more than they cost the operator, and premium tiers at less, usually being positioned as an 'incre- ment' on top of the basic price. This meant that, paradoxically, pay-TV operators have tended to make most of their money on basic.

The tiered buy-through model is of benefit to the programme supplier, too. If every one of a platform operator's subscribers takes the programming in the basic tier, then the supplier of a basic tier channel knows what its reach is: and can sell this reach on to advertisers. This provides a much clearer basis for negotiations than a situation in which both sides have to guess what the take-up of a new channel might be.

Despite these advantages, the classical two-tier structure has been undergoing a metamorphosis in recent years, as pay-TV operators seek to expand penetration to wider reaches of the population (in terms of the demographic model outlined on page 187) by encompassing the 'early majority' and 'late majority' segments. This has led to the introduction of lower-priced 'mini-basic' tiers, to 'thematic' tiers, and to 'big basic' and 'extended basic' tiers. The thinking is that by offering a greater and more flexible variety of packages, consumers who are put off, either by the price or by having to purchase 'bundles' of channels, many of which they are not interested in, will be more prepared to subscribe.

A mature example of this development at work is DirecTV's complex subscription offering, which allows the service to be configured in many different ways for many different prices. Currently, the greatest degree of experimentation in this area is taking place within the UK cable market, where penetration levels have remained stubbornly low, generally at below 30 per cent.

UK cable's pricing structure is representative of what the industry generally tends to provide. There is usually a low-priced tier, together with a set of thematic tiers. Would-be cable subscribers might get a mini (or sub-) basic tier which, in addition to telephone rental, offers the terrestrial channels plus at most five or six channels as an entry level. Subscribers can then choose from any three or four thematic packages for an additional payment and then add any of Sky's premium film and sports channels as they see fit.

If it is true that the more flexibility the operator allows the consumer, the more that market penetration can be extended, then, in theory, the more revenue can be obtained. However, even if there is a net effect on penetration levels, the net effect on revenues remains in question. Just as new subscribers can be attracted by low entry-levels, existing subscribers may be enticed to trade down to obtain only those channels they want. The net effect, then, could be neutral or possibly even negative.

Taken to its logical conclusion, the 'flexible' multi-tier model eventually turns into the 'à la carte' model.

'À la carte' model

At the other end of the marketing spectrum from the tiered system is the 'à la carte' model. Although it exists on some modern analogue cable systems, it is much rarer in territories with mature, low-capacity networks. The idea inherent in 'à la carte' is that the viewer is free to choose any mix of basic and premium channels required, and is charged accordingly. This concept extends into pay-per-view, where the viewer chooses and pays for individual programmes rather than channels, and has its ultimate expression in the video-on-demand concept, where, effectively, there is really no such thing as a channel at all.

One reason why à la carte offerings have been held back is a technological one. In many cable systems, the 'basic' offering is transmitted 'in the clear' down the cable system to the home: the set-top-box supplied to the cable subscriber as part of his subscription simply 'converts' the signals from the cable frequency to the one used by the television set (one reason why cable set-top boxes are still often referred to as 'converters'). The premium channels are the only ones that are scrambled. For true à la carte facilities to be offered, every channel would need to be scrambled, and the software in the home and at the cable head-end would jointly have to be capable of unscrambling only those channels that the subscriber had requested. This entails a set-up termed 'addressability': the ability of the service-provider to identify a particular box at the other end of the cable network, and configure its service accordingly.

À la carte causes other complications from a business point of view. First, from the point of view of the pay-TV operator, billing is much more complicated and requires much more sophisticated back-office software. Second, and rather more significantly, a true à la carte offering disables 'buy-through'. If a subscriber is free to take any mix of channels desired, he or she can elect just to take the premium channels (and therefore, for the operator, the less profitable ones), reducing the pay-TV operator's margins.

The à la carte model is arguably problematic for the channel provider, too. First, it involves increased risk. At the point where a deal is being negotiated with a pay-TV operator, the channel provider cannot know in advance precisely how many subscribers will be opting to take his service. He thus has to take an educated guess, based on his own knowledge and what the pay-TV operator tells him, as to what the likely subscription and advertising revenue potential will be, and negotiate a price on that basis. When negotiating for inclusion in the basic tier, matters are much more straightforward.

When the time comes for re-negotiation, however, the problem becomes transparency, rather than opacity. By then, each side will know exactly how many subscribers chose to include the channel in their à la carte choice. This knowledge is much more difficult to obtain when a channel is sold into basic, since the only gauge of viewing preferences within the basic tier is audience research, which is often inaccurate for small niche channels, and sometimes inapplicable (where a channel provider cannot afford to pay to be included in the television research panel).

While transparency is an advantage for channels which are popular, giving them increased leverage in contract negotiations, it disadvantages minority ones, and may even make them economically unviable. In a tiered system, basic channels not only subsidize the premium ones, but also each other: the strong channels carry the weak ones. In an à la carte system, weak performance is exposed, and the tendency is for revenue to flow away from the least popular channels towards the most popular ones. In a way, à la carte – a system whose flexibility seems to work entirely in the consumer's favour – could be seen as undermining the very diversity of choice that might make a consumer opt for a digital multi-channel offering in the first place.

Pay-per-view, and true on-demand television, take this tendency to its logical conclusion. An example of the phenomenon at work is provided by the experience of pay-per-view football in Italy. According to Telepiu, the three top clubs (Juventus, Internazionale and AC Milan) were responsible for around 80 per cent of the subscriptions to its Telecalcio pay-per-view package (*Financial Times,* 10 March 1997). This package offers a season ticket to the away matches of Serie A and B teams to those living within the team's home area, and the entire schedule to those living elsewhere.

The economic risks of such a system were highlighted when Telepiu's marketing boss at the time said the number of people paying to view some of the less important matches meant 'it would have been cheaper for us to take them individually by helicopter to ground to watch the match'.

Economic logic would dictate (and some of the top clubs have been implying) that the lion's share of the money that Telepiu pays in rights to Italian football should go to the three top teams, and that those clubs with few or no subscribers should not have any of their games broadcast on Telecalcio. In the words of Luigi Predeval, general manager of FC Internazionale, speaking at a time when the revenue concentration effect was not quite so marked, 'Inter, Juventus and AC Milan fans provide 64 per cent of subscriptions for pay-per-view but don't get 64 per cent of viewing rights' (*Financial Times*, 23 November 1996).

Contrast this with the situation that existed before, where every subscriber to the Telepiu football channel would have been able to see every match shown, whether involving the top clubs or the lesser ones. In such a situation, soccer fans end up watching club matches they might not opt to watch in a 'free-choice' environment, simply because 'that's what's on'. It is arguable that in such an 'opaque' environment, pay-TV sports rights will actually be worth more overall to the clubs than they will be in a 'transparent' pay-per-view one.

Despite these difficulties, there is no doubt that the trend is currently away from rigid tiers towards a much more fluid situation, with à la carte facilities, including pay-per-view, being offered alongside tiers. Digital television offers a strong imperative for this, since as channel choice multiplies and the potential for ever more complex tiering arrangements increases, the digital offerings will become increasingly confusing to new entrants, and increasingly difficult to market. The advent of the Electronic Programme Guide (see below), which forces programme-based rather than channel-based choices on viewers, will also help to speed this trend, but regulatory pressure will do more to promote this development than anything else. Athough this issue is dealt with at greater length in Chapter 9, the impulse for this pressure comes from the fact that regulators, rightly or wrongly, regard it as 'unfair' for consumers to be forced to purchase channels they do not want to watch. A recent statement from the UK's Independent Television Commission (Independent Television Commission, 1998) epitomizes this approach. Concluding that 'channel bundling' in the retail pay-TV market entailed a number of anti-competitive practices, it proposed:

- the prohibition of minimum carriage requirements and tiering obligations by programme providers, which, it stated, would enable satellite and cable operators to offer basic channels either à la carte, or in mini-basic or 'big basic' packages;
- a measure allowing consumers to buy through to premium channels from any basic package;
- making bundling of more than one premium channel (excluding bonus channels) permissible only where the channels were also available à la carte.

All of the above regulatory measures would impose greater tiering and à la carte flexibility on pay-TV operators, whether they wanted it or not. In the UK, this measure would prevent BSkyB's digital service from offering NVOD only to premium film channel subscribers; BSkyB would have to offer the facility to any basic subscriber. In other territories where pay-per-view is available, this has now become accepted practice, whether for regulatory reasons or otherwise. This development has significant implications for the continued viability of premium programming tiers. Consumers, particularly those with low video consumption habits, may be reluctant to pay for a movie channel when they can purchase occasional films on a one-off basis. With sports, meanwhile, the ability to show a live event and make people pay for it implies that that same event has to be withdrawn from the schedules of the premium sports channel – or at least shown at a later time.

Channel or service branding

It is axiomatic that, as the number of television channels increases, it becomes successively more and more difficult for each additional channel to establish its 'share of voice' or 'shelf space'. The web provides a ready illustration of this phenomenon: faced with a near-infinite number of sites to access, Internet users navigate in three principal ways:

- they instantly 'jump' to sites with which they are already familiar;
- they use a navigation service;
- they start with the default site set on their browser.

One of the reasons UK digital television operators such as BSkyB and ONdigital have been courting the BBC is precisely because it has one of the world's best-recognized programming brands. In an environment where much of the programming is characterized by low production values and where programme costs are being driven inexorably downwards, being able to be associated with a high-profile, high-quality programming brand is clearly an enormous advantage, and will help to drive consumer choice to the extent that it is programming-directed.

It is possible that these brands may not need to be television-related ones. In a sector where sponsorship is increasingly being used to bridge the gap between programme budgets and commissioning fees, non-TV brands such as Coca-Cola or Levi may be used to enhance recognition. Indeed, the phenomenon of 'disintermediation', through which product manufacturers bypass the middleman to address their preferred customers directly, suggests that well-recognized brands such as these are able to rise above the prevailing level of 'noise' in a digital universe, to a point where they may well become programme-makers themselves (regulations permitting).

As the importance of brand allows advertisers to become programmers, it is equally likely that programmers will be forced to behave more and more like advertisers. In the words of a senior executive at Discovery Networks Europe, taking a direct analogy with the supermarket, the challenge is for every channel to justify its place 'on the shelves'. He believes that if conventional television companies are to survive, 'they have got to stop seeing themselves as TV brands but more as brands that happen to be in the business of TV'.

It is probably also true that the advent of digital television will see the branding of individual programmes becoming more important than the branding of individual channels or broadcasters. Much depends on how electronic programme guides (EPGs) are configured. If choices are grouped by broadcaster or programmer ('click here to choose from the BBC bouquet'), this matters less; but if grouped by theme ('click here to go to the comedy zone'), then programme brands become much more important. In a true video-on-demand environment, 'channels' as such disappear altogether, and, once the consumer has chosen a genre, programme brand is everything.

The second category of the web analogy list (jumping to the navigation site) can be likened to the electronic programme guide, clearly now a ubiquitous feature of digital television platforms. Time and technology will tell whether digital set-top boxes will eventually contain a multiplicity of different electronic programme guides – one per 'bouquet'. Should this prove to be the case, the EPG itself will not be the reason for consumers purchasing a particular digital television service. However, once the consumer decides to subscribe, it may well determine which channels he decides to tune into, or which programmes to buy. Thus, consumer awareness of the EPG, which is likely to be promoted by being associated with a particular service-provider, will be critical, as will how these EPGs are used within services to market particular choices to consumers.

The third web analogy category – the correspondence with default browser settings – is clearly akin to the case where only one electronic programme guide exists: in this case, the fight is not so much to achieve brand-recognition for the electronic programme guide, which is 'default', but for the channels and programmes positioned within it.

Drawing on the two latter analogy categories, the key issues for the marketer are therefore exposure and sign-posting, both of which are dealt with in the section on electronic programme guides below. At this stage it is sufficient to say that brand will become more important in determining the success of competing pay-TV packages in a digital television environment, rather than less. If the comment from Discovery Networks is correct, this would also imply that the roles of advertiser and programmer, which were formerly quite distinct, will increasingly overlap, with the dividing-line between the two becoming increasingly blurred.

Pricing

Vital to the success of digital television is the perception of value-for-money. For instance, some companies prefer the Canal+ set-top box rental model, in which the subscription includes a hidden price for the set-top box, to one involving an up-front purchase, even if the total year-one cost is actually more. When considering the price being requested for a particular option, they will weigh up what they are already paying for entertainment, and whether the extra expenditure is justified by such benefits (real or imagined) as enhanced picture and sound quality, improved programme choice, exclusivity of access to premium material, inter-activity and so on.

Other broadcasters have decided to give the box away, modifying the highly successful cellular telephone business model, which assumes a low-cost of entry and subsequent annual subscription. BSkyB has adopted this model, and since May 1999 has given the set-top box away 'free' in return for a one-year payment. Thereafter the box can be kept by the viewer. The rival ONdigital model is different, where the box is given away 'free', again in return for an annual payment, but must be returned if the subscription lapses. In reality, the box is loaned to the viewer and the set-top box remains an asset of the broadcaster.

Promotions

Special promotions historically have had a central role to play in encouraging the take-up of pay-TV, and this is likely to remain true in the digital television domain, especially when the entry-price remains high. During 1997–8, in response to an apparent plateauing of its analogue subscriber base, BSkyB was offering a new stereo satellite system for £49.99, a saving of around £50. This included installation, but was only available when the customer agreed to subscribe to all the Sky channels for 12 months (at that time £29.99 per month), and pay a one-off connection charge of £12. At the same time, in the USA, EchoStar was running a promotion in which, if an existing cable subscriber bought a digital satellite system before a key date and mailed in their last cable bill, the subscriber received a US$40–60 credit against their first EchoStar bill.

What generally characterizes such promotions is some sort of hardware discount in exchange for a commitment to an upfront subscription. There are parallels here with the mobile phone business, where cellular phones are effectively given away in exchange for the consumer agreeing to a lengthy contract with high billing-rates. This is, in effect, the so-called 'Gillette' marketing model: the razor itself is the loss-leader, with the money made on a continuing requirement for razor blades that will only fit that particular razor.

This model has been deployed to great effect in the games console business, where hardware devices which have processing-power equivalent to high-end PCs are heavily subsidized in order to tie in the buyer to proprietary, high-priced games software. The digital television industry has not yet reached the stage where the equipment is given away, but as Moore's Law (which states that memory chip performance doubles every 18 to 24 months) and mass-production together continue to bring down the price of processing-power and memory storage, the free-of-charge business model becomes more affordable, especially with sub-US$100 set-top boxes. Giving away US$100 in order to win a subscription income of US$300–400 is good business, especially in the second and subsequent years.

The hardware give-away model should, however, not be confused with the Canal+ rental model. In the type of promotion being discussed here, the hardware belongs to the subscriber. In the Canal+ model, the pay-TV operator continues to own it. The exigencies of the rental model have compelled Canal+ to develop other forms of promotion which are not hardware-dependent.

In Spain, it has had particular success through a marketing campaign launched in September 1997, where existing subscribers to its analogue Canal+ service were offered a free subscription to the Canal Satelite digital basic tier until August 1998. According to Canal+, this led to a 'significant increase' in the proportion of digital subscribers, which by year-end accounted for nearly 20 per cent of its subscriber portfolio. By the end of 1997, just over half a million subscribers had signed up for the Canal Satelite digital package, 51 per cent of whom had been supplied with a digital set-top box.

In France, Belgium and Poland, Canal+ has also experienced some success with what it describes as a 'cash-and-carry' subscription process, in which visitors to hypermarkets or shopping centres can sign up for the service on the spot. In Belgium, this was said to have accounted for 20 per cent of new subscribers in the final months of 1997. In Poland, this was supplemented by efforts to enhance customer loyalty and improve service, such as a commitment to 24-hour set-top box delivery and the ability to sign up for subscriptions via the Internet. Canal+ says that these promotional efforts together resulted in a 45 per cent increase in Polish subscriber recruitment for 1997.

In 1999 ONdigital in the UK placed large numbers of its set-top boxes in supermarkets with a ticket price of £119 to include 'the box, and a one-year subscription' to ONdigital's basic tier of channels.

What is critical to the success of such promotions is their visibility. Ownership of a pre-existing mass-market window, whether on television, radio or in the press, is crucial, as is ownership of a pre-existing customer base. A large measure of BSkyB's success in the analogue market can be traced to the fact that it was strongly cross-promoted (and continues to be in the digital era) in the News International stable of newspapers which News Corporation controls. News Corporation holds a 40 per cent stake in BSkyB.

Canal+'s success in managing the transition to digital has also been based on the existing terrestrial window it enjoys in the analogue pay-TV market, and its exclusive ownership of French pay-TV customers. The Canal+ premium channel had nearly 600 000 digital subscribers at the end of 1997, an increase of some 380 000, yet during the year the total number of Canal+ subscribers (analogue and digital) increased by only 103 000 (figures taken from Canal+ report and accounts of 1998). This suggests that most digital subscribers to the channel were former analogue subscribers, rather than new digital ones. Much the same argument applies to BSkyB, which with its digital product is clearly converting plenty of its former analogue subscribers, but not so many new entrants.

The Electronic Programme Guide (EPG)

In a digital television environment, Electronic Programme Guides (EPGs) are essential. Without an EPG, it is very difficult for broadcasters to attract viewers to their channels and almost impossible for viewers to access the channel they want to view out of the hundreds of channels available. Although the consumer's purchase of a digital decoder is unlikely to have been driven by the navigation system, he or she will very quickly find that zapping or teletext is quite inadequate to navigate within digital packages, especially once exposed to advanced interactive services.

The EPG's strategic role is primarily to act as the main gateway to multi-channel bouquets (packages of services). For the consumer, the EPG is the answer to the questions: 'Where am I?' and 'Where should I go?'. For the service provider, the EPG is the answer to the question: 'How do I tell them about my service?'. For the platform provider, the EPG answers the question: 'How do I gain and keep my customers?'.

In most EPGs across the world, the design is a 'menu-driven' system. There is usually one main entry screen providing all the options in the full bouquet, followed by layers of sub-menu screens providing access to the option selected in the higher-level screens.

For broadcasters, bouquet and platform providers, the EPG offers a wide range of marketing opportunities. The various screens at different levels of the EPG offer ideal locations for logo, caption and corporate design, as well as marketing and promotional messages.

On each of these screens there is a marketing opportunity. The main entry screen is clearly the place that the platform provider will use most. Here is the ideal location for logo, caption, corporate colours, corporate design, fonts and symbols. Since this is the first 'face' of the EPG, it is also the ideal area for marketing and promotional messages. For instance, a specific area on the screen can be updated regularly with fresh and relevant messages.

As the user moves into the lower, deeper levels of the menu structure, he or she will use more service provider-related information and thus these pages or screens should not be taken up by the platform provider's marketing messages. This space is potentially ideal for the service provider to use for its own marketing purposes. The service provider, like the platform provider, can also use the EPG screens to display logos, use its brand colours, and use allocated areas in the EPG screen for marketing and promotional messages. For example, where there is a list of channels or services to select from, the channel and service logo can be used. Once the consumer reaches the screen for that channel's information, the background of the screen can be changed to that of the service provider's house-style.

The area on the screen allocated for marketing and promotional messages can also be used for cross-promotion of all services offered by a service provider. For example, a service provider could choose to promote a prominent event or new service within its total product range. However, it is worth noting that the cross-promotion of different services by a service provider and the manner in which this is effected in the EPG is likely to be subject to close scrutiny by regulators in certain markets and is almost certainly going to lead to commercial disputes between different service providers and the platform provider.

Currently (2000), most EPGs carry the services of one bouquet, even though the bouquet may contain many channels. In the near future, EPGs are likely to become more and more the gateway to multiple bouquets – packages of multiple channels offered by different bouquet providers. The consumer will then be presented with a choice between different bouquets and will have to decide whether to subscribe to all or to some only, selecting his own combination. Two terms are particularly relevant to this discussion: position and positioning.

- The position of a service means the 'ranking order' of the service within a list of options. Positioning, therefore, means the way in which a service provider markets or promotes itself, its products or services; the brand image it projects; the qualities and concepts it is associated with; the expectations created in the market about what and who it is.
- In the case of a single bouquet, the actual position of a service or a channel is very important, since it can easily get lost among the multitude of service or channel options available.

When EPGs become the gateway to more than one bouquet, with different packages offered by different service providers, then the positioning of the bouquet becomes the important issue, since now it is the bouquet which can become lost among the other bouquet options.

In the EPG both these issues are very important to the individual service provider, since both can work favourably or unfavourably for him.

Position and positioning are also very controversial issues, not only in the EPG business but in the digital television business as a whole. It is proposed that every service, bouquet or platform provider should have an equal opportunity for promotion and receive the same amount of prominence in the EPG. However, some service, bouquet or platform providers may want to be 'more equal than others'.

Take the case of a digital television channel. Why is its position so important? The answer is that in a multi-channel bouquet the consumer has a very wide choice, one that will grow wider over time. There is a battle for eyeballs. How can a broadcaster attract more viewers to his channel? As already argued in previous sections of this chapter, to be attracted, viewers have to know about your channel and find your brand image and service information appealing.

It is important to underline that the EPG is not used like a channel. If a channel can be compared to a destination, the EPG is the route that takes the consumer to that destination. The consumer will not spend a long time within an EPG; it will be used to make a quick decision on what to watch or as confirmation that the right choice was made. Then the consumer quickly moves out of the EPG and back to channel viewing again. The opportunity for making an impression and drawing viewers to your channel or programme are therefore limited and of short duration. First impressions are critical!

Every channel wants to be at the top of the position list when there is a selection to be made, or on a ranking position which matches their station identity: for instance, Channel 4 wants to be at position four in the list but RTL4 wants to be on position four as well. This is obviously not possible, so the EPG operator has to make a decision based on other factors: for instance, whether the preferential position should be available at a premium charge, whether channels can be rotated between preferential positions, or whether to adopt a random allocation procedure of 'first signed up, first served'.

Should channels become treated equally in this way, it will be even more important for a channel or service to increase its prominence on the EPG screen to maximize its positioning. EPG operators will have to ensure additional marketing and promotional space on the screen is available for channels and services.

For the consumer the EPG not only leads the way to a pre-defined destination on a pre-planned route, but it can provide new and interesting routes with information about the path being travelled, enticing the traveller to try alternative routes and gain new experiences. In the digital television world, the use of the EPG is not only essential it is also enjoyable in its own right.

Initially a digital decoder user may be content to use the EPG to gain programme listings information. The user is then likely to take advantage of the opportunity offered to find a particular programme or channel by genre. Gradually the consumer may use the EPG in a similar way to the web by simply exploring possibilities or options as an enjoyable experience in its own right. Ultimately the EPG may be enhanced to alter fundamentally the way the consumer selects television programmes by means of user recording and scheduling.

Future developments

The EPG is likely to develop in a number of areas, which will have additional implications for the marketing of digital television and consumer benefit. The key development is a move to user behaviour recording and scheduling, whereby data representing viewer behaviour is captured and stored over a period of time and then analysed to determine whether there is a pattern or model which can be used for forecasting future viewing preferences. One absolute precondition is that the service should only be made available with the very definite consent of the viewer.

The requirements include specific software which can interface with the EPG application, a minimum definition of viewing and household member identification enablement. Given the memory constraints in the decoder, the data would be sent back by means of a modem to a central database where all viewing data would be recorded and analysed. It would then be sent back, stored in the decoder and would interface with the EPG data as it is being broadcast. The on-screen application would check whether the user wished to have any recommendations 'pushed' at him and if so how these recommendations should be implemented: display or video-recording.

Would fluctuating human moods and preferences make it difficult to derive a statistically reliable forecast? Would the primary use be for immediate viewing or for planning future viewing? Would audience measurement agencies and the broadcasters that fund them wish to help finance such an application? Whatever the answer to such questions, there are, regulations permitting, rich marketing opportunities to be reaped from the advanced EPG. In fact, the model adopted in the UK by Open. . . (the interactive service backed by British Telecom and others, which markets itself as Open. . ., but is controlled by British Interactive Broadcasting Ltd, BIB) depends heavily on the ownership of subscriber data for marketing purposes. The idea is that Open. . . will sell access to its subscribers to retailers and advertisers on the basis of being able to tell them precisely which programmes they prefer, and even which advertisements they watch. This would then provide the springboard for one-to-one marketing.

The advantage for the advertiser or retailer is that they target their promotional and marketing messages very precisely. The advantage for BIB is that it is able to charge a premium for such a service, and also use such data to its own advantage, either to help it fine-tune its own programming and promotions, or to sell on additional programme-related merchandise.

An obvious example would be, for instance, where Open. . . knew which PPV films a particular subscriber had recently watched, so that they could market the sell-through copy of those films (or films like them) at a discount. Alternatively, BIB could alert the viewer to appropriate upcoming pay-per-view events or films and offer discounts on these. Such promotions could be pro-active; as soon as the subscriber logged on, there could be a message flashing on the EPG screen.

Though the EPG, as the recorder of viewing choices, is theoretically an extremely powerful marketing tool, relatively few companies, even where they do own such information, make use of it particularly effectively for one-to-one marketing purposes. This is a discipline still in its infancy, as demonstrated by a survey carried out in Germany and published in March 1998. Commissioned by Gemini Consulting (a unit of Cap Gemini Group), Computer Zeitung (a German IT journal) and the University of Freiburg, the study found that only 28 per cent of companies surveyed used their own customer data to produce more targeted marketing; moreover, 55 per cent were unaware of the potential benefits such an approach could bring to their businesses. Clearly, it is one thing to own the data, quite another to know how to use them effectively.

Can the EPG help sell digital television?

Is it only *after* the purchase of a digital decoder that the EPG plays a marketing role? Is the EPG simply a means of enhancing the purchaser's experience of digital television once he or she starts to use the digital decoder? In markets such as the UK, where a digital broadcaster is seeking both to upgrade its existing analogue installed base and to attract consumers who have had no experience of multichannel television, which group might be most influenced by the benefits of the EPG? These questions are more complex than they may appear at first sight and require analysis.

Consumers who have no experience of digital television are most unlikely to understand or appreciate the nature of or benefits from an EPG. Many may have experience of Teletext programme guides; those with experience of analogue multichannel television may have used full channel programme guides offered on cable systems such as Channel Guide in the UK or TV Vandaag in The Netherlands. However, these guides function simply as electronic listings, alternatives to printed programme guides. In the digital television arena, the EPG is much more than this: it is a navigator and it is in this full functionality, as a marketing tool, and, from the consumer's point of view, its convenience, that its power lies.

Can navigation be promoted as a potential consumer experience that could influence a consumer to purchase digital television? There are two reasons to believe this may be the case.

First, where digital decoders are offered for sale in retail outlets, the retailer will seek to differentiate this new product, not simply by using the digital broadcaster's point of sale promotional material but also by linking digital decoders to ordinary television sets to provide a display of one or more digital television channels. The problem is that such channels are likely to appear to potential purchasers as identical to analogue television channels. One option is for the retailer to simply switch on the decoder and television set and allow the screen to show the EPG with its range of different options.

Digital broadcasters may even create a retail digital channel that demonstrates via the EPG the range and depth of the digital package. Promotional videos using the EPG as the central theme to a presentation of the appeal of the digital package could also be used. Once digital television receivers are manufactured in volume and reach the high street outlets, then apart from picture quality (always a difficult feature to convincingly demonstrate in a shop crowded with other electronic products and with television sets wired to a communal antenna) it will be the EPG that will make the most differentiating visual impression.

Second, it is clear that many purchasers of new products – excluding innovators and perhaps early adopters – often consult friends or colleagues before making a final purchase decision. With an electronic product the simplest method is to visit another household and examine the product or how it is used. Just as in the retail context, the feature of a digital television installation that is likely to make the most lasting visual impression is likely to be the EPG.

Can the presence of the EPG in the electronics retailer, or the neighbouring household, visited by a potential purchaser, contribute significantly to a positive purchase decision? If it is concluded that it is the range and depth of digital packages that will be the key driver to the uptake of digital television, then there is every reason to believe the EPG can be the most efficient medium to demonstrate this. Additionally, if the web-surfing paradigm has a strong appeal to a particular demographic group (the 16–34 age group for instance) then the EPG can function as a familiar indicator of the potential of surfing or navigating in the television field.

As argued earlier, digital television is, and will continue to be, principally a point-to-multipoint technology. However, as the hybridization of television and online progresses through the provision of increasingly sophisticated set-top boxes with integrated modems, obvious marketing opportunities arise which are not dependent on conventional banner or display advertising.

The possibilities here do not greatly differ from those offered by the EPG, but there are some aspects that need to be drawn out. First, EPGs are proprietary; the web is not. Second, the degree of interactive communication afforded by the web is currently much greater than that offered by a typical EPG. Early digital television boxes, particularly those developed for the mass-consumer market, are not generally fully Internet-capable (although there have been a rash of analogue PC/TV hybrids at the high end of the market which purport to be). E-mail and 'chat' facilities on EPGs are either not available or difficult (both requiring the purchase of an additional keyboard), or what is being offered is not the 'open' web, but a subset of it which is more or less difficult to opt out of.

These aspects of the web have advantages and disadvantages in marketing terms. From a marketing point of view, it is in fact preferable for the EPG to be a proprietary, closed environment, since the audience remains captive within it. If there is 'entertainment' of one kind or another available out on the web, and the EPG links seamlessly to it, then the audience can 'leak' away from the digital television environment, at least in principle; and as argued elsewhere, just as the domestic television set may not be the ideal environment for viewing web-based entertainment, the web may not be the ideal environment for offering TV-like programming based on linear video.

There is evidence to suggest that such 'leakage' is a real possibility. PricewaterhouseCoopers, in a consumer technology survey published in June 1997, found that one third of respondents admitted they substituted television viewing for Internet usage. In another major survey published in April/May 1997, 35 per cent of respondents reported that the web had replaced television daily and 27 per cent stated it had done so at least once a week.

The possibility of substitution taking place where there is a seamless link from television to web (i.e. where a television set-top box offers web access) is, presumably, much greater. This means that the opportunities available for the digital television operator to promote the service and market its features to its own subscribers are correspondingly lessened. In a way, this is an extension of the problem of fragmentation in a multichannel audience. In this situation, the web creates another universe of 'channels' which the viewer can be drawn into, inevitably eroding the 'viewing-time' – and therefore, the marketing opportunity – allocatable to each individual channel, including that of the digital television operator.

The advantage of true web functionality, on the other hand, is that it makes it possible for digital television operators to enter into a dialogue with their audiences (and potential audiences) which is not possible when operating in the traditional one-to-many broadcast mode. A good example of this is Fox Home Entertainment's *The X-Files* web site, where fans can register their interests, enter competitions, order videos and other series-related merchandise, look up plot details and information about the main actors, and even download clips from the series.

The purpose of the site is two-fold: it creates and reinforces a 'community' of interest around *The X-Files* series, and drives users back to the video material, whether on television or otherwise. In an ideal world, this becomes a virtual cycle: *The X-Files* fans use the web site to expand the ingredients of their interest, have an upcoming series or episode promoted to them, watch the episode, and then bounce back to the site. Other reinforcing mechanisms can be added in, such as being able to e-mail the actors, to 'chat' with other fans about the latest episode, and so on.

The creation of such a cycle is obviously vital if the audience is not to 'leak' away in the way described. If such a cycle can be created, then the marketer can derive all the benefits of the web experience (one-to-one interactivity, marketing and communications), without any of the disadvantages. But it is a delicate balancing act, for the TV-to-web part of the cycle is so powerful a conduit that it is in danger of becoming a one-way street for the viewer.

A recent study, for instance, found that the percentage of web users who discovered 'new' web pages through promotion of the URLs (Uniform Resource Locator, or web site address) on television is rising, to 38 per cent at the end of 1998. This finding is supported by more objective evidence about the most popular content sites: many of the most-visited correspond to real-world television brands (CNN, ESPN, etc.).

Without such a loop already being established, it is open to question whether attempting to convey the consumer in the other direction (i.e. from web to television) is an effective marketing strategy, such as might be used to promote a digital television service to new subscribers. This is because the most effective model is clearly one in which the television viewing experience is central: the web site is used to expand the television experience, but also ultimately to promote it, so that viewers are driven back to it. The web is therefore a 'supplementary' marketing tool for the digital television operator, not a primary one.

In any case, using a web site as a primary marketing-tool produces a number of difficulties. In the TV-to-web direction, the group of web site users is self-selecting: they regularly watch the relevant programme or channel, they happen to be connected to a PC, and they know where the site is (the URL is promoted on the television screen or on the EPG; eventually, it may even be embedded in the television picture, so it can be clicked on to take the viewer direct to the site).

Moving in the opposite direction presents difficulties; while the web is increasingly mass-market, its demographics are skewed, so 'picking' up the type of web user who might want to watch a particular type of programme or to sign up for digital television is more difficult (outside the USA, web access is frequently still a minority interest: the cross-over with would-be digital television subscribers is even more marginal). Moreover, if the digital television brand is a new one, it will be difficult to construct an online brand so visible that the web site will act as a conduit to the new service. In other words, new digital television entrants have a higher entry threshold to cross than existing, established ones, whose brand is already visible on the web.

Finally, such web-based marketing strategies ultimately face a technological constraint: bandwidth. The most effective medium for promoting television is television, as any scheduler knows. Moreover, since air-time is always restricted, on-air television promotions are reduced to a series of brief, fast, intercut video clips showing the principal highlights of the programme or channel.

As at early 2000, standard dial-up Internet access (which is all that most digital set-top boxes offer, if at all) is not able to handle video in such a way as to have a great deal of impact. Frame-rates are slow, the video is not full-screen, and the colour is muddy. The sound quality is also usually blurred. There is a way round this, which is to download the promotional video-clip (the model used in *The X-Files* site); but this inevitably takes time (particularly outside the USA), and the clip cannot be very long.

No doubt advances in digital compression technology will improve this situation over time, but it is doubtful whether broadcast-quality video will ever be available in real-time over an ordinary phone-line (although technologies such as ADSL, cable modems, and ultimately fibre may make such a facility available to a minority).

8

The economy of niches

Where are the new digital channels and services coming from?

'What is happening is this. The more the unit cost of producing and delivering content is coming down, the greater the number of people are interested. The market, like Moore's Law, is growing, and competition helps it grow even more,' says Antonio Arcidiacono, who runs EUTELSAT's new products division.

EUTELSAT, based in Paris, is a group of satellites, owned by Europe's various telephone companies. It is currently in the process of privatizing itself, and expects to be fully independent by mid-2001. EUTELSAT is in the front line when it comes to new broadcasting opportunities, and Arcidiacono (in 1999) said that consumers only have a limited amount to spend on new broadcasting inventions: 'But for business use I see an enormous growth for the near future. For the consumer the scope for new entrants is limited unless you start seeing the pro-sumer emerge. Then you produce wealth out of the use of your existing bandwidth.'

Niche channels, multiplexed channels, skip-hour channels all play their part in the expansion of choice, and the key to these new broadcasting niches is digital transmission. Claire Leproust runs Canal+ interactive division. She says broadcasters must ask what constitutes a new niche channel: 'A broadcast shouldn't just come as pictures with sound. It should also include questions like: should there be a teletext service attached to it, a web site promoting it, an interactive game supporting it, a home-shopping element as part of it, and asking third-party companies to be part of that, as another revenue stream, on your behalf. It is thinking of the whole package.'

Leproust suggests that each broadcast channel should be treated as its own portal site. 'Because to offer a complete service, with games, or merchandising, or news, or pictures within the TV guide. [A portal] also changes the broadcasters' relationship with advertisers which will no longer be passive, but active. We allow them to suggest direct mail or coupon-response, but also those advertisers will also become potential merchant-partners with us.'

The power of a pay-TV broadcaster in controlling the market, manipulating its subscriber base, is immense. 'We have the database, we have the information a commercial broadcaster does not have. We can now e-mail all of our subscribers across the world, and this will become increasingly important as all free-to-air broadcasts become part of the pay-TV offer,' added Leproust.

In November 1999 Canal+ celebrated its fifteenth Anniversary and on 4 November added 'i>television', a 24-hour news channel that takes its model from NY1, an innovative news channel from the USA. Unfortunately, NY1 also inspired the Channel One service in the UK, which failed in 1998. Canal+ seem to have recognized the risks. i>television promises to be truly revolutionary, sending out its video-journalists not with a bus-pass and ENG camera, but fully-equipped Satellite News Gathering (SNG) cars with self-tracking roof-mounted satellite dishes.

Allied to i>tv is 'Le Journal de Chez Vous' ('Your Hometown Newspaper') which delivers highly localized electronic news coverage. Viewers can pre-select their 'favourite' pages and regions, for example, looking at 'Paris' for national headline news or another town for its local news. Le Journal is also designed to provide regional classified ads, and earn itself a few francs. This is enhanced teletext and some.

Canal's new on-screen activity extends to its 'Foot+' service which has expanded dramatically for the 1999–2000 soccer season. Foot+ helps combat rival Television Par Satellite (TPS), which can also show some live matches. Canal+ aggressively adds value with on-screen extras, video-in-video replays through its 'interactif notepad' device, and a fascinating 2–3 minute video-in-video summary, with commentary, of the missed action.

'ZapFoot' is the name given by Canal+ to its soccer service, which helps pay-per-view subscribers to monitor goal-scoring action on seven live channels. While watching one game a text message pops up saying a goal has been scored at another match, which the viewer can then instantly join.

Canal+ has more than news and sport on its channels. Its electronic wizardry is used on its flagship nightly entertainment show, *Nulle Part Ailleurs*; here viewers can call up a menu of what has happened and, again through picture alongside picture, watch a missed interview, musical number or the popular *Les Guignols de l'Info*, the Spitting Image-type latex puppets, who deliver their comic spin on the day's news.

Leproust says an increasing number of Canal+ channels have sophisticated interactive overlays. Efforts include *La Chaine Meteo*, Canal Satellite's own weather channel and Eurosport, Fox Kids and Canal J that shows *Pikto Rezo*, a bouquet of interactive kids' games. Up to four players can interact from different locations via telephone or Minitel (France Telecom's interactive mini-TV monitor in many French homes). Half a million people a month are using *Pikto Rezo*. 'Being able to play friends across town adds a completely new dimension to the experience,' says Leproust in 1999.

However, E! Entertainment's head of international, Jon Helmrich gives this view:

> There are undoubted opportunities in the digital world, but we have to weigh the economics in the digital world and many of the channels that are springing up are just multiplexes or quasi-channels especially those coming from the music industry where they have a couple of extra staff reformatting a signal. They're not real channels.

Helmrich agrees, though, that personalization and localization has always been the name of niche broadcasting.

> Localization is absolutely vital, and it is the core of our international strategy. It's why in some territories we have moved a little slower than expected. I will be blunt in saying that we were offered several years ago in the UK a channel that was just the imported US domestic signal and we said that was not good for the long term. Viewers might appreciate the novelty [of E!'s American-led content] at first but in the UK they would want a behind-the-scenes show on *Eastenders* or *Ruby Wax*.

EUTELSAT's Arcidiacono comments on the economics:

> There are some important economies of scale. When you pass 1 million users, you enter the consumer market. But if you cannot exceed 10 million consumers you do not survive for long in the consumer market. The advantage of using common technologies makes these targets easier, because you can have any number of 1 million niches. It is clear that multimedia and Internet by satellite is not yet in the consumer market, while DTH is very much in the consumer market. Likely in the next few years multimedia and Internet by satellite will be in the consumer market.

Those multiple small niches have been exploited, certainly in Europe by Ynon Kreiz, president of Fox Kids Europe. In addition to being present in almost every major European market, Fox Kids added Russia, Ukraine, the Czech Republic, Slovenia, Lithuania and Bulgaria between 1999 and 2000. 'Our strategy is to be present in every country in Europe; we are now in 23 markets in Europe. The two key markets where we are not present at the moment are Germany and Italy. It's not that we have been slow in getting into these countries, but we thought these two markets were unsettled with a lot of moving elements.'

Kreiz says each market must be taken on its merit. 'In the UK to multiplex was an easy decision to take, where you have already over 1 million digital subscribers on Sky. Our pan-European strategy allows for this sort of flexibility, saying for example that the UK will have two feeds but France for the time being only one. It totally depends on the market, and the evolution of the market.'

Evolution was also on Gerry Glover's lips. Glover runs National Geographic UK and a second channel from Nat-Geo is imminent. 'We have a lot of original material we have commissioned, and that could allow us to offer a couple of different genres if we choose to do so.' Glover added: 'We seem to do well linked to the relative maturity of the market, for example in those markets where we came on to the scene reasonably soon after pay-television launched. In Poland, South Africa and Australia we are in the top five channels. Usually it is us and Discovery, switching positions, and then movies and sport ahead of us. But mainly it is the two documentary services that rate very highly. In Australia we have been in the top two or three since launch, and in Poland we are in the top six or seven channels. They are places where competitors didn't have anything like the head start.'

In other words, you should get your channel idea in quick, but not so early that you are ahead of the market, and that 'magic million' subscriber base.

In France Canal+ is now (2000) carrying a test channel from banking group Credit Agricole. Claire Leproust suggests that this bank's entry into digital broadcasting will be the spur to bring in most of its competitors. 'It will provoke other banks to run similar channels, and also hypermarkets like Carrefour and other major retailers. Retailers especially want to ally their brand and get much closer to TV channels. The problem is that these people must create good quality material and not just propaganda. That's a challenge. Look at the banks, where the real added-value is to develop their home banking and the value of a TV set is to give them the ability to humanize this relationship.'

Localization, personalization, and now humanization. That's what the new breed of television is all about. Whether it's allowing viewers to choose their 'own' camera angles or calling up 'Your Hometown Newspaper' on the television, producers are continually seeking to drill down to their niche audiences. It's what digital television is all about.

Twenty years to become clear

It has taken twenty years for the thematic channel picture to become clear. On 1 June 2000 CNN will celebrate its twentieth anniversary. Although HBO launched first – and films and sport are the foundation of any thematic platform – it was really CNN that broke the mould of broadcasting. The changes established by Ted Turner are now taken for granted, and most recognize that the world of broadcasting is changing. However, there are noticeable examples of even more dramatic shifts in the growth of niche and thematic channels. They are proliferating at a breathtaking pace, and there are other developments as seemingly every broadcaster on the planet starts offering web-based channels to the users, spawning a new word in some circles, hence 'viewsers'.

News is just one sector. Documentary is another, and viewers are beginning to see a rapid deployment of new and fascinating 'doc-channels'. There are few platform broadcasters which have not partnered with, or imitated, the Discovery model; but it seems every niche and sub-niche is being examined or developed for exploitation into a thematic channel. This dramatic shift to new content is confirmed by Michael Wolf, media consultant at US creative giant Booz, Allen and Hamilton. Speaking to journalists after a presentation at the 1999 International Media Forum in Berlin, he said that the future of television belongs to viewers, allowing them to use interactive technology to call up programming that suits their interests and schedule. 'In five years, the television of today will look like black-and-white television to us. TV networks will only prosper if they adapt to TV's new age.'

Wolf suggests that television by the year 2004 will be unrecognizable compared with what exists today, with more than 1000 channels commonplace in viewers' homes and video-on-demand, game-order services and the Internet on television creating ever-greater choice.

As if to confirm the trend, Europe's two giant satellite players have recently confirmed just how important the explosion in digital choice has been. SES/Astra claim more than 800 video and audio channels, and promise another four satellites by the end of 2001. Romain Bausch, Astra's director general says in his view the future programming will follow two styles: 'The first being more TV channels where the programmer is packaging content for viewers but offering it a straightforward broadcast format. The second group will come from the electronic supply of all sorts of content, video, entertainment, education . . . in other words there will be the prepared, structured type of channel and the unpackaged style.'

His opposite number at EUTELSAT, director general Giuliano Berretta, claims more than 550 television channels plus another couple of hundred radio stations and says another type of channel is going to emerge. 'We now have a total of 37 [digital] multiplexes. In fact, there is nobody more experienced in developing niche markets than EUTELSAT. There are new niches coming up every day but they need to find carriage and sell themselves at a much lower price. I can predict plenty of new niche channels if the price is right and it is my job to create gateways so that channels can get on the air.'

Berretta's concept comes from technical improvements benefiting digital broadcasters all over the globe. He says that digital compression ratios are improving all the time, and with low-cost noise-reduction technology, further improvements will follow. 'In the near future, thanks to these improvements, [we will] provide television channels at slightly lower video quality at a 2 Mbps bit-rate and at that level our prices would be extremely attractive and yet still provide acceptable video quality', says Berretta.

Berretta calls this new television model, 'micro television'. 'RAI's Net Uno is today transmitting perfectly acceptable pictures at 1.8 Mbps and there are many channels that we broadcast today at 3.2 Mbps. I see considerable scope for regional channels where viewers do not necessarily want entertainment in the conventional sense but news and information from their region. I also see another level of broadcasting emerge and I call this Industrial Television where companies need to talk to their customers or their own employees.'

EUTELSAT is boosting the number of opportunities for micro-stations. In early 2001, EUTELSAT will launch a new satellite (EUTELSAT Hot Bird 5-R) with space for at least 18 individual 2 Mbps channels. 'We are currently in discussion with a major group who see great potential in bringing together single niche channels and who see a business in creating packages from them,' says Berretta.

Choice – or a 'heart attack within a year'

However, German network broadcasters seem not to share these predictions. Georg Kofler, who retired as CEO at Germany's Pro Sieben Media Group in 1999, dismisses the '1000s of channels' argument and says technology will not change the inherent laziness in most viewers. 'Even in a multimedia market, people will continue to follow the laws of sloth,' he says. 'If a super-user for all this new media does exist in the future, he'll be ready for a heart attack in a year.'

Kofler said most people would still want to use their free time to relax and would consider too many choices for entertainment stressful rather than exciting. Nevertheless, Pro Sieben was due to launch N24, its 24-hour news channel on 24 January 2000.

Three other German broadcasters also shared their views of the future shape of television at Berlin.

■ SAT1 CEO Juergen Doetz says he is confident that network TV in its current form would remain central to the market. 'Our core business will remain television, television and again, television', he said, adding that the major networks were only using the Internet to enhance their programming with sites linked to popular shows and news broadcasts.

■ Gerhard Zeiler, the head of RTL, Germany's largest and most profitable network, admits the market will fragment but that RTL would rely on its strong branding: 'The value of the brand will only grow more important.' RTL, in exploiting the brand name, has promised four thematics, centred on soap operas, news/magazine programmes, action and a 'best of RTL' channel.

■ Dieter Hahn, deputy CEO of the media conglomerate Kirch Group which in September 1999 re-launched its DF-1 digital multichannel direct-to-home package as Premiere World, said that because it had interests in commercial, pay-TV and digital TV, it could wait to see whether the passive or the active viewer won out. 'It does not matter how we reach our viewers, whether it is over the Internet, via satellite, cable or antenna,' Hahn says. 'Just as long as we reach them.'

Canal+ Leproust recognizes the problems. 'It is important we hold the subscriber's hand. The TV is a passive media for entertainment. If we look at consumer habits, with our 60 thematic channels, most consumers have the ability to manage that offer. But some people have difficulty coping which is why it is important we help them navigate.'

Microsoft's WebTV does take viewers by the hand, with its core business designed to add value to established programming and channels. Jim Beveridge is WebTV's business development manager for Europe, and he predicts explosive growth in web-streamed channels. 'There is no stopping it. In fact it reminds me of the evolution of radio and the early days when people had to use a primitive crystal set to start off with, then it got better and better. It's junk today and one would have to be pretty keen to sit and watch or listen at these wonderful 2-inch-sized windows, but it is going to get much better.'

The key niches

Kids

Considered a vital element in any multi-channel bouquet, the kids segment is especially important because of the spin-off licensing and merchandising benefits. Whether Nickelodeon, Disney, Fox Kids, Kermit, Canal J or the other clones, kids are big business. As this book is written, the BBC is planning a pair of children's channels (pre-school and general) while many thematic providers are extending their brands into directly adjacent age-groups (Noggin, ABC, Nick Jnr).

News

CNN set the pattern, since when practically every national broadcaster has launched its own stand-alone news service. CNN has extended its franchise with joint-venture channels in Spain (CNN+) and Turkey (CNN-Turk). Besides BBC World, EuroNews, CNBC, Bloomberg and Sky News, recent competitive offerings have come from Italy (Stream's 'Class Financial Network'), Turkey's NTV, and Kanal EE (Economy and Entertainment). We are also beginning to see 'foreign' broadcasters attack CNN's home ground, in other words an increasing number of channels are using the English language to break into the global news/business news market (Turkey's NTV-I, Dubai's Business Channel).

Documentary

Discovery Communications created the genre by taking the BBC/PBS model and beautifully packaging documentary and natural history into highly appealing niches. Arts & Entertainment's History and Biography have also carved out a slice, as has National Geographic, France's Canal+ (Multithematiques) and TPS, Italy's RAI, Telepiu and Stream, and Spain's TVE (TVE Tematica). But the past year or two has seen Discovery segment itself even further, into travel (acquiring The Travel Channel in the process) as well as science, adventure and history strands. Amsterdam-based UPC has launched a clutch of factual channels including Avante and Expo: The Design Channel, which are being rolled out to their cable systems across Europe.

Music

MTV was first – and no other sector has seen as many imitators. Even MTV has spawned sub-divisions (Rap, Country, Blues) together with localized versions all over the planet. The next step might be to bring these distant relations back under one all-embracing MTV digital platform, containing MTV Asia, Latino, India and Russia. Some of the competitors have made significant progress, not least Germany's VIVA and Channel [V]/Zee Music.

Exporting and importing niches

Niches can also travel from one region to another. For example, there is no shortage of European channels exported to Asia, or Far Eastern products exported to other parts of the globe. However, with precious few exceptions this international trade is limited to the state-backed broadcasters like the BBC, Italy's RAI, France's TV5 and Germany's Deutsche Welle. Each of these broadcasters reflects in one form or other a wish to reach their own expatriate audience as well as portray something of a shop-window for viewers wanting entertainment, news and some cultural exposure from the broadcasting country. Other channels falling under this general heading, including Turkey's TRT and a channel from Greece. Currently only the BBC makes any effort to produce local-ized content in an overseas market, of which more in a moment.

There has been little movement in the export of other, more commercially orientated channels from Europe. Most of the running has come from channels that are clearly identified as 'American' in origin, even if content has been localized for regional audiences. Indeed, one television insider described the prospects of sending more European channels to the Far East as 'problematic', adding that audiences for language-specific channels were so fragmented, and cable and satellite delivery systems so numerous, that any immediate plans to expand services were 'questionable'.

One exception is the Granada Television-backed UKTV channel on AsiaSat and ArabSat. This channel should not be confused with the similarly named UKTV channel available to Australian viewers, which is part-owned by BBC Worldwide.

The Granada channel may well benefit directly from a new venture announced in August which sees a new production company (GB Productions) formed with the BBC to develop jointly a new crop of dramas and situation comedies for the American market. If these concepts come to fruition, it is quite likely that both 'UKTVs' will benefit over time from fresh programme ideas.

The Granada/BBC effort is seen as a positive move to not only exploit the existing libraries of both broadcasters, but to create programmes that compete more effectively on a global scale. Scott Siegler (who is also president of Granada Entertainment USA) heads up the venture and said at the launch that the UK broadcasting scene was rich with high-quality concepts, citing *Cosby* 'which is directly modelled on a ratings-winning BBC comedy show (*One Foot in the Grave*).

Another British broadcaster that attempted to get a foothold over the Far East and Japan was Carlton Communications. Their KTV (Karaoke) channel, in which they had a 31 per cent stake, was a financial 'fiasco' which they closed in 1997 having sustained 'significant losses' according to the company. A few months later, Carlton retreated even further, selling its interests in Home TV, a joint-venture Hindi channel launched with Pearson, the *Hindustan Times*, Hong Kong media group TVB and investment bankers Schroders. Mumbai-based Sahara Group picked up the shares.

While Granada's plans might take time to mature, and Carlton is itself concentrating on expansion in the UK and Spain, two other European outfits have been aggressive in their export thrust. The first, BSkyB has placed a few channels in front of Far Eastern, Australian and Middle East viewers. Sky News, for example, is widely available throughout Asia/Pacific thanks to Star TV's feeds from AsiaSat 3S and ArabSat (as part of the Star Select bouquet). Though clearly targeted at UK expatriates, it is available and redistributed for Australian and New Zealand multichannel viewers.

BSkyB is also exporting its UK-produced [tv] computer channel to the Middle East, alongside Granada's UKTV and the Arts & Entertainment-backed The History Channel. According to Altaf Alimohammed, chief executive at Star Select, The History Channel's Middle East programming has already been localized for his region's audience.

The History Channel is a classic example of how to create a documentary product that appeals to local audiences. This winter it will announce three key broadcasting distribution partnerships for India, Japan, and what they call 'greater' China and South East Asia. Whitney Goit, Arts & Entertainment's executive vice-president for its television networks, expects services to start early in 2000. 'The core of the content will come from our own archives, and that product will be dubbed into local languages with some interstitial material and possibly hosting inserted to make the channel appeal to local audiences. We strive to put a [suitable] product out there, so that the viewer sees us as an international channel with an obvious effort to relate closely to that local market.'

Goit says the Indian market is the easiest to adapt to, thanks to its English-speaking traditions and Anglo-American influences. 'However, in China we are having to send every piece of material into the country in advance of being shown on air where it is checked. The mechanism is in place, but we are keen to create with the authorities a reputation for being ultra-sensitive and reliable to their needs. We want them to have programming that they are comfortable with, but it is a different market. We will start with a block of programming so that they can see how serious we are.'

The History Channel is most cautious about how it presents its programming. Goit says 'Chinese audiences might know about Marilyn Monroe within our Biography strand, but there would be other key figures in our history that they would not be aware of. But we can turn this to our advantage, by hosting the show with a little introduction setting up the item, saying 'This week we are going to explore great American film stars', and then explain why John Wayne or Gary Cooper or Joan Crawford mattered so much. They might not know each individual but the theme will be appealing, same with musicians or politicians or generals. It is for us to tell the story and make the item interesting.'

By 2000–2001, Goit expects to have doubled The History Channel's global distribution. 'China alone should give us coverage on larger cable systems and a block on provincial TV stations. It's been a long haul, but they are such huge markets with such long-term potential and we have been able to learn a little from those who have gone before us.' Next on the list for History are similar deals in Turkey, Israel and in time Pakistan.

BSkyB is also firmly behind (with the NBC network of the USA and Fox) the remarkably successful National Geographic channel, Nat-Geo. BSkyB owns a 50 per cent stake in National Geographic's European operation, and this includes the Middle East service. National Geographic has been a resounding success globally, even though it has yet to launch in North America. Sandy McGovern, president of National Geographic Channels Worldwide, speaking at the MIPCOM programming market in September, was especially optimistic about National Geographic gaining further carriage in the Far East. 'In Australia for example we are in the top five channels. Usually it is us and Discovery, switching positions, with movies and sport ahead of us. But mainly it is the two documentary services that rate very highly.'

Nat-Geo has just multiplexed its digital service for the UK (Nat-Geo+1hr) and over time, and where digital capacity allows, this policy might be extended. Nat-Geo has extensive distribution in the region (mainly on AsiaSat 3S and Palapa C2) and is one of the few international channels to gain total acceptance in China, where it has more than 12 million homes viewing. McGovern says Nat-Geo's roll-out has been one of the fastest-ever in cable and satellite history, now topping 13 million homes (plus China). Besides the Asian region, Nat-Geo is also concentrating its sights on the USA where it plans to launch later in 2000.

Nat-Geo's concept, in the words of chief operating officer Ken Ferguson, is straightforward, and includes localizing content for the 57 countries it is now available in: 'We're not just about the animal kingdom. We're extending subject matter to include modern culture and religion; one programme examines why 30 million people visit Rome and the Vatican. But we are also reaching new audiences, in India and several Asian markets either via various licensing deals or new channel launches.'

As part of Nat-Geo's global awareness programme it has created a competition where filmmakers from all over the world are invited to submit ideas for 'Blue Planet Heroes', a series of four-minute documentaries.

The other European outfit which is beginning to make a considerable noise throughout the Far East is a little-known Paris-based company which has created two fascinating entertainment niches. MCM International is now making its signals available throughout the region and already successfully exporting its Fashion TV and MCM (music) channels. Indovision, for example, carries Fashion TV while Indonesia's embryonic cable systems (Metra and Kabelvision) additionally carries MCM as well as Fashion TV.

The Fashion TV concept is so easy; it is a never-ending line-up of attractive models displaying the latest from the world's top fashion houses. Broadcast without commentary, the images are universal and easy to absorb. Its sister-channel MCM is France's unashamed alternative challenge to MTV. No specific changes are made to either Fashion TV or MCM to suit local audiences. Indeed, it is the very nature of the programming that it is left untouched.

BBC Worldwide

The BBC is largely recognized from its BBC World flagship news channel, but much more is happening under the BBC banner. 'By 2006 we will be contributing around US$300+ million to the BBC's commercial activities,' says BBC Worldwide's chief executive Rupert Gavin, speaking at a television programme sales market in Cannes in October 1999. Gavin added that by 2006 BBC

Worldwide will be a 'very large organization' in its own right, 'because to deliver a US$300 m cash flow benefit our sales revenue will be something around US$1.9 billion, which contrasts with the BBC's current licence fee which draws in around US$3.5 bn.'

BBC Worldwide was formed in 1994 to develop a co-ordinated approach to the commercial activities of the otherwise publicly funded BBC. BBC World operates from within BBC Worldwide. It is also home of the 50/50 joint venture with Discovery Communications to launch a number of channels (marketed in the Far East by Discovery Networks Asia or India). One of these channels is Animal Planet, which over the past year or so has gained almost immediate acceptance by cable and satellite operators within the Asian region. Some 5 million Indian viewers receive Animal Planet.

BBC Worldwide's vision, in the words of chief executive Rupert Gavin, is to be 'recognized in our own right as one of the UK's leading international consumer media companies'.

Its flagship channel, BBC World, is already well known around the world. Patrick Cross is BBC World's MD, charged with taking BBC World to every corner of the globe, and he explained in 1999 why the channel's existing distribution success is soon to get a boost:

> We will be introducing a new programming schedule in April 2000, which packages news at the top of the hour and documentary material at the half-hour. It becomes a very tidy schedule, easy for viewers to understand. But news always takes priority, and we will always stay with important breaking news.
>
> In India, at 10 p.m. every evening we have our 'made in India' slot, which features programming from India about India. The highlight of the week is Friday's *Question Time India* show. We were coming under increasing ratings pressure from the other competitive news channels, and Star News started up in April last year, so these slots were created and have enabled us to regain control of that key 10 p.m. slot. Our reach has

been maintained, with around 10–11 per cent viewership from the available audience of around 8.5 million connected television households.

Cross says the Indian model is one the BBC would like to replicate to other major markets, 'Except to say this sort of programming is expensive. We are very careful to maintain BBC editorial control, which means close liaison with the local production company. *Question Time* is especially onerous because it's an unashamed political programme with all the special needs of balance and fairness.' Cross admits that maintaining a balance has often been hard work, with the show regularly creating fireworks of its own.

The BBC were planning a similar opt-out programme for Pakistan, but the October political changes have placed that concept on to the back burner for the time being. 'But we can only consider these sorts of special shows where there is a viable local audience,' says Cross.

Japan is a case in point for the BBC. 'We do some "opting in" shows in Japan. They draw down the signal from PanAmSat and insert programming from the BBC archive specially for the Japanese audience on satellite and cable, which carries Japanese advertising.' These seasons of shows have tended to be on wildlife and a series on English gardens.

All this activity has raised BBC World's profile. According to PAX 99, the latest survey (as at January 2000) conducted in seven cities in Asia-Pacific by Asia Market Intelligence Ltd, BBC World is the fastest growing news channel in South East Asia, with a daily reach which has increased 23 per cent among business decision makers and 31 per cent among affluent adults since 1998. The weekly reach for the same demographic groups has increased by 15 per cent and 12 per cent respectively, while BBC World's total viewership has grown by 44 per cent among business decision makers and 46 per cent among affluent adults over the same period. BBC World now claims it reaches a total of over 155 million homes in 200 countries and territories world-wide.

China is the largest missing market for the BBC. Although BBC World is available in Hong Kong, other than hotel distribution there is no formal re-distribution of BBC World into China. Cross expects that to change. 'We have no authority to market in China, since they objected to a programme we ran in the UK on Chairman Mao's private life. We are working very hard to get those permissions and we have had some signs of softening towards us.'

Table 8.1   Niches in Asia

Channel	Language	Description
BBC World	English	'The BBC's flagship news channel'
Animal Planet	English/local	Animal documentary
Deutsche Welle	English/German	News and features about Germany
History Channel	English/local	History and biography documentaries
RAI International	Italian	Entertainment and news the Italian way
National Geographic	English/local lang.	'A passion for adventure'
Sky News	English	'Comprehensive news in a popular style'
TV5 International	French	'Best of French broadcasting'
MCM Music	French	Music videos
Fashion TV	No language	Non-stop fashion from the catwalk

There are, seemingly, a million other niches. A quick glance at any major digital satellite will show how esoteric some minority interests can be. However, whether a Russian channel broadcast to émigrés living in Brooklyn, New York, or a Vietnamese channel beamed to expatriates in California, these niches can only grow and become increasingly important in a digital age. How they are best delivered is something we examine in the next chapter.

9

Web-casting to the TV, or TV on the PC?

According to Peggy Miles, president of on-line broadcasting specialist Intervox Communications, in mid-1999 there are in excess of 2000 radio stations broadcasting full-time programming on the Internet. There are also, she says, 'well over 100 television stations doing much the same thing' and many more broadcasting part-time segments, usually news or current affairs. Miles also admits that the number of new web-streamed networks entering this arena means it is now almost impossible to provide up-to-the-minute figures.

However, anyone who doubts the impact web-casting is having on the Internet has only to dip into the Broadcast.com web site (www.broadcast.com) where in late July 1999 they boasted having 410 live, continuously transmitting, radio stations and 49 television channels, as well as on-demand music from their CD Jukebox with 3000 titles.

Much stock-market action is focused on the book-buying habits of the customers of on-line bookshop Amazon.com, but early in 1999 Broadcast.com saw its Nasdaq-listed stock price rocket 44 per cent in a single day. Even Rupert Murdoch issued a warning, saying that at that time the euphoria accompanying web stocks was overstated.

As many engineers know, and a quick glance at Broadcast.com will prove, it is easy to dismiss the 28.8 Kbps delivery technology as crude and far too clunky to meet any sort of critical acceptance. By any measure, it is not the same product as that available on a television set. The dilemma for conventional broadcasters is coping with Broadcast.com's 'hit-rate', which is claimed to be 'many millions' a day, and rising only slightly slower than their stock price.

Stories abound of people viewing and listening to their 'favourite' television and radio stations over the web for hours at a time, albeit an easier story to accept in countries which pay little or nothing for local telephone calls. These 'stations' have their appeal because they deliver a product that is *not* available on the living room television.

Whatever happens to Broadcast.com's stock price, the company will probably go from strength to strength. At a London conference (Broadcasting @ Internet/IBC, 1999) speaker after speaker demonstrated, with some powerful arguments, that web-cast programming is here, is happening and thanks to technology improvements underway, is going to get much more important. In fact the long-awaited multi-channel future may already exist, but on the web. Moreover, web-delivered 'programming' has some important advantages over conventional broadcasting.

Marcus Bicknell, once SES/Astra's commercial director but now (1999) president of CMG Information Services in Europe, says with more homes hooking up to cable and satellite, each with 'massive bandwidth available ... therefore joint online and TV services are beginning to trigger demand.' He argues that the era of restricted 28 800 Kbps delivery is over. Bicknell, not for the first time, is right. Cable companies, such as UPC's impressive 'chello' interactive service, show that bandwidth restrictions are a thing of the past.

Perhaps the most high-profile supporters of web-enhanced television is WebTV, the start-up that Bill Gates acquired three years ago for US$425 million. Today WebTV has more than 1 million subscriptions with over 50 per cent of them logging in every day. WebTV uses an ordinary telephone connection running with its own proprietary software to 'add value' to conventional television images as well as to access the world wide web.

WebTV's software converts all on-screen text (normally PC-sized) to a size and format that is specifically designed to be read on a television set, and at an 'ideal' viewing distance from the set. The format also lends itself to the 'lean back' needs of normal entertainment, as distinct to 'lean forward' computer use. WebTV overlays its own user-friendly software with consistent functionality to its web access, but viewers can keep their favourite channel in one portion of the screen, and with certain partner channels, hook up to specially created data specific to that channel's output.

Critics of this sort of US-inspired functionality are quick to remind WebTV that most Europeans can overlay this sort of data, albeit more crudely, thanks to Teletext-type services. Nevertheless, WebTV is a major advancement in bringing Internet and broadcast television together, which might prove to be a useful stepping stone.

Infotainment

However, Jan van Lier, chairman of the Teleweb Project steering board (and standardization manager at Philips Consumer Electronics), says Teleweb is the natural extension of Teletext. 'Teleweb allows the content provider to deliver interactive "infotainment" to a wide audience or to individually addressed consumers.' Van Lier says Teleweb brings together programme-related content, advertising and Internet-style information packages. Moreover, he says Teleweb can run on today's television networks, in parallel to Teletext and other data services.

For analogue television, the Teleweb data can be transmitted via independent Teletext data lines (IDLs). He says that while the Teleweb pages are unlimited in size and their greater graphical content needs more channel capacity than Teletext's usual VBI delivery, this problem is easily solved by using otherwise wasted Teletext transmission capacity. Van Lier also suggests using overnight 'down time' to feed data to TVs in stand-by mode. Teleweb, he says, is a natural for DVB-compliant and other digital delivery systems including DAB, with a cost of around US$25 to integrate into TV sets.

Teleweb has the look and feel of Internet, tailor-made to the television screen. Viewers can browse with the TV remote control, and the technology, says the Teleweb steering group, can give interactive television with instant access as well as integrating Teletext and EPG-type information. Teleweb project members include Philips, Grundig, Sony, Seimens and others, while on the content side the German Axel Springer Verlag group, ProSeiben, TDF and others.

No more channels, every programme is a portal

Gary Arlen, president of Arlen Communications, of Bethesda, Maryland has for 20 years predicted greater convergence between television and computer industries. He says we are all well on the way to becoming 'viewsers' and suggests the needs of the consumer now go beyond the usual clichés of couch potatoes and are no longer age or gender-related. He quotes MTV research (July 1998) which claims 'heavy usage of one medium begets heavy usage of new media'. He adds that we are in the middle of a blending process, where Internet and broadcast television are seen as overlapping, with 'video portals' creating an evolutionary process for the Internet, with significant risks for conventional broadcasters.

Barclay Dutson, of Vision Research, a UK consultancy, also warns broadcasters that they ignore the Internet at their peril. In research published in 1999, his organization states that, despite the growth of digital television in Europe (almost 3 million subscribers at December 1998), Internet usage is higher, and forecasts 'consistently higher growth for Internet than for digital television.' He warns that digital television is 'launching into a much more Internet-aware and Internet-trained audience than broadcasters thought when first commissioning set-top boxes.'

There's also a new satellite kid on the block, in terms of Ka-band. Operating near the more commonly used Ku-band frequencies, Ka-band has been earmarked for two-way traffic directly between the satellite and home or business-based dish, and back to the satellite.

Dutson also suggests that the exploitation of satellite-delivered Ka-Band means 'You ain't seen nothing yet!' in terms of bandwidth available to broadcast Internet applications. Vision's forecast is that satellite Internet will have between 14.1 m and 37.1 m users by 2010, out of a total of between 240 and 400 million global Internet users. In other words, 6–9.5 per cent of the world Internet population will get their signals from satellite. These 'viewers' will not be limited by 28.8 baud clunky delivery; they will be unfettered by any sort of bandwidth restrictions.

Advantages

There are some recognized advantages to web-casting and one obvious type of channel to benefit profit-wise is one not recognized by most conventional broadcasters: pornography. Whether we like it or not, it is a fact that live (or 'as live') pornographic images via the web are commonplace. Moreover, neither the ITC or other Euro-regulators can or seem to want to do much about this unsavoury content.

Julian McGougan is ITC (the UK broadcasting regulator) policy advisor, responsible for developing regulatory policy in relation to convergence and interactive broadcasting. In a 1999 paper he says 'Because of its limitations as a delivery medium for audiovisual services and low Internet penetration, it is unlikely that the unregulated nature of such services . . . will be a major cause of concern.' He describes the ITC's 'hands off' approach as 'pragmatic' and suggests that if any regulation is required over Internet-delivered audiovisual service, the ITC will start 'with a light touch' and become heavier later 'if audience research suggests that it is required'.

There are a host of other 'advantages' to web-cast television: gambling and betting, unlimited advertising, product placement, unrestricted price control, zero 'windows' or territorial limitations and no compliance culture, absence of controls over bias or balance and unfettered access to home shopping.

John Ensor, a partner at London-based media law firm Olswang, shrewdly suggests that this absence of control is one of the appeals of the web. However, he also warns that even within this highly anarchic model, there should be the normal controls over credit-card purchasing of products and services, common-sense rules over data protection and consumer protection should be enacted and copyright protection should be provided for.

That viewers will gravitate towards 'quality' content is not doubted, and is already proved. The most popular web sites come from those who have most experience in broadcasting, whether CNN.com, msNBC or newspapers with a high degree of commit-ment towards web-created material. Today's 28.8 k baud rates will soon be replaced by greater bandwidth, however, and while many of us will continue to seek our entertainment via the televi-sion, there is now little doubt that the PC or Internet-connected television might soon be providing Broadcast.com's output to us. And zip will go another one or two per cent per annum of network television's audience.

Earlier in this book I have quoted from interviews conducted with some key leaders in the industry, each prophets in their sectors. One such individual is Jim Beveridge, Microsoft's busi-ness development manager (Europe) for their WebTV Networks. Asked specifically whether web-streaming was going to be impor-tant, Beveridge answered: 'Absolutely. There is no stopping it. In fact there's something quite nice about it. It reminds me of the evolution of radio and the early days when people had to use a Crystal Set to start off with, then it got better and better. It's junk today and one would have to be pretty keen to sit and watch or listen at these wonderful little 2 in windows, but in time. . . .'

Beveridge continued: 'Clearly there are bandwidth restrictions on the Internet and I see the Internet almost like a sea of technology and services. What people will do is take elements of that which is offered and build into their own networks what they believe is worth including. So you are going to see live streamed media across from Australia to California then it is not going to be a great experience. But if you have servers where the material has been cached locally and in addition have access to cellular bandwidth then you will be able to receive the video without problem at all.'

He also saw an increase in business-to-business web-streaming, and intra-business possibilities: 'I think we are the model. For example, whenever someone gives a presentation within Microsoft, and I am not just talking about Bill [Gates] here, the presentation, it might be on the potential for video-streaming, is recorded and people can then go into the file-server at any time and view the presentation or elements of it when it suits them. It is almost like training on the job, and this could be used by any company. We believe in this because we are the best user of our products. But I think most people would love to have this sort of stuff. It's wonderful.'

But Beveridge also issued a warning as to how broadcasters would see their roles by 2003–4.

They are all going to have to re-think their business plans. You are going to get a huge cross-over between those who say they are just programme-providers, and those who say they are transmission specialists. And everything in between. It comes down to the basic argument of who controls the distribution channel, and the big boys like to have it all. Look at Rupert [Murdoch], where Fox makes the movies, NDS encrypts the material, and Sky shows the stuff on boxes Sky has given away. It's perfect. It works. And no-one knows better than Murdoch how to squeeze value out of every link in the chain. On the other hand there are broadcasters who seem to want to back away from technology, they just want to stay in their niche as programme providers.

> The suggestion of every channel being a portal and every programme a sub-portal is a smart way of looking at it. Everyone is getting hung up on the portal, one gateway that everybody has to delve through to get the stuff. In reality anything you are watching could become a portal in its own right and give access to stuff from that. One problem is that a lot of people in the programme-making arena do not understand what is going on [in technology]. And a lot of people in the technology areas don't know a thing about programme-making!

Another acknowledged expert is Steve Billinger, who was until the end of 1999 BSkyB's director of interactivity. He too has some clear ideas about the role of web-casting. In his opinion all the major digital platforms now transmitting will continue and have a viable future.

> Every future platform will be digital and interactive as matter of course. It doesn't matter where or what it is. I am including digital radio, all forms of wireless, all forms of broadband. In my view television will continue to be used to build the primary compelling brand position, and that all of those platforms will deliver slices of the content pie. I use the term 'content continuum'. A perfect example: somebody who thinks of family entertainment thinks of Disney – we may think of the BBC here but in the USA it's Disney – when they want to experience family entertainment they need to be able to find a Disney-branded product, and I think they will be able to find that brand and product on every available platform. There'll be times when they are on the radio, and the Theme Park, and on Broadway, and the hockey team in the park on a Saturday night. Each will continue as viable-share businesses, they will be the first choice for building that primary brand value. They will almost certainly be the starting off point. However, all of these platforms must be seamlessly integrated to present a kind of content continuum.

Elsewhere in this book I have stated the oft-repeated phrase that 'content is king'. Billinger does not agree:

I don't necessarily believe content will be king. My view is that the blur between content and technology, or content and utility, is going to be so fuzzy that it will be difficult to differentiate what is what. For example, in any interactive space, what is e-mail? I call it non-category specific content. It isn't news, sports or entertainment, but it's a critical part of the customer offering, and this is the main thing that so-called new media guys don't get. Because increasingly the technology is king, they are both kings.

I asked him how, if content allied to the brand is important, and the brand and its content was what viewers sought, how could a new content provider break in to the market?

Look at the three most recognized brands that have emerged recently, none of which are in the 'content' business that you and I would recognize: Amazon, e-Bay and Yahoo!. All three represent utility, and utility has become content in that environment, and that has built their brand value. We all thought that 'content was king' meant CNN and the like. My view is that these are now irrelevant and that customers in an interactive technology-based market, which is what every future platform will be, cannot tell the difference [between CNN and Yahoo!]. One way to do it is to supply better features, better technology, than anyone else or package those utilities, features or technologies better than anyone else, which is what the portal-play is all about, or create platform-specific via the usual types of media structures. To that end it is more like [web site] Intertainer, which is a broadband player in the USA distributed on the RoadRunner platform in the USA. It doesn't represent anything I have ever seen before but is specifically targeted at the broadband platform.

Billinger took his argument further, saying that the Yahoo! and Netscape-type portals would be the expected route to our traditional video content: 'You have only to look at Yahoo!'s strategy in acquiring Broadcast.com and rumours that they also want @Home/Excite. I have absolutely no doubt in five years, but pick a date, it doesn't matter but sooner than you and I think, AOL and Yahoo! will be competing head-on in the network business against Fox and everybody else. There's no doubt about that. Some people say they have no content, and that's rubbish. They are inundated with content, and utility and most importantly, with audience.

(Perhaps Billinger was perceptive, but as the world now knows, in January 2000 America Online bought Time Warner in a US$135 billion deal, the world's largest-ever combination in the media industry. AOL now have content.)

Are new services emerging?

Some of them. People park their brains when they face new media. How often have you heard that shopping is the new theatre, or something similar. This is a utility that is perceived as content, and things like this, which we would never have thought of as content, i.e. e-commerce or shopping are content. QVC for example. The notions of what content is are going to change. There will be new content brands that will be an amalgam of technology features or utilities. MSN.com is a very good example.

Billinger described how set-top boxes are far more than dumb, passive terminals.

Our service, the Sky Interactive service, has no need for a modem link whatsoever. Yet it is an entirely interactive experience. It's totally in the box. It's the same with TiVo and Replay, where you have all this interactivity but no back-channel at all. It's a complex series of equations that have to be figured out and there's frankly a lot of [hype] in the market right now, and you have to constantly ask yourself who benefits from what is said. The cable industry benefits by saying the back-channel is critical because journalists say they are the natural home of interactivity. It seems to me that a satellite broadcaster with a TiVo-type interactive box is in a pretty interesting space.

On the question of web-streamed audio and video content, Billinger has few doubts:

> It is definitely going to have mass-market appeal. I see this happening once broadband has decent penetration. If you are asking whether the mass-market sees it as desirable, I'd also say yes because I do not see it as a nurdish, anorak-type niche, or even a high-end user niche. But it will remain a niche until the platforms get their bandwidth together.

Steve Billinger left Sky towards the end of 1999, but his comments are valid as pointers to the way digital television will change our lives. In the next chapter, we examine more specifically the prospects for digital television, where that over-used word 'convergence' fits in, and the 'blue sky/jam tomorrow' hopes and aspirations of some of these specialists.

10

The future: brave new world or just more of the same?

The new millennium has given every press and broadcasting pundit the opportunity to sound off on pet futurology theories. There are, however, one or two voices that should be listened to, the first coming from the cutting edge of the business marketplace and one global company who is well known for its sharp appreciation of customer trends and developments.

PricewaterhouseCoopers (PwC), in a report they called 'A gaze into the crystal ball', published in late 1999, speak optimistically about our digital future. Author Saul Berman says the Digital Age of television is upon us. '3-D, 360-degree audiovisual experiences are all the rage at theme parks ... and the Internet has spawned a vital new home information, education and entertainment paradigm'. While no one can know for sure what the frenetically evolving, consumer-entertainment landscape will look like in the twenty-first century, Berman's views of how his crystal ball is appearing makes interesting reading in the context of this book.

A future scenario

PwC supply some educated hypotheses about the near future of consumer entertainment, both within and outside of the home.

Hypothesis no. 1: Consumers and then technology (in that order) will determine the future entertainment environment. As consumers display an ever-increasing interest in, and demand for, active stimulation, companies will create innovative, 'high-tech' content and software to satisfy those desires. But woe to those corporations that get caught up in the 'gee whiz' of the laboratory and fail to properly monitor the market. PwC say both will be needed to produce the 'cha-ching' of the cash register.

Hypothesis no. 2: Consumers will experience more stimulating content, audiovisual sophistication and interactive technology in their entertainment choices. Interactive technology will be prominent both in and out of the home. Within the home, consumers will take a hands-on role in creating new and differentiated content, with programming presented in menu-driven format. Outside the home, they will also be afforded new and distinguished choices to interact with and actually create content. Companies will extend their corporate and product brands into these new entertainment choices. A good example is Disney's plan to spend more than US$1 billion over the next 10 years to build as many as 30 DisneyQuest centres, equipped with virtual reality, Internet and computer-based gaming.

Hypothesis no. 3: Consumer electronics, high-tech and gaming companies will become major players in alliances and partnerships set up for content creation, a space currently dominated by the purveyors of more traditional, passive entertainment (for example, studios, broadcast networks, cable MSOs and publishers). Examples of this trend include Sony's foray into video games with the Sony Playstation and Microsoft's significant presence in CD-ROM titles.

Hypothesis no. 4: A more interactive, sophisticated entertainment model will spawn greater two-way interaction with the Internet and online services, and diversified programming options. The big question is: who will take us to the broadband promised land, providing us with the fat communications pipeline to make our twenty-first-century dreams a reality? The answer is a yet-to-be-determined combination of telco, cable and wireless companies with each pushing one another to innovate and to cut costs and inefficiencies from their business. Emerging players such as satellite companies and potential new players such as utility companies will join the race in the future.

Hypothesis no. 5: Once we have achieved this new, open, multi-channel environment, distribution will become increasingly 'commoditized', with money made on a volume rather than a quality basis. The creation and presentation of content will assume an even higher place on the entertainment 'value chain'. Thus, in the end, content will indeed be king.

Hypothesis no. 6: PwC suggest that an ironic trend in mass consumer entertainment advertising will intensify as an increasing proportion of the US population reaches senior citizenship. These arguments also apply elsewhere in the developed world. Consumer entertainment offerings will skew toward (at least the perceived) tastes of the 18–35-year-old demographic. The younger generation is typically the most influential age group, as it is most likely to try out new products and to adopt new trends. Even as this younger demographic shrinks, it will be prized as the most desirable target group and aggressive marketing efforts to win its favour will dominate in this new century. Advertising dollars will flow to where the young eyeballs are.

Hypothesis no. 7: The proliferation of consumer devices and appliances will decrease as the features they offer start to overlap. However, the television in the living room and personal computer (PC) in the home office will continue to maintain their separate identities, albeit with more similarities than the current environment.

For example, television will offer interactive, menu-driven features through sophisticated set-top boxes as well as Internet access devices (for example, WebTV). Personal computers, in turn, will be able selectively to access programming from broadcast, cable and satellite transmissions.

Hypothesis no. 8: PwC says that digital television will eventually succeed in the USA, although the US government may have to push back its 2006 mandate for majority conversion to digital broadcast. Costs of consumer equipment and upgrades are not expected to drop as quickly as needed and the economics of digital television are in question. Moreover, it is unclear whether broadcasters will use the digital spectrum to offer one high-definition channel or multiple low-definition channels. That aside, broadcast television has clearly entered a new phase and will never be the same.

Hypothesis no. 9: Purveyors of today's relatively passive, traditional entertainment content must – and will – adjust to the new environment by melding their traditional and new media production capacities. In a PwC survey of 1010 consumers, 35 per cent of respondents said that the time they spend on the Internet comes at the expense of watching television; and 31 per cent said their Internet time comes at the expense of reading a book, newspaper or magazine. Traditional forms of entertainment clearly are losing eyeballs and mindshare, but traditional entertainment companies have recognized this shift and are leveraging their brand and resource power to create ancillary products (for example, consumer products, interactive software).

Hypothesis no. 10: Mergers and alliances between the traditional and non-traditional entertainment players will proliferate. Computer hardware and software, consumer electronics, Internet service and digital broadcast satellite companies will broker deals with their traditional entertainment brethren, seeking those oft-touted, sometimes elusive synergies.

It is worth remembering that these ten hypotheses are somewhat USA-focused. PwC rightly talk about 'convergence'. It's an overused word, but anyone who doubts the linking together of broadcast television, telephony and computing has only to look at how digital compression technology has been overlaid onto the new generation of cell phones to deliver breathtaking possibilities. The likes of CNN have provided a 'direct to cell-phone' service for some time. They, and others, see consumers as always ready to consume more hard news, whether it is stocks and shares, sports or just a missed recipe from yesterday's cookery show.

Radio is also going to be important in the home, whether from one of the established services or new technology standards, such as 'Bluetooth', for in-home appliance control. Bluetooth is the snappily named creation of the cellular telephony industry (in particular Nokia, Ericsson, Intel, IBM and Toshiba, and about 800 other industry members) which is designed to provide standards-agreed, enabling link technology between various modem-linked items in the home. Bluetooth was a tenth-century Scandinavian king, who united various warring groups in his region. The comparison with 'warring cell-phone companies' is perhaps apt.

A home today might easily have a television that is linked to the Internet (for example, Canal+'s MediaHighway system, or BSkyB's Open . . .), together with a desktop PC with a modem, a portable PC with a modem, and a Palm Pilot or Psion organizer-type device with a built-in modem. If we look a little further ahead, the home might also have a refrigerator with bar-code scanning, linked to a modem (Ericsson is working with Electrolux on a range of next-generation products including refrigerators, washing machines and other home appliances).

How would Bluetooth work in this sort of environment? The theory is that the white goods-buying population, which in Europe spends around US$15 billion a year on refrigerators, cookers and the like, will be increasingly tempted to buy equipment with this sort of extra functionality. A refrigerator, with a flat-panel screen, for example (ideal for calling up a recipe, or maintaining the kitchen diary) would monitor, via a bar-code scanner, what is placed in it and removed from it. Making up a shopping list becomes easier, and ordering the replacement items via the television or PC-link for home delivery even more so. Bluetooth technology, when linked to a central processor unit (CPU) in the home, gives users the ability to 'talk', via a cellphone, to and between these devices.

Bluetooth works in the 2.4 GHz band, and is designed to operate at low power but also to 'see' around corners and through walls, to a range of about 10 m. Amplifiers can be used to boost this signal range. Bluetooth's main advantage, however, is that there are no wires or cables. Aside from the high-tech applications, there are companies working on other, fundamentally useful interpretations based on Bluetooth, for example, an alarm device that is worn, which immediately notifies the central processor of a problem with an elderly or infirm person?

This book is not about kitchen appliances or heart monitors, but one can see how the various emerging technologies are coming together to provide greater control and linkage within the home. Meanwhile, as far as digital television is concerned, the greatest interest remains in the clear and obvious developments in the entertainment sector.

Technically, in the same way that PC users are increasingly using neat, flat-screen digital displays in place of bulky, cathode-ray tube PCs, so home users will soon be buying large-area, flat-screen monitors for home use. At 1999–2000 prices, around £8000–10 000 (US$12–15 000) in Europe, they are simply too expensive for mass-market adoption, but there are increasing signs of these prices softening as quantities increase and development costs are amortized. As a guide, prices have halved since 1997, and this trend shows no sign of slowing.

Nevertheless, in the following sections are the core products and industry sectors that concern us in this summary chapter.

1 VOD/NVOD and PPV – we cannot avoid it

We're not looking for other businesses to launch on the back of VOD and our movies.

> Jack Waterman, president, worldwide pay TV,
> Paramount Pictures Television Group

> [VOD] is no longer rocket science, needing an army of
> technicians. It is a straightforward plug-and-play system.
>
> Yvette Gordon, vice president of interactive
> technologies, SeaChange International Inc.

In May 1997, when Time Warner pulled the plug on its much-hyped Full Service Network (FSN) system in Orlando, Florida, the picture looked very different. At the time, in May 1997, many observers questioned the wisdom of cable operators or broadcasters in general investing heavily in the complex and expensive head-end kit needed to supply viewers with everything from the instantaneous delivery of programming – video-on-demand (VOD) – to the speedy delivery of a mozzarella-heavy pizza.

Even Time Warner chairman Gerald Levin, in a widely published interview in 1997, admitted at the time that FSN was 'off the mark,' and that 'he who makes a living from a crystal ball must learn to eat ground glass'. The costs of the experiment were reportedly in the US$100 million range.

To give credit to Time Warner, and other similar VOD tests and trials that have taken place over the past few years, many were deliberately designed to put leading-edge technology through its paces. The technologies worked just fine, but the business models all too frequently failed to match expectations.

Despite enormous optimism about VOD's brightening picture, there are some who question whether or not all the ground glass has been swept away. Among those concerned about getting cut by a sliver or two is Hollywood. Some movie studio executives express large reservations about how VOD is developing. At the same time, the lowered cost of technology and the roll-out of digital systems that enable two-way communications are making operators and technology companies much more optimistic.

'VOD is the killer application,' Leigh Wood, chief operating officer of Britain's largest cable operator NTL Inc, says as she talks about the company's roll-out of digital services during 2000. In her opinion, VOD is the application 'that differentiates us wildly from the competition'. By competition, she is referring to not only the direct-to-home platform British Sky Broadcasting plc, but digital-terrestrial television as well.

Get it right and the prize, according to estimates from a leading research company (Forrester Research Inc.), is a glittering share of the US$8 billion-a-year video-rental market. Forrester predicts that by 2005 cable's VOD efforts will reap around US$3.1 billion of that market. Direct-to-home satellite 'buys' will only add to that revenue stream.

Further understanding of VOD's potential comes from the US programmer Showtime Entertainment Television (SET). It reports that in the first six months of 1999, the US-generated PPV revenues of US$267 million from 'events' alone, up 114 per cent more than in the same period in 1998. Boxing and wrestling made up 98 per cent of the total.

Helen Britton is the Los Angeles-based vice president of programming for yet-to-launch (as at May 2000) VOD service DemandVideo Corporation. She notes that there is a 'huge' difference in buy-rates when operators move from PPV to Near-Video on Demand (NVOD), which is a middle-ground between PPV and the instantaneous delivery of programming afforded by VOD. But how much will the buy-rates increase when systems move from NVOD to pure VOD? 'That's a question that nobody knows the answer to right now', she says.

Britton explains that large distributors of programming pose a number of questions about the future of VOD. Needless to say, most queries have to do with revenue. 'Right now, there are very few VOD households, and it costs [the studios] probably US$25 000 to US$500 000 just to do one of these [VOD distribution] deals. There's costs like staff time, lawyer time, tape transfer,' she says. While the studios have participated in several VOD tests, 'it's cost them a lot of money, and so far they haven't gotten anything in return. Now they need evidence of [subscriber levels], effective technology and a business strategy that indicates that the VOD companies will produce revenues back to the studios.'

'Is there a need for VOD?' Jack Waterman, president of world-wide pay TV for Paramount Pictures Television Group, asks when speaking about NVOD versus VOD. Paramount, through parent Viacom, has ties to home-video giant Blockbuster, another firm that has reason to consider VOD a potentially huge threat to the bottom line. 'What does a consumer get from VOD that they don't get from NVOD?' Waterman questions.

The opportunity does exist to exploit library product in addition to just new movie titles, but 'it costs a lot to convert to the VOD environment,' Waterman says, speaking not about his own studio's costs, but about the cost to operators.

Perhaps of even more crucial concern to Waterman is how cable systems will package VOD services with other interactive offerings made possible by two-way digital technology. 'We're not looking for other businesses to launch on the back of VOD and our movies,' Waterman says. 'A lot of companies are looking to do e-commerce or repeat viewing of [regular TV programming].' He contends that operators need to build firewalls between those businesses and VOD so they don't cannibalize the VOD revenue stream for studio product. 'I'm looking to sell movies in the most effective way we can.'

Technology companies contend that programmer concerns about the economics of VOD have been resolved. For example, SeaChange International (based in Maynard, Massachusetts) says it has more than achieved operators' objectives of lower-cost servers that do not require an army of technicians.

Yvette Gordon, vice president of interactive technologies for SeaChange, says today's VOD is very different from the Time Warner FSN trial in Orlando, particularly when it comes to cost. 'If you looked at the FSN or Omaha trial, they were far too expensive. There were two parts to that expense – first with the capital costs, and second the operational costs of the trials – in other words the number of people needed to keep the trials up and running.'

Gordon contends that costs have declined so much that it now makes it possible for a business plan to work. VOD 'is no longer rocket science, needing an army of technicians,' she says. 'It is a straightforward, plug-and-play system. It's a huge difference.'

SeaChange in 1999 said that this reduction in costs and overall flexibility provides a very real option for modestly sized systems to climb aboard the VOD train. 'We calculate the breaking-point system as being 1000 streams, which is 10 000 subscribers. Below that figure, the break-even into profitability might be longer than our two-years-or-so ideal. But above 10 000 subscribers, we are very comfortable about a two to three-year payback,' adds Gordon.

SeaChange file-servers have been selected for a VOD trial conducted by UK MSO Telewest Communications plc. Competitor nCUBE Corporation is also involved with the Telewest trial with one of its MediaCUBE scalable video servers initially supplying 825 simultaneous streams for a 20 000 households split across two franchises. SeaChange has also been picked for China's Guandong GDCATV system. Guandong province is one of China's richest regions, and the system there plans to use SeaChange hardware primarily for educational services. GDCATV is providing 'a large library of educational programming' to serve some 400 000 households by the end of 2000, according to SeaChange. The systems integrator is Guangzhou-based Global Net Broadband Industry, which has also developed specialized set-top boxes for the scheme.

Clearly, companies like SeaChange and nCUBE are gearing up for big business ahead. Another rival is Concurrent Computer Corporation, which was recently selected for a Time Warner trial in Tampa, Florida, involving 877 000 households. The test is 'three times the size of the [SeaChange] Austin trial. We were competing head-to-head with [SeaChange], waiting to see who would be selected, so we consider Tampa a big win,' brags Andrea Ariza, Concurrent's vice president of corporate communications.

Concurrent's stock price doubled in November 1999 after the company acquired competitor Vivid Technology in a stock-and-cash deal valued at some $US20 million. 'Vivid was attractive because even though it was a small company, it had an excellent video server, and in addition they have an excellent relationship, and technology solution, for General Instrument [Corporation] equipment,' says Ariza. She adds that because GI equipment is in some 70 per cent of US cabled homes, it was vital to come up with server solutions for GI customers.

Also looking to cash in on VOD is California-based Diva Systems Inc., a full VOD system provider offering everything from equipment to programme content. Diva normally expects cable operators to pay it a flat amount per subscriber to cover hardware and installation costs. Then, once VOD revenues hit a pre-agreed level, revenues are split between Diva and the cable operator.

Once installed, Diva offers viewers a large roster of VOD programming, including movies, children's shows and speciality programming, along with the ability to pause, fast-forward and rewind the programming.

Diva has struck programming deals with almost every major American content provider, including Hollywood studios Warner Bros, Walt Disney Co., Sony Pictures Entertainment, Universal Studios, Twentieth Century Fox, Dreamworks SKG, MGM International TV Distribution, New Line Cinema, and Polygram. It also has agreements with channels such as Home Box Office, ESPN, Discovery Communications, National Geographic TV, PBS and Playboy Entertainment.

Diva says its research indicates that operators can expect typical buy-rates of 3.5 to 4 purchases per subscriber per month. However, SeaChange's Gordon predicts that European buy-rates won't hit the four-a-month level that VOD consumers in the USA are expected to reach. She suggests that, as VOD moves away from the mainstream programming that has dominated PPV in the past, such as adult, movies and sports, and moves into genres such as children's shows, it could bump up the buy-rates.

Clearly, Diva is about to test the predictions in both the USA and Europe. In September 1999, it struck a major agreement with MSO MediaOne Group for a number of markets in the United States. Additionally, Diva confirmed a relationship with UK-based set-top maker Pace Micro Technology in May 1999 that allows

Pace to integrate Diva's solutions for two giant MSOs in the UK, Telewest and Cable & Wireless Communications. NTL (which is in the process of absorbing Cable & Wireless's systems) has also contracted with Diva for a trial in Woking, a large commuter town south-west of London.

Diva is working closely with Yes Television, a regional VOD operator in the United Kingdom, which has a VOD trial in Cardiff, South Wales, using Scientific-Atlanta boxes. Yes Television isn't limiting itself to the UK; it plans to roll out in Thailand (with local partner Broadcasting Network Thailand) to around 800 000 passed homes. The technical trial is taking place in early 2000. A similar deal has been struck with South Korean Internet-service provider, ThruNet.

One of the most advanced VOD projects occurring in Asia right now is in Hong Kong, where the telco Cable & Wireless HKT has provided genuine VOD since March 1998. It operates its asymmetrical-digital-subscriber line-dependent (ADSL) VOD service through subsidiary company IMS. That unit's spokeswoman, Anna Ngai, says the service began with just 200 hours of material, and has now grown to well over 1000 hours of programming.

IMS is getting added strength from a news-on-demand deal with Reuters, and a recent agreement for multimedia services with programming platform STAR TV, which is backed by News Corporation. It has also linked up with Microsoft, which will use the system as a main test-bed for software merging television and PC technology. Microsoft chairman Bill Gates, in a local Hong Kong report published in March 2000, stated that Hong Kong's ADSL system is 'the best place in the world' to try true video-on-demand over the Internet.

Subscribers to the service, which uses the brand name iTV, pay about US$35 a month, a figure said to be some 50 per cent of what it actually costs IMS to provide the service.

However, local industry insiders are highly critical of iTV. Its business plan originally promised 250 000 subscribers by March 1999. The actual numbers were closer to 80 000 at that time.

Allen Ma, head of iTV, has rolled back his projected break-even date by two years to 2003 and freely states that VOD movies, Karaoke and horse racing are not enough to drive the business plan forward. In his view, the killer application will be Microsoft's content input.

The picture is just as confused in Singapore. Magix, Singapore Telecom's brand name for its VOD service, was launched in November 1997 using ADSL technology at speeds up to 8 mbps. It had only signed up 14 000 subscribers as at April 1999 – far fewer than Hong Kong's iTV. Yet observers say Magix's technology is impressive. Singapore Telecom acknowledges mistakes were made during the initial learning curve, and now states that it is concentrating on sales and marketing.

Another company heavily committed to VOD is British Telecommunications (BT). It is backing a major West London VOD trial using ADSL technology, and it has a buoyant view of its prospects. BT says it will upgrade 400 local telephone exchanges, covering about 6 million homes, to supply VOD, interactive and Internet content, starting in the spring of 2000.

Graham Mills, BT's director of visual and broadcast services, is closely involved with the trial. He predicts a healthy future for conventional movies shown in a VOD system, but also suggests spectacular growth possibilities thanks to Internet-protocol-based, web-streamed content (of which more in a moment).

Mills reckons that once viewers become accustomed to programming-on-demand, they will quickly expect increasing flexibility and sophistication in what is offered. 'I can easily see the Hong Kong community in London having all the Hong Kong channels and services available to them,' Mills says. 'The same would apply to Brits who want to hook into the Los Angeles area or elsewhere in the world. It will mean TV is available anywhere, anytime.'

Such rosy outlooks are tempered not only by the historic results of VOD so far – but also by those who are trying to troubleshoot the issues up ahead. 'There's side issues like copyright protection,' says Britton. 'Also quality of picture issues, the rate for data transfer.' Most Hollywood studios, for example, won't allow VOD streams below 4 megabytes per second, according to Yes TV's head of marketing, Steve Garvey.

These are issues that VOD providers and programmers have talked about until they are blue in the face. But trying to avoid such shards of ground crystal that could deflate the VOD promise is likely to make the reality a lot more solid.

To glibly suggest that all these issues can be ignored would be foolish. There may well be technical problems as well as problems of customer use. However, this writer firmly believes the days of the video rental store are numbered. PPV, in all its different guises (VOD, NVOD and instant response) is here to stay, and will capture a growing slice of our previous leisure time.

2 E-commerce ... another unavoidable trend

E-commerce is a hugely diverse area of goods and services, where the PC (and therefore Internet-based) world of on-line shopping has, thanks to digital television, begun to migrate to the television set. It seems there is no end to the global services that can now be shopped for on-line.

From the embryonic ground work undertaken by suppliers such as Amazon.com (books), CDs, clothing and specialist suppliers of seemingly every product under the sun, the television-based retailers are building their own operation. However, the revolution is not as dramatic as one might think; in the UK, a huge proportion of family holidays (especially last-minute vacations and weekend break bookings) are prompted by Teletext-based advertising.

Teletext is the brand name of a UK news/information and advertising television service that uses the analogue vertical blanking interval of a TV picture. Other broadcasters use the technology for similar text services. A matching, and visually improved, system exists in the digital world usually incorporating graphics-rich information, pictures of holiday destinations, houses or cars for sale, clothing for sale, etc.

Consequently, travel is an area where broadcasters see considerable revenues being generated off-the-screen. TV Travel Shop in the UK (a Flextech subsidiary) launched in 1999 and similar operations exist in mainland Europe. They allow viewers on one level to view a travelogue programme about this or that destination; if they delve deeper they can look at a specific hotel, perhaps even a hotel room. Either on-line or via the interactive digital television, viewers can even call up a 'virtual' tour of the location, booking it if they want and adding flights, car-hire, insurance and all the other revenue generating elements of a typical holiday.

But 'Open . . .', the interactive television service from a consortium that includes BSkyB, sees us using our digital television sets for much more. It has tied up with supermarkets, travel service companies, music and video retailers and many others to create a complete shopping centre experience 'all from the comfort of your armchair'. Sending and receiving e-mail is also possible.

Open. . . opens its doors

October 12 1999 saw Open. . .. come alive. Trials at the midday launch on 12 October were impressive, with speedy e-mail access and rapid access to the various vendors. Open. . . chief executive James Ackerman was buoyant about the number of sales already completed, with 10 000 homes ordering the interactive keypad (at £34.99) within the first few hours.

Ackerman announced that confectionery retailer Thorntons had joined the scheme, together with UK savings and loan company (building society) The Woolwich. Firstcall Direct joined a few days, later offering viewers tickets for theatre, music and sports events.

However, there were early reports (since cured) of clogged telephone systems, especially on the BT-supplied Talk 21 e-mail link. One report published in October 1999 spoke of 'thousands of people who cannot get a connection' and attempts over the first weekend to gain access to the system were totally fruitless. Other additions were made. The wireless keypad arrived in time for Christmas 1999 with Open. . . levying a 1p a minute charge for its e-mail service, in addition to on-line telephone costs.

While the undoubted attractions of up to eight e-mail accounts per home cannot be denied, some might argue that those pennies will quickly add up, especially in an age where 'free' Internet is increasingly available.

The Open . . . High Street

Woolworths	Dixons	W.H. Smith
Domino's Pizza	Carphone Warehouse	Somerfield
Manchester Utd	Kitbag Sports	Yalplay
HSBC	First Call	Argos
Gadget Shop	Gameplay	Iceland
Next	Going Places	Abbey National
Woolwich	e-trade	Hasbro
Shop!	*Yellow Pages*	

The Open. . . service is not the Internet, but what is called a 'walled garden', a safe area where there will be reliable retail names and no surprises or shocks. Many of the retailers offer matching services on the Internet, using the same back-office fulfilment systems. Open. . . sees the day when there are four million or more subscribing homes, able to address its offerings. Like Internet-based services, it sees viewers using Open. . . to book their travel tickets, cinema and theatre bookings, holidays, and the like. Time will tell if it is successful in its aims.

The growth in the Internet is by now well-known. Some statistics are given in Table 10.1.

It is undoubted that the Internet will increase in importance. Indeed the highly regarded USA-based Forrester Research organization predicts that by 2003 some 9.7 per cent of all US business will be conducted through the Internet. Jupiter Communications predicts that Internet penetration in Europe will rise to 31 per cent by 2003, by which time some 47 million households, some three times higher than at the end of 1998, will be online. The European IT Observatory suggests an even higher number, predicting that by the end of 2002 some 93.3 million users in Europe will be regularly accessing the Internet, a compound growth of some 26 per cent per annum, which is nothing short of staggering.

Table 10.1   European household online penetration*

Country	1997 (%)	1998 (%)
Norway	13.7	26
Sweden	12.5	23.8
Denmark	11	20.7
Finland	12.3	18.3
Austria	7.5	16
Switzerland	10.1	15.6
Netherlands	6.6	12.7
UK	6.9	12.7
Germany	7.2	11.5
Belgium	4.3	6.5
France	2.6	5.9
Spain	2.5	4.5
Italy	1.3	2.7
Rest of Europe	0.9	2.6
Central Europe	0.6	1.3
Russia	0.1	0.5

*Source: Dataquest (mid-1999)/Merrill Lynch

To what extent television-based e-commerce will encroach on this potential market is as yet unproven. But BSkyB has, from its own market studies, created an attractive business plan for future business.

Digital television has another Internet-based role, however, already described in a previous chapter. Many broadcasters and programme makers see their channels and individual programmes as portals to further information, extra levels of data and the inevitable opportunities to earn more cash, or at least retain viewer loyalty.

The big changes

This brings us to our 'top four' predictions for digital television and its next stages, drawn from previous chapters.

1 Personal video recorders (PVRs)

Put any two so-called experts together and you will have two different views of where the next television revolution will come. Few doubt, however, that one important development is the new generation of set-top boxes now beginning to emerge, which essentially allow viewers to throw away the VCR. The new personal video recorders (PVRs) have computer-type hard drives of some 15–25 Gb, which is probably five to ten times the size of the hard drive in use on most PCs. Moreover, their recording capacity will increase dramatically over the next few years, with some experts predicting over 100 Gb of storage within five years or so. If correct, this places a high-capacity file-server in every home.

These PVR set-top boxes, as well as picking up satellite and cable signals, allow viewers to record programmes, just like the VCR. The key difference is the 'intelligence' built into the PVRs. This 'fuzzy logic' intelligence monitors a user's viewing habits, and if the pattern is to watch *Friends* every Thursday evening, the equipment can automatically record an episode if the viewer forgets to set the equipment. Two systems (TiVo and Replay) are already on sale in the USA, and other broadcasters plan their own launches during 2000.

2 ADSL technology

Another favoured option is ADSL (Asymmetrical Digital Subscriber Line) telephone technology. Utilizing digital technology, telephone companies can supply almost any number of channels down an 'ordinary' telephone line. The line is transformed into a fast, two-way pipe capable of running video, interactive games and television on demand. It will have been significantly upgraded, vital if bothersome (and technically disastrous) pops, clicks and static stay on the system. The line is also enhanced at the telephone exchange, with the telephone company supplying a choice of channels just as if it were a satellite or cable company. These ADSL technologies are now being widely converted from trial status to full implementation.

3 Web-casting

'Television' is already available on the Internet, and outfits like Bill Gates' WebTV are increasingly seeing the power of using web-based technology to marry Internet-delivered signals with the television set. Though it is generally accepted that the PC is being used for 'lean-forward' activity, while the TV set is 'lean back' or relaxation mode, the lines are being blurred, with television increasingly being seen as the most attractive device in supplying home-shopping, banking, and, for many people, e-mail. Most European and United States broadcasters now have a wide selection of 'tele-shopping' options.

The Internet is fighting back, though; awash with online shopping opportunities, the Internet is becoming increasingly sophisticated about the entertainment it can supply. Have a look at www.broadcast.com if you have any doubt.

4 Micro-television

Broadcasting is expensive. Besides making or buying programmes, there is the cost of transmission. Sending the signal up to a satellite is also costly. Digital transmission helps cut these costs, but there is a new twist emerging for would-be broadcasters. By 2003 satellite transmission will, in the words of EUTELSAT'S director-general, Giuliano Berretta, 'be democratized'. Transmission bit-rates of about 2 Mb will increasingly be used – at least for some services – squeezing 18 channels into the space normally occupied by one analogue channel.

More channels mean dramatically less expensive transmission charges, and there is talk of even further cost-savings down the line. Such technology developments will change our television lives, no less dramatically than they have been changed since 1990. What has not changed that much is the amount of time viewers spend watching television, and few doubt that television will continue to be our prime supplier of leisure entertainment. What is already changing – and we have examined the trends in other chapters – is the number of niche and minority channels that tempt us to tune in for a few moments. Whether Discovery Wings is that different to a Military channel, or whether Discovery Civilisations will appeal more than The History Channel is a matter of consumer choice. What is inviting is a Discovery Kids channel that gives youngsters something other than a non-stop diet of animation.

If nothing else, then we must welcome the digital broadcasting entrepreneurs who are creating these new television opportunities. Are these actually new channels, or just a rehashed packaging of old repeats? I prefer to think of them not only as genuinely new, but as a real opportunity to see material that is near-perfectly packaged for a viewer's specific taste.

What is also fascinating is the amount of live, brand-new television that we might now get an opportunity to see, thanks to multi-channel television. During 1999, as well as the end-of-year Millennium celebrations across the world (and how many viewers in Britain saw the Jean-Michel Jarre concert from the Pyramids?) we were able to dip into the Venetian gondoliers race, live thanks to Italy's RAI TV, and to a wonderful fiesta in Catalonia – no fighting bulls but teams of youngsters building human towers with everyone standing on each other's shoulders to seven and eight levels of humanity. Simple, yet captivating TV.

I see no reason why other viewers should not share these moments.

Final health warning

While talking of these 'big changes' in digital television, I am reminded of a conversation I had with a senior executive of a UK television rental company (the UK has a tradition of people renting their television sets) who pointed out that they still had more than 20 000 people paying for 'black-and-white' (monochrome) television sets, a generation or two after the introduction of colour television. Indeed, these customers had to be issued with colour sets that had been deliberately degraded to keep them within the government regulations on colour television reception (the UK government allows a licence fee discount for monochrome reception).

I make the point if only to remind ourselves that for every dynamic early adopter of these technologies there will be a matching laggard, and as Europe moves towards totally embracing digital broadcasting, not all viewers will be enthusiastic about a multi-channel future promising dozens or hundreds, let alone thousands of potential channels. Politicians everywhere will have to face the electoral consequences of balancing their enthusiasm for these new technologies while at the same time paying due regard to those members of the population who are less than enthusiastic for such social changes.

References

ABN-Amro (1999). Into the second phase. *Digital TV*, June.

Brinkley, J. (1997). *Defining Vision*. Harcourt Brace.

Collins, R. (1992). *Satellite Television in Western Europe*. John Libbey & Co.

Hammond, R. (1984). *The Online Handbook*. Hodder and Stoughton.

Hammond, R. (1996). *Digital Business*. Hodder and Stoughton.

The Independent Television Commission (1998). *Competition investigation into channel building in the retail pay-TV market*. The Independent Television Commission, 1 April.

Smith, A. (1995). *A Television History*. Oxford University Press, pp. 69–83.

Index

Focal Press

http://www.focalpress.com

Visit our web site for:

- The latest information on new and forthcoming Focal Press titles
- Technical articles from industry experts
- Special offers
- Our email news service

Join our Focal Press Bookbuyers' Club

As a member, you will enjoy the following benefits:

- Special discounts on new and best-selling titles
- Advance information on forthcoming Focal Press books
- A quarterly newsletter highlighting special offers
- A 30-day guarantee on purchased titles

Membership is FREE. To join, supply your name, company, address, phone/fax numbers and email address to:

USA
Christine Degon, Product Manager
Email: christine.degon@bhusa.com
Fax: +1 781 904 2620
Address: Focal Press,
225 Wildwood Ave, Woburn,
MA 01801, USA

Europe and rest of World
Elaine Hill, Promotions Controller
Email: elaine.hill@repp.co.uk
Fax: +44 (0)1865 314572
Address: Focal Press, Linacre House,
Jordan Hill, Oxford,
UK, OX2 8DP

Catalogue

For information on all Focal Press titles, we will be happy to send you a free copy of the Focal Press catalogue:

USA
Email: christine.degon@bhusa.com

Europe and rest of World
Email: carol.burgess@repp.co.uk
Tel: +44 (0)1865 314693

Potential authors

If you have an idea for a book, please get in touch:

USA
Terri Jadick, Associate Editor
Email: terri.jadick@bhusa.com
Tel: +1 781 904 2646
Fax: +1 781 904 2640

Europe and rest of World
Christina Donaldson, Editorial Assistant
Email: christina.donaldson@repp.co.uk
Tel: +44 (0)1865 314027
Fax: +44 (0)1865 314572